The FATAL GIFT *of* BEAUTY

NINA BURLEIGH

The FATAL
GIFT *of*
BEAUTY

The Trials of
AMANDA KNOX

BROADWAY BOOKS   NEW YORK

Library of Congress Cataloging-in-Publication Data
Burleigh, Nina.
The fatal gift of beauty: the trials of Amanda Knox / by Nina Burleigh.
—1st ed.
1. Knox, Amanda. 2. Murder—Italy—Perugia—Case studies. 3. Homicide
investigation—Italy—Case studies. 4. Trials (Murder)—Italy—Case studies.
I. Title.
HV6535.I83P438 2011
364.152'3092—DC22   2011012669

ISBN 978-0-307-58858-6
eISBN 978-0-307-58860-9

Printed in the United States of America

Design by Ellen Cipriano
Map and diagram by Mapping Specialists, Ltd.
Photographs by Erik Freeland
Jacket design by Daniel Rembert
Jacket photograph by Daniele la Monaca/Reuters

1 3 5 7 9 10 8 6 4 2

First Edition

In memoriam:

female victims of sexual violence

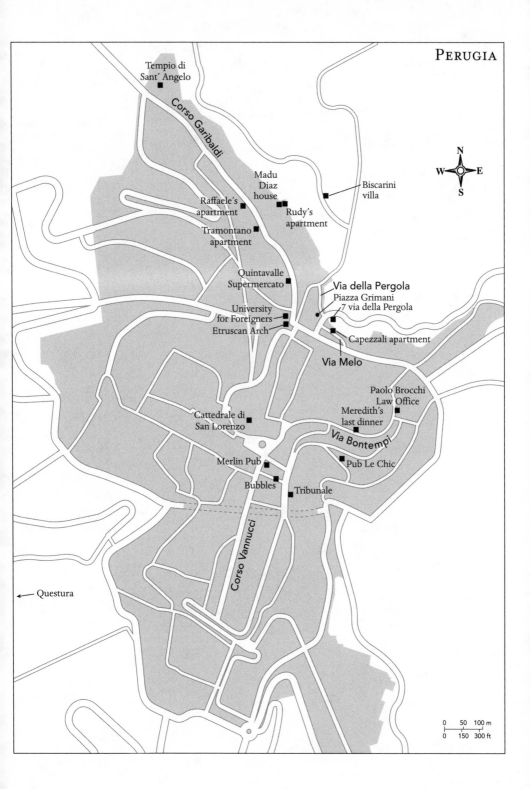

PERUGIA

Tempio di
Sant' Angelo

Corso Garibaldi

Madu
Diaz
house

Biscarini
villa

N
W   E
S

Raffaele's
apartment

Rudy's
apartment

Tramontano
apartment

Quintavalle
Supermercato

Via della Pergola
Piazza Grimani
7 via della Pergola

University
for Foreigners
Etruscan Arch

Capezzali apartment

Via Melo

Paolo Brocchi
Law Office

Cattedrale di
San Lorenzo

Meredith's
last dinner

Via Bontempi

Merlin Pub

Pub Le Chic

Bubbles

Tribunale

Corso Vannucci

← Questura

0   50   100 m
0   150   300 ft

7 VIA DELLA PERGOLA

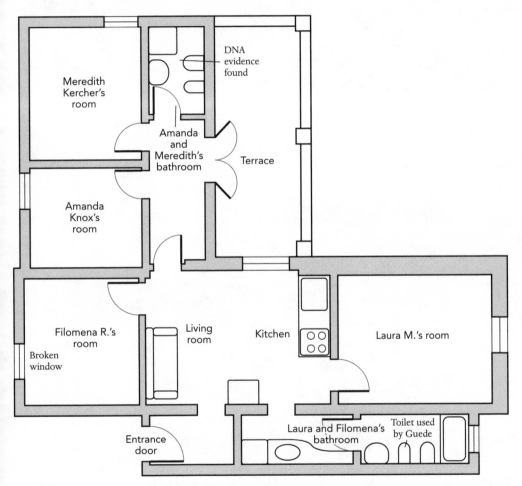

Meredith Kercher's room

DNA evidence found

Amanda and Meredith's bathroom

Terrace

Amanda Knox's room

Filomena R.'s room

Broken window

Living room

Kitchen

Laura M.'s room

Entrance door

Laura and Filomena's bathroom

Toilet used by Guede

Italia! Oh Italia! Thou who hast
the fatal gift of beauty.

LORD BYRON

CONTENTS

DRAMATIS PERSONAE

THE VICTIM

MEREDITH KERCHER. Born December 28, 1986, in the United Kingdom. Died November 1, 2007, in Perugia. A student at Leeds University, she was in Italy on an Erasmus scholarship, studying political theory and history of cinema, when she was murdered.

THE DEFENDANTS

AMANDA MARIE KNOX. Born July 9, 1987, in Seattle. A junior at the University of Washington, she was in Perugia studying Italian at the Università per Stranieri when she was arrested in November 2007.

RAFFAELE SOLLECITO. Born March 26, 1984, near Bari, Italy. A student at the University of Perugia, he met Amanda Knox on October 25, 2007, and became her lover that night. He was two weeks from getting his degree in virtual reality computing when he was arrested in November 2007.

RUDY HERMANN GUEDE. Born December 26, 1983, in Agou, Ivory Coast. His father, Roger Guede, brought him to the outskirts of Perugia when Rudy was five years old. He was later adopted, as a teen, by one of the richest families in Perugia. A high school dropout, he had no occupation when he was arrested in Mainz, Germany, in November 2007.

THE FAMILIES

JOHN AND ARLINE KERCHER. Meredith's parents.

CURT KNOX. Amanda's father, an accountant at the time of the murder, working in the finance department of Macy's in Seattle.

EDDA MELLAS. Amanda's mother, a Seattle elementary school math teacher.

CASSANDRA KNOX. Curt's second wife, a housewife and the mother of their two daughters, Ashley and Delaney.

CHRIS MELLAS. Edda's second husband, an IT professional.

DEANNA KNOX. Amanda's younger sister.

FRANCESCO SOLLECITO. Raffaele's father, a urologist based in Bisceglie, Italy, with his second wife, Mara.

VANESSA SOLLECITO. Raffaele's older sister, a Rome-based carabiniere who lost her job after her brother was arrested.

ROGER GUEDE. Rudy's father, a bricklayer born in Ivory Coast and living in Bastia, Italy.

THE HOUSEMATES AT 7 VIA DELLA PERGOLA

FILOMENA ROMANELLI. Intern at a Perugia law firm, age twenty-six at the time of the murder.

LAURA MEZZETTI. Intern at a Perugia law firm, age twenty-six at the time of the murder.

STEFANO BONASSI. Student from Marche, lived in the downstairs flat.

MARCO MARZAN. Student from Marche, lived downstairs.

GIACOMO SILENZI. Student from Marche, Meredith Kercher's lover in the two weeks before her murder, lived downstairs.

RICCARDO LUCIANI. Student from Marche, lived downstairs.

PERUGIANS

DIYA "PATRICK" LUMUMBA. Congolese immigrant, musician, bar owner, and Amanda's employer.

PAOLO CAPORALI. Wealthy Perugia businessman, owner of the Lio-matic vending company and the Perugia basketball team; adopted the teenage Rudy Guede, then disowned him.

ILARIA CAPORALI. Paolo's daughter.

IVANA TIBERI. Rudy's first Italian teacher and de facto Italian mother.

NARA CAPEZZALI. Elderly woman neighbor of 7 via della Pergola who testified that she heard screams on November 1.

ANTONIO CURATOLO. Homeless heroin addict who testified that he saw Amanda and Raffaele near the murder scene on November 1.

MARCO QUINTAVALLE. Perugia grocery owner who testified that Amanda entered his shop as it opened the morning after the murder.

HEKURAN KOKOMANI. Cocaine dealer and Albanian immigrant who testified that he saw Amanda and Raffaele together with Rudy in the days before the murder.

BISCARINI FAMILY. Wealthy villa owners who found Meredith's phones.

FRANK SFARZO. Perugia-based blogger whose case files were confiscated by police.

FRANCESCA BENE. Reporter for the Perugia daily *Il Giornale dell'Umbria,* detained by police for her investigation into the witnesses.

THE "BRITISH GIRLS"

SOPHIE PURTON. Leeds University Erasmus student in Perugia, the last person to see Meredith alive.

SAMANTHA RODENHURST. Erasmus student in Perugia, friend of Meredith.

AMY FROST. Erasmus student in Perugia, friend of Meredith.

NATALIE HAYWORTH. Erasmus student in Perugia, friend of Meredith.

ROBYN BUTTERWORTH. Erasmus student in Perugia, friend of Meredith.

FRIENDS

BRETT LITHER. Amanda's elementary and high school friend, West Seattle.

MADISON PAXTON. Amanda's University of Washington friend, Seattle and Perugia.

DAVID "DJ" JOHNSRUD. Amanda's Seattle boyfriend.

THE POLICE

MONICA NAPOLEONI. Head of the Perugia homicide squad, among the first on the murder scene, present at the November 5–6 interrogations of Knox and Sollecito.

MARCO CHIACCHIERA. Head of the Perugia anti-Mafia section, present at the interrogations.

GIACINTO PROFAZIO. Perugia police chief superintendent, present at the interrogations.

EDUARDO GIOBBI. Chief of the Serious Crimes Unit, Rome-based national police, observed the interrogations.

RITA FICARRA. Interrogating officer.

LORENA ZUGARINI. Interrogating officer and one of the first on the crime scene.

IVANO RAFFO. Junior member of the national police, among those present at the interrogation.

AIDA COLANTONE. One of two main civilian translators who worked with the police interpreting Amanda Knox's speech and writing in 2007 and 2008.

ANNA DONNINO. Part-time English translator for the Perugia police, present at the interrogation of Amanda Knox on November 5–6, 2007.

PATRIZIA STEFANONI. Head of the Rome police crime lab.

THE LAWYERS

GIULIANO MIGNINI. Perugia magistrate in charge of investigating and prosecuting the Kercher murder.

MANUELA COMODI. Perugia magistrate, assisting Mignini in the trial.

LUCIANO GHIRGA. Perugia lawyer representing Amanda.

CARLO DALLA VEDOVA. Rome lawyer representing Amanda.

LUCA MAORI. Perugia lawyer representing Raffaele.

GIULIA BONGIORNO. Rome lawyer and parliamentarian, representing Raffaele.

VALTER BISCOTTI. Perugia lawyer representing Rudy.

NICODEMO GENTILE. Perugia lawyer representing Rudy.

FRANCESCO MARESCA. Florence lawyer representing the Kercher family.

CARLO PACELLI. Perugia lawyer representing Patrick Diya Lumumba.

TIMELINE

2007

July 9. Amanda Knox celebrates her twentieth birthday and soon afterward leaves Seattle for Europe.

July. Rudy Guede moves back to Perugia and rents a studio apartment on via Canerino.

August. Rudy Guede tells a friend he can't sleep alone at his own apartment because he sleepwalks and wakes up far from home.

September 10. Meredith Kercher moves into 7 via della Pergola.

September 20. Amanda Knox moves into 7 via della Pergola.

September 27. A weekend. Christian Tramontano wakes up in his Perugia apartment between 1 and 4 A.M. and confronts a man he later identifies as Rudy Guede who has broken into his apartment.

October 6–7. A weekend. Someone breaks into a private English nursery school operated by Maria Del Prato in Milan, cooks a large meal of pasta and spinach, and steals 2,000 euros from a cabinet.

October 13–14. A weekend. Someone breaks a second-floor window and enters and robs the law offices of Paolo Brocchi and Matteo Palazzoli on via del Roscetto in Perugia.

October 20. Meredith and Giacomo Silenzi become lovers.

October 23. The Madu Diaz home on via Canerino in Perugia is burglarized and severely damaged in a fire by a burglar who "feasted" in the kitchen. Among the items stolen are a woman's gold watch.

October 25. Amanda and Raffaele meet at a concert in the Aula Magna of the Università per Stranieri and become lovers.

October 27. A Saturday. Rudy is arrested inside the Milan nursery school owned by Mrs. Del Prato. Police find Paolo Brocchi's laptop and cell phone, a woman's gold watch, and a sixteen-inch knife belonging to the nursery school kitchen in his backpack.

November 1. All Souls' Day, a national holiday in Italy. Meredith Kercher is murdered.

November 2. Police discover Meredith's body. Police question Amanda Knox and Raffaele Sollecito for the first time.

November 3. Police question Amanda Knox.

November 4. Police question Amanda Knox. Coroner completes autopsy and cannot confirm sexual assault of Meredith. Amanda and Raffaele are videotaped shopping for underwear.

November 5. Police summon Raffaele for questioning. Amanda joins him.

November 6. At 8:45 A.M., Amanda provides police with a hand-written note in English, describing a "vision" of herself sitting in the kitchen of their house and hearing Meredith screaming while

Patrick attacked her. Amanda, Raffaele, and Patrick Lumumba are arrested.

November 6. Edda Mellas arrives in Perugia by train from Rome.

November 7. *Il Giornale dell'Umbria* publishes the first reference to the students' "erotic game."

November 9. Judge Claudia Matteini rules that the three can be held in preventive detention.

November 15. Police announce that the murder weapon is a knife they found in Raffaele's house, with Amanda's DNA on the handle and Meredith's on the tip.

November 19. Police announce that Rudy Guede is a suspect.

November 20. German police arrest Rudy in Mainz; Perugia police release Patrick Lumumba.

December 6. Rudy is extradited to Italy.

December 17. Giuliano Mignini interrogates Amanda in the presence of her lawyers, who halt the proceeding.

December 18. Rome scientific police reenter the murder house and retrieve Meredith's bra clasp for testing.

2008

February 8. Mignini and Napoleoni interview the "British girls" in Bergamo.

May 15. Rudy admits to Mignini that the bloody Nike shoe prints in the murder house are his.

July 11. Mignini formally asks a judge to charge Amanda, Raffaele, and Rudy with Meredith's murder. He also requests a slander charge against Amanda regarding Patrick Lumumba.

September 19. Perugia Judge Paolo Micheli grants Rudy a "fast-track" trial.

October 28. Micheli convicts Rudy and sentences him to thirty years in prison. Micheli upholds the murder charges against the two students and sends the case to trial.

2009

January 2. Amanda Knox is voted Italian television's "Woman of the Year," edging out Carla Bruni and Sarah Palin.

January 16. The trial of Amanda Knox and Raffaele Sollecito begins.

February 6. Prosecution witnesses Antonio Curatolo, Nara Capezzali, and others testify.

February 13. The "British girls" testify about Amanda's strange behavior and Meredith's unhappiness with Amanda.

February 14. Amanda appears at trial in a sleep T-shirt reading "All You Need Is Love." Giacomo Silenzi testifies about his affair with Meredith.

February 17. Perugia police officers testify.

March 16. A Perugia appeals court awards Patrick Lumumba 8,000 euros for slander.

April 4. Rudy Guede appears at the students' trial but refuses to testify, exercising his right to remain silent.

May 22. Patrizia Stefanoni testifies about the DNA on the knife and the bra clasp.

June 12–13. Amanda Knox testifies.

July 6. Defense expert testifies that the kitchen knife cannot be the murder weapon.

July 18. The trial is suspended for a two-month vacation.

September 14. The trial resumes.

November 21. Prosecutors conclude closing arguments.

December 2. Defense concludes closing arguments.

December 4. Amanda and Raffaele are convicted and sentenced to twenty-six and twenty-five years in prison, respectively.

December 16. Donald Trump urges Americans to boycott Italy.

December 22. Rudy Guede's sentence is reduced to sixteen years on appeal.

2010

January 22. A judicial panel in Florence convicts Mignini of abuse of office in the Monster of Florence investigation and gives him a sixteen-month suspended jail sentence.

June 1. Amanda appears in court on charges that she slandered police and is photographed for the first time since her conviction. She has cut her hair short.

November 24. Amanda and Raffaele's appeal begins.

2011

January 22. Appeals court appoints independent experts to review DNA evidence against Amanda and Raffaele.

February 15. Italian Prime Minister Silvio Berlusconi is indicted on charges of frequenting a teen prostitute.

February 23. Perugia court indicts Amanda for slandering police officers.

March 24. Italian press publishes leaks that independent experts can't find incriminating DNA on the bra clasp or the knife.

The FATAL
GIFT *of*
BEAUTY

PROLOGUE
MEZZANOTTE

BY DECEMBER 2009, THE SECOND anniversary of Meredith Kercher's murder had come and gone and the trial of her roommate Amanda Knox and Amanda's boyfriend, Raffaele Sollecito, had reached its final act, a crescendo of argument, personal rancor, and notoriety. In the United States, Thanksgiving had been celebrated, turkeys carved and consumed, college ball games watched, as lawyers half a world away shouted and droned their final arguments, galloping along with barely a *pausa*. In chilly Perugia night fell a little earlier each day. Time, an element that had always seemed as dispensable in that courtroom as the sunny hours of an Italian afternoon, was finally constricting, pressing down, yielding to gravity. The hourly gonging of church bells from the gloom outside the brick walls only accentuated the strange isolation of the participants and spectators within. The spectacle possessed a life force of its own, constructed from the egos and emotions of all the people involved but now beyond the control of any individual. It was becoming clear that the Tribunale building had been gestating something, dying to be born. In the final hours, it was quickening.

The frescoed medieval courtroom itself and the stairwell outside it began to stink of sweat and tension and other things. Cigarette smoke;

cheap espresso from the Liomatic vending machine (the property of the wealthy Caporali family, which had disowned the third murder defendant, Rudy Guede, as a liar some years before); the never-cleaned single bathroom behind it, damp of floor, without soap or toilet paper; the exhalations of the smokers and coffee drinkers, the alkaline smell of the crumbly ancient brick walls that left white streaks of dust on the clothes of anyone careless enough to lean against them. The policewomen and female lawyers and journalists were now ferociously outdoing one another in terms of boot selections—kitten heels, cowboy boots, suedes, patent leathers, motorcycle boots, Gucci, Ferragamo, Prada—every conceivable style was banging up and down the metal steps to and from the courtroom. Nerves were frayed to breaking. Journalists and cameramen snarled at one another in a tiny pressroom piled with coats, video equipment, old newspapers, and half-broken chairs, vying for a view of the fuzzy television screen that monitored the courtroom. A British documentary filmmaker buzzing around was under threat of legal action from at least two members of the press who expected to be badly portrayed in his final product. A reporter for one of the British tabloids had nearly punched out one of the documentary's cameramen. Rumors and threats of lawsuits involving journalists, lawyers, family, and police filled the chatter during breaks.

Wandering around in this sweaty, smoky haze, the Knox family, radiating hope and that quality that so differentiates the American from the European—enthusiasm, and especially Amanda's mother, Edda's, persistent chirpy cheer and quivery emotions—were now grating badly, because everyone except them understood that the beast was being born and there was nothing they could do about it, their daughter was going to be convicted of murder. Only the most sadistic or ratings-desperate could hold a gaze on these fish in a barrel for long. The American television network producers, all vying for the big "get"—Amanda herself—circled incessantly, not daring to let the family out of sight for fear of missing some competitive moment, pouring money into pricy dinners with ample uncorkings of the finest limited-edition local red, the Sagrantino. Only they among the journalists were still maintaining the facade of the possibility of an acquittal. And their efforts would be for naught: the Italian judiciary would deny all reporters access to the beauty behind bars. In the end, the winner of the Amanda interview prize would be a right-wing Italian politician named Rocco Girlanda, who used his unfettered parliamentary access to prisons to enter Capanne Prison twenty times, plied Amanda with a laptop and fatherly male attention (although he admitted to having some vaguely romantic dreams about her), and eventually published a book about these encounters titled *Take Me with You*.

After they filed their nightly stories, the anglophone press gathered to compare notes, share gossip, and quaff the cheaper local *rosso* at the *enoteca* near the Porta del Sole, a hundred yards from a postcard-perfect overlook point with a grand view of the roof of the murder house, and, in the distance, the same panorama of violet Umbrian hills the girls— one murdered, one on trial—had once enjoyed.

On the morning her lawyers began to present their final arguments, Amanda shed the talismanic red Beatles hoodie she'd worn to every hearing since summertime cooled and donned a wrinkled green blazer, grass green, the color of hope, the color of the Madonna del Verde, frescoed on the wall of a strange round neo-Christian church at the highest point of Perugia, believed to have originally housed a pagan temple. A cell mate had done up her hair into a tight French braid. It was a nice gesture to *la bella figura* but not enough, and everyone knew it. "An American journalist observed that Amanda's new conservative look was 'too little, too late,'" reported the London *Times*.

One of her lawyers, the white-haired, gap-toothed former local soccer star Luciano Ghirga, tried a folksy appeal to the civic pride of his fellow Perugians, imploring them not to fear that an acquittal would hurt their fair city's image. "He has changed the motive," Ghirga complained of Prosecutor Giuliano Mignini. "In the beginning, it was just: Sex! Now it's not an orgy, now it's money, and now it's anger. Look, these girls were both in love with Italian men, they were having the time of their life here, where is the anger? . . . Come back with a sentence that reflects the prestige of this court and this city. Do not think that our beautiful city will lose with an acquittal. You must set Amanda free. Her family, you see them here, is not a 'clan.'"

He finished his statement in a fit of weeping.

In the waning hours, as the afternoon turned dark, the legal women finally got their turn to speak. Knox's chief attorney Carlo Dalla Vedova's assistant, Maria Del Grosso, a girlish thirty-five-year-old with beautiful dark hair pulled back into a ponytail, gave a spirited defense, going on for hours trying to drive home the inconsistencies in the case. At the end she pointed to Amanda and implored the jury, "Is this the witch you're going to burn?"

Each lawyer concluded his or her remarks with appeals to God, as is customary in Italian trials, but really they were talking to six citizen jurors and one very human man, the deceptively genial Woody Allen look-alike in the middle of the dais, Judge Giancarlo Massei.

"The judge is not God," Sollecito's lawyer Giulia Bongiorno proclaimed.

"I would like to refer to the law of the church before you go in and decide the sentence," Dalla Vedova concluded. "You need a moral certainty to convict. In the Church there is a law of moral certainty that has a spiritual meaning, and it is compatible with Italian law. You need a moral certainty. In your soul, you need a tranquillity, and only then can you be sure of judgment. Moral certainty is personal. Some have it, some don't."

As the translator repeated his words to her in English, Amanda's mother, Edda, was awash in tears.

Then the civil lawyer Carlo Pacelli rose. He was a tall, brisk man with a gray crew cut, representing Patrick Lumumba, the Congolese bar owner Amanda had falsely accused of being in the murder house. Shouting, he reminded the jury of Amanda's behavioral anomalies, the outrageous cartwheels at the police station, the kissing of her boyfriend while the corpse cooled, the blithe lack of concern, the particularly female duplicity on display before them.

"She has never shown true grief for the death of Meredith. Actually, all to the contrary, she would kiss and cuddle joyfully with her boyfriend. She goes out and buys sexy lingerie at Bubble and talks about having mad sex with him. So who is Amanda Knox?" he shrieked. "Is she the angelical Santa Maria Goretti that we see here today? Or is she the diabolical Luciferina, the explosive concentrate of sex, alcohol, and drugs, dirty in her soul, just as she is dirty on the outside?"

Prosecutor Giuliano Mignini got in a few final words: "I have been observing the defendants through the trial, trying to determine if violent acts are in accordance with their characters. I have had a graphologist look at their handwriting, and that man confirmed that Amanda Knox is aggressive, narcissistic, manipulative, transgressive, and has no empathy; she likes dominating people, she doesn't like people to disagree with her, and she's very negligent overall. Her behavior in the police station proved this. As for Sollecito, the graphologist says his handwriting indicates that he is a person who seeks approval from others."

As if in despair, he burst out, "If these kids were innocent, how could they sit here and bear listening to this?

"Don't forget the victim. A victim of sexual violence, a young woman who would go home and visit her mother on her birthday, who should have gone back to London to look after her mamma instead of being dead. Now the Kercher family can only go to the cemetery to see her. As for Rudy, he didn't bring the murder knife to the scene, and he tried to clean up the blood. These are attenuating circumstances. There has been a lot of lobbying in America by people who think she's not guilty, but remember that in this moment, the function of justice is consistence. From Roman canonical law: you should give to all what comes to them. They need to pay. I am finished."

When he asked for *ergastolo,* a life sentence, spectators gasped.

. . .

THE TWO DEFENDANTS TOOK it in quietly, Raffaele gnawing at his cuticles, Amanda squirming in her chair and occasionally weeping. When Raffaele rose to make his last spontaneous declaration, he tried to clarify that he wasn't his codefendant's slave. "You are about to decide my life. I am living in a nightmare. Discovering that I have been pulled into this dramatic situation of which I know nothing. I have listened to the prosecutors, yet I haven't understood what they think my role is. I have heard that Amanda killed Meredith for a matter of personal hygiene and then because of . . . men. I am not clear why they think I killed her. They think I am a sort of dog on a leash, dependent on Amanda. I met Amanda just a few days before, and I got very attached to her. But it was just the beginning. In such a relationship you cannot create dependence. If Amanda had asked me to do something I disagreed with, I would have said no. Imagine if she had asked me to kill a young girl! I am not a violent person, I have never been and never will be a violent person. I did not kill Meredith, and I was not in that house. Each day that goes by I hope the real killer confesses. I still strongly believe in justice. Thank you for listening."

Amanda rose, quivering from head to foot, her confidence finally shaken. "Meredith was my friend, and it is impossible that I could have wanted revenge against such a kind person. I do not know Rudy at all, and all that has been said about me here is pure fantasy." She protested against the "mask of an assassin that has been burned onto my face."

The trial adjourned on the morning of December 4. Lawyers and spectators were told to expect a verdict by the next day at the latest. For the first time in the trial, the jurors would not be allowed to go home for dinner until they had finished deliberating. The jurors and the two judges who had been their guides in law for eleven months and who would guide their deliberations and later pen a four-hundred-page document explaining the verdict as well, retired to a room within the bowels of the Tribunale (courthouse) to decide the students' guilt or innocence.

At nine in the evening, BlackBerrys and iPhones lit up. The court had reached a verdict, and would deliver it without delay, precisely at *mezzanotte,* midnight. It was a wet, chilly night, and fog snaked through the dark cobbled streets as on a horror-movie set, but the revolving yellow star of a Christmas Ferris wheel perched at one end of the hilltop gave the evening a festive glint. By ten-thirty, a crowd was already mobbing the doors of the Tribunale. Security, which had been present in the form of two languid guards sitting at a table near the entrance throughout the trial itself, seemed to have evaporated. Townspeople, students, all the followers of this salacious crime story who had stayed up late and ventured out in the midnight fog for its denouement, crushed against one another, crowding the door, shoving and cursing. Lawyers, family, press fought their way through the mob to the front door, where a clerk could be seen trying to hold back the crowd.

Finally the doors opened, and the mob surged inward and clattered down the stairs. The courtroom looked the same as it had for the past year, peeling madonnas on the walls lit with fluorescent lights. But there was an unusual spareness to it. The spectators' chairs had been removed. Everyone would stand.

Edda wore a scoop-necked little black dress and makeup, looking ready for a Christmas party. Her second husband, Chris Mellas, stood to one side of her, looking grim, and, on the other, Amanda's younger sister, Deanna Knox. Amanda's father, Curt, and his second wife, Cassandra, stood beside them. Curt's two younger daughters were too young to be allowed inside the courtroom, so they were stationed in the anteroom, through which their big half sister and her onetime boyfriend were delivered by guards to their fates.

The jurors filed in. In the same small, uninflected voice he'd used all year, the judge began reading the verdict. *Condanna. Condanna.* Guilty. Only when Raffaele's relatives began to sob did the Knox family understand that their daughter had been convicted.

The reading of the verdict was over in a matter of minutes. Amanda Knox was led back past the little sisters who had been positioned to greet her in freedom. Instead, her sobbing and shrieks of "No! No! No!" echoed long after the doors had slammed shut behind her.

Meredith Kercher's mother, Arline, stood still amid the commotion and fixed a long glare on Edda Mellas from across the room.

CNN and the other American networks interrupted programming to bring the news live to viewers back in the United States, where it was approaching dinnertime.

In the fog, back up at street level, Curt Knox clung to his teary-eyed younger daughters' hands and marched them defiantly into a scrum of backward-walking photographers and television camera lights. The gaggle moved as a group across the long piazza to the luxury Hotel Brufani Palace.

Lawyers drifted out of the Tribunale doors toward waiting cars, lighting cigarettes and dropping quotes to the media pack en route. Within a few hours, U.S. Senator from Washington Maria Cantwell had issued a press release condemning the verdict and calling upon Secretary of State Hillary Clinton and the U.S. State Department to take a closer look. The Italian press treated the mere mention of Clinton's name as a sign that the American secretary of state was on her way to Italy to spring Amanda Knox, providing the Italian talk shows with hours of material on Yankee heavy-handedness. Clinton refused to comment.

Not much later, Donald Trump urged a boycott of Italy.

ETRUSCAN GATE

PART ONE

1
CRONACA NERA

As I began studying postwar Italian history it became obvious that
surrounding any crime or political event, there are always confusion,
suspicion, and "the bacillus of secrecy." So much so that dietrologia
has become sort of a national pastime.

—*Tobias Jones,* The Dark Heart of Italy

IN ITALY, THEY CALL NEWS of incidents like the Meredith Kercher murder
cronaca nera.

A black chronicle.

Murder is common enough in Italy—the Mafia commits hundreds,
common criminals and domestic violence have carried off thousands
more. But a *cronaca nera* possesses an element of the macabre, diabolical,
or obscene that journalists instantly recognize. The annals include mur-
derous mothers; cold, calculating killer boyfriends; scorned women an-
nihilating errant men; female rivals killing each other; and maybe best
of all, the eyes-wide-shut bloody rites of deviant cults. If the murderer

is especially prolific, he (all have been male so far) becomes a "Monster." In recent years, Italy has had a Monster of Florence, a Monster of Foligno, a Monster of Genoa.

Death distinguishes a *cronaca nera* from the relatively lighter but equally popular Italian newsprint fare involving rare sexual tastes—pedophilia, DIY prostitution rings involving housewives and children, or the surprisingly common and blackmail-able preference among some ranking politicians and denizens of the Vatican for Brazilian butt-implanted transvestites. *Cronache nere* are so popular in Italian newspapers and on television that they have their own page or segment, like soccer, the weather, and business news.

Most black chronicles remain within the Appennine peninsula, but this particular black chronicle, the *"caso Meredeet"* (as the Italians said, "Meredith case"), had it all, every single lurid element, whereas most black chronicles only have one at best. It went global faster than tiramisù in the 1980s, faster than pricy super-Tuscans before the crash.

Almost everyone in the world with access to television or the Internet has heard of one of the alleged murderers, Amanda Knox. People around the world have seen her on CNN—often smiling, sometimes perplexed, peering anxiously from behind iron bars, rarely collapsing in tears. Hers is a pretty face, one of those faces made more, not less, beautiful by the camera, and it is mostly speechless. Her parents, friends, and lawyers speak for her. Millions of Americans watched her extended family on *The Oprah Winfrey Show* or caught her mother, Edda Mellas, in tears, opining "This case is crap" on one of the national television networks.

The face, placed next to the depraved crime, is one element that makes the story intriguing. The mass media cliché machine went into fifth gear when she was arrested in November 2007, churning out descriptions. She was "angel-faced" or "fresh-faced," the eerily smiling "soap-and-water" girl who went mad one night—moved by psychopathy or erotic mania of the sort that afflicts nymphomaniacal cheerleaders in Hollywood slasher films or under the morality-frying influence of drugs and alcohol—and stabbed her pretty, young British roommate to death with the help of two young men, who were so besotted with her that she was able to manipulate them into committing rape and murder.

In the course of a *gioco erotico*. A sex game.

The story came to resemble a fairy tale about things that happen to bad girls and to good girls. It had strains of Franz Kafka and the *Malleus Maleficarum*, an Inquisition-era witch-hunting guide. It resonated with the churning fear of parents whose children are far away; of young women in houses alone after dark; of older women remembering their own ill-spent youths, their own date rapes and other regrettable incidents after midnight. The story titillated men habituated by Internet porn to the real possibilities of group sex and the slithery catfight. It was and is drenched in local superstition, misogyny, mistranslation, and deliberate misinformation, magnified and distorted by the mass media, monetized by lawyers and filmmakers, and analyzed in scholarly papers. The worst inclinations, prejudices, and stereotypes of three different cultures—American, British, and Italian—are knotted up in it. It's been spun into an Internet spiderweb by a band of bloggers who have microanalyzed every element and threatened one another to the point of involving lawsuits and police. Aficionados and armchair CSI experts have been known to spend hours, days, weeks debating the facts and suppositions.

In Perugia, the medieval hill town in Umbria where Meredith Kercher was murdered and where Amanda Knox was tried and convicted and sentenced to spend twenty-six years in prison, even before the guilty verdict on the cinematically foggy midnight of December 4, 2009, it was almost impossible to find a person who would consider the possibility that the narrative of the crime, which they had been reading about and discussing since the fall of 2007, might not be the truth. "It was a game, *un gioco,* that got out of hand," Perugians would say, or "She's an American college girl, and those girls can be very mean, very competitive." Or "she's witchy." Or, especially, "She's a white American, and white American girls *always* blame the black guy."

The Italian, British, and American reporters who covered the case from day one, the ones presumably holding all the information the various lawyers revealed in bits and chunks of comment and digital document over the course of the past three years, from Amanda Knox's prison diary to the actual videotape of police working at the blood-spattered crime scene, were a little less sure. Having sat through the trial and heard the evidence that the prosecutors presented to judge and jury, they were not sure that Amanda Knox had personally wielded the knife that killed Meredith Kercher. In fact, neither was the jury, which decided that Amanda Knox and her boyfriend, Raffaele Sollecito, were guilty of aiding the main perpetrator, "the author of the evil"—as the judge wrote in the document explaining the students' convictions—Rudy Guede, the African-Italian man whose prints were on the walls of the dead girl's room, inside the dead girl's purse, and whose DNA was on her clothes and inside the dead girl's vagina.

But, they reasoned, Amanda Knox still deserved to spend twenty-six years in jail for following sadosexual urges to their utmost degree of depravity, by spontaneously and without premeditation helping Rudy rape and then kill her roommate.

There are many "facts" and voluminous "evidence" in the complicated story of this crime. The problem is that many reported facts are actually bits of rumor or unverified statements by lawyers, by police, by journalists, and all are subject to debate. The only indisputable truths are these: On the morning of November 2, 2007, in the presence of a police officer, a strong young man kicked down a locked door in a house perched on a ravine at the edge of Perugia's city center. Besides the man and a cop, there were three young women and two men inside the stone cottage. Two of these people would ultimately be convicted of murder.

On the floor, inside the tiny locked room, they found the dead body of Meredith Kercher, twenty-two, a foreign exchange student from the University of Leeds, the fourth and youngest child of John and Arline Kercher of suburban London. Her long brown hair was stuck with dried blood to a gaping stab wound on the left side of her neck. Her eyes were open. She was covered with a duvet that, when removed, revealed that she was naked from the waist down, her shirt pulled up to her neck. A pillow had been placed under her hips, directing her pelvis upward, a leg splayed outward. Blood splattered the wall near where she lay and smeared the floor, as though she had been dragged or rolled a few feet through her own blood.

Those are the facts, and they are almost the only facts that no one disagrees about. Almost everything else—from the number and nature of her wounds, to when she died and when her roommate called the police, to who saw the body and the wound and when, to what people said about the body and when they said it, to the exact size and owner-ship and placement and substance of the shoe prints and the bare foot-prints and fingerprints in the house, to the DNA traces on walls, knife, toilets, and clothing, to the bloodstains and possible semen on Mer-edith's pillowcase, to exactly where she last used her cell phone—has been endlessly debated, both inside the courtroom and outside, around the world.

THE FACT THAT MEREDITH Kercher was found nude from the waist down, with DNA inside her vagina belonging to a man she was not known to have had a sexual relationship with, immediately suggested to the police and prosecutor that she was also a victim of a male sexual assault, but medical experts never conclusively determined that the DNA arrived there *against her will*. There was no sperm inside her, just the skin cells of a young man named Rudy Guede, a break-in artist and sleepwalker who turned into a dog or a professor or a businessman in the middle of the night, who had a habit of waking up in the dark to find himself out of bed and walking miles from home. Rudy Guede has insisted that she wanted him there, and there wasn't enough bruising on her labia and thighs to prove forcible sex. If she was raped, according to the European

Council, she was among the one in five European females between the ages of two months and ninety years old who are victims of a sexual assault at some point in their lives.

Ninety-eight percent of their aggressors are male.

To meet one of the 2 percent that are female is a rare thing indeed. To meet one who is beautiful, in a city and a nation renowned for all that Western civilization deems fine, is rarer still.

SLAVE

The fact that woman is the predominant character of Italian life,
even if not the most conspicuous, can be read in many small signs.
Almost as many popular songs are dedicated every year to La
Mamma as to voluptuous hussies or romantic beauties. "Mamma
mia!" is the most common exclamation. What other people call for
their mother in time of stress or danger?

—*Luigi Barzini*

November 2, 2007

AT AROUND 10 A.M. ON November 2, 2007, a strange cell phone in her
garden disturbed the otherwise leisurely morning of Signora Elisabetta
Lana Biscarini. The Biscarinis are people of wealth, and their property is
well shielded from unexpected intrusions. The three-story yellow brick
villa is perched on a steep incline outside the northern wall of Perugia,
surrounded by an impenetrable brick wall with a tall electric steel gate.
Thornbushes line the wall on all sides, and graceful cypresses sway in

the breeze, surrounding and further shielding the villa. In the distance, on three sides, are the serene violet Umbrian hills, familiar the world over as the backdrop of some of the greatest Renaissance paintings.

Beyond the gate, the Biscarinis' short driveway enters the via Sperandio, a ring road that hugs the city wall and swoops steeply down toward the verdant Tiber Valley flatland and Perugia's shabbier sister village of Ponte Rio, on the banks of the Tiber River, here shallower and muddier than it becomes farther south in Rome.

The Biscarini villa is isolated. No one would think of strolling past it on via Sperandio, because drivers are speeding and there is no sidewalk or even shoulder. To the north and east lies savage, brambly, untamed ground, too steep for olives or grapes or hiking. But across the road lies the ancient wall of the city and, beneath it, a large, scruffy, needle-filled city park, a haunt of Perugian junkies.

On the morning of November 2, La Signora, her two teenage children, and their maid were slightly on edge because of an unsettling incident the night before. An anonymous caller had phoned at around 10 P.M. and warned them that there was a bomb in their toilet. Wealthy Italians take such calls seriously, and the Biscarinis alerted police. The Biscarinis had a special reason to obsess over security: thieves had broken into their villa at least three times in the preceding decade.

Police investigated and assured the family that the anonymous caller had been a mere prankster, perhaps motivated by the mischievous spirit of Halloween.

Coming within twelve hours of that threat, the discovery of a strange cell phone in the garden frightened La Signora. She called the police emergency number and was connected to an Italian police agency known as the Postal Police. The Postal Police handle Internet crime, mostly pedophilia, financial crime, and online frauds and scams. It is their duty to know and understand electronic gadgetry, computer software, mobile phones. Their symbol is a winged @. The Postal Police told Signora Biscarini to bring the mystery mobile phone down to their office, a fifteen- or twenty-minute drive away on the flats below the medieval city.

Signora Biscarini got into the family car, clicked open the gate, and steered out onto via Sperandio. It was approximately 10:30 in the morning. The clocks had been turned back an hour for fall a few days prior, and people were still not used to the extra hour, so it still felt later than it actually was. Traffic was lighter than normal, as usual for a Friday after Thursday's national holiday, All Souls' Day. Most Italians were "making the bridge"—that is, extending their holiday, taking an unofficial day off to make a four-day weekend of it.

At two minutes to eleven, Signora Biscarini turned the mystery cell phone over to the police, who logged it and asked her to wait. Half an hour later, the police had identified the owner of the Italian SIM card— the phone's chip—as a woman named Filomena Romanelli. Signora Biscarini knew no one of that name, and she left the phone with the Postal Police.

Just as she was driving off to do some morning errands, her daughter, Fiametta, called to say that another mystery cell phone was ringing in the garden. Signora Biscarini told her daughter to meet her, and together they brought the second phone to the Postal Police headquarters, where it was logged in at 12:46. At 1:00 P.M., the police determined that the second cell phone was British and registered to a British citizen named Meredith Kercher. Romanelli and Kercher, according to the phone records, both lived at 7 via della Pergola, just a half mile up the road, even closer as the crow flies directly across the wild hillside from the Biscarini villa.

Postal Police officer Michele Battistelli was dispatched to return the phones to their rightful owners.

Unlike other Italian police officers, Officer Battistelli and his partner in the winged @ brigade didn't have timing devices inside their vehicles. Their duties generally kept them at their desks and required knowledge not of road maps but of computers. On the morning of November 2, the

Postal Police officers also had no GPS device in their car, and they had a hard time finding 7 via della Pergola.

Via della Pergola or via Sant'Angelo, a road with either name depending on the map, is a main artery just outside Perugia's city walls. Via Sant'Angelo runs a curving line uphill to a mysterious temple, consecrated as a church in the sixth century but built on the foundation of a round Roman temple, with basins for sacrificial blood or ritual ablutions still in place on the floor and twelfth-century Madonna frescoes on the walls. Until recently, the neighborhood it traversed was known as the Borgo Sant'Angelo, "whose people were always considered the wickedest and most desperate in the city," according to an eighteenth-century English travel writer. Like via Sperandio, into which it leads, via della Pergola is now a blacktop without sidewalks, a road designed for impatient drivers finally putting the pedal to the metal after inching through the narrow medieval lanes of the city.

Officer Battistelli eventually located 7 via della Pergola after parking his car, walking down a hill, and crossing the road on foot. The house was gray stone with a red-tiled roof, two stories high, set below the street and just a minute's walk from the Etruscan arch, one of the landmark gates of the city, an ancient engineering feat of massive stone blocks, cut and laid by the slave-owning, pleasure-loving Etruscan founders of what they called Perusia. The stone house was perched on the upper edge of a wilderness ravine, and the walled Biscarini villa far below was barely visible. Like all houses built on hills, the upper half of it is above ground, the lower half embedded into the earth. The north-facing windows have fantastic views of the glorious Umbrian *campagna*; the south-facing half fronts the busy street and looks out on a charmless but much-used concrete parking lot with an automatic ticket-spewing machine, an electric gate, a shadowy underground level, and a video camera, built just beneath the city walls.

A short, gnarled *cachi* tree heavy with ripe globes of orange persimmon fruit tilted over some stone steps leading down to a door on the first floor. That afternoon, the absorbing gray of the sky and foggy, bone-chilling humidity muted those spots of color and that of the fading red-and-yellow foliage on the hillsides in the distance beyond the ravine.

Walking down the driveway to the house, Battistelli saw an attractive young couple standing together near the gravel driveway. The girl had on a white skirt and hiking boots; shanks of straight dark blond hair framed her wide cheekbones, small nose, heart-shaped face, clear blue eyes. She was very pretty but looked startled, troubled. The boy, Battistelli immediately pegged as coming from money. He sported class symbols known to all Italians: yellow cashmere scarf knotted around his neck, rimless glasses, high cheekbones, expensive jacket, pale hair and eyes. And he had his arm around a blonde. Battistelli identified himself. The officer would say later that the young people seemed shifty and surprised to see him.

In some tellings of the story, Battistelli also encountered them holding a mop and bucket, but police never brought the cleaning tools into the trial as evidence. They were an important part of the story told *before* the trial, the essential but extralegal narrative that would help convict the students.

The boy was Italian, and he did the talking. He explained that his girlfriend, an American student, lived in the house with three female roommates. He said she had returned home in the morning to find the door unlocked. One bedroom appeared to have been broken into—Officer Battistelli could see the broken window above them as they spoke—but, the boy said, nothing appeared to be missing, even though everything was in disarray. No one else was home, but one of the roommates' doors was locked, and they had been trying to phone her all morning.

Battistelli walked inside. The hallway was tiny. The Italian boy showed him the locked door and another room in disarray. Did the roommate normally lock her door? Battistelli asked. The American said something he couldn't understand, and the Italian boy said, yes, she locked it regularly when she took a shower.

As they talked, another group of young people showed up, two boys and two girls. One of the girls, a thin, pretty, finely dressed young woman with long brown hair, was in a state of panic. The room with the broken window was hers, said Filomena Romanelli. She was also the owner on record of one of the missing phones—but she explained that she had given the phone to her roommate, Meredith Kercher.

Now the officer understood that both the mystery phones belonged to this same Meredith, whose door was locked and whose failure to appear during the morning now seemed more worrisome than before.

As Battistelli stood by, Filomena Romanelli fluttered past him into her room and walked around it, nervously moving objects around, checking for missing belongings. She was shaking with the sense of violation: someone had emptied her closets, strewn clothes around on the floor, moved shopping bags, even thrown her laptop on the floor. But her jewelry was still intact in tiny velvet bags and little boxes, all the gold bracelets and necklaces and earrings safe.

Attention turned again to the locked door. The pale boy with the glasses said he had already tried to break it down, with no luck. Battistelli was reluctant to damage property. It was not clear to him that a crime had even occurred. Romanelli had said that nothing was missing. He was not authorized, as an inspector of phones and Internet crime, to wreck a door in the process of an unauthorized investigation. The state of alarm was growing, though. Filomena Romanelli stated that, contrary to what Battistelli thought the American girl had said, Meredith never locked her door. He later said he found this contradiction strange.

Luca Altieri, a friend of Romanelli's boyfriend, who had arrived on the scene with him, agreed to break down the door. Luca was a big young man. Six hard kicks and a shoulder, he estimated later, broke it down. Those looking on from the corridor registered the scene inside the little room in different ways. Some recalled only the disorder; others, a bare foot sticking out of the blanket on the ground; still others, the smears of blood on the wall, and the white bedsheet and the ghastly puddle of red pooling in the back of the room.

"*Un piede! Sangue!*" Someone shouted. *A foot. Blood.*

The boys grabbed their girls and backed out, crashing together in the tiny hallway, gasping for air once outside. Filomena's boyfriend, Marco Zaroli, stayed behind long enough to see Officer Battistelli, wearing Adidas sneakers, walk into the tiny bloody room, squat down, and lift the bloodstained blanket. Battistelli would later say he never looked at the body.

Marco suddenly felt sick and fled outside to be strong for his hysterical girlfriend.

Marco did not see what Officer Battistelli later claimed he never saw. It was a sight no member of the Italian Postal Police is really trained for: a pretty girl's face smeared with blood, her long hair sticky with blood, eyes wide open, glassy and dull, like a hooked fish's eyes, drained of the life that had exited, obviously, through a deep, still foaming gash on her neck. *Sgozzata*, Battistelli would later say, as would all the others—police, lawyers, Italian kids. *Sgozzata:* an Italian farmyard word meaning slaughtered with a knife to the neck, butchered like meat.

Alerted by the police activity, the local press was on the scene within the hour. Photographers gathered across the street and massed on the broad, curving stone steps high above the murder house, above the picturesque spray of pinkish terra-cotta roofs of the houses spilling onto one another down the hill toward the columned bulk of the University for Foreigners and the Piazza Grimana. The national newspaper *Il Messaggero*'s local photographer with his long lens captured the first pictures—click, click, click—of Amanda and her boyfriend, the pale boy named Raffaele Sollecito, sitting apart from each other on the backseat of Luca Altieri's car, headed to the police station. Raffaele, closest to the camera, is white and slack-jawed, practically walleyed, looking sick. Amanda stares straight ahead, poised and grim.

"See that," said the photographer, showing off his prize catch two years later, jabbing his finger at the digital image on his laptop. "See that? It's in his face, you can see it. He makes the perfect slave."

Schiavo. It's Italian for "slave" and the root of the all-purpose greeting *Ciao. Ciao-ciao,* Italians say, bye-bye, *I am your slave.* In macho Italy, to call a man a woman's slave is a serious charge, a low insult indeed.

ON THE RIDE TO the *questura,* the police headquarters, a modern turquoise-and-sand-colored complex at the bottom of the Perugia hill usually surrounded by lines of Africans, Albanians, South Americans, and Arabs seeking to legalize their immigrant status, Raffaele, from the backseat, asked Luca Altieri if he knew how Meredith had died. "I told him her throat was slit. *Sgozzata,*" Luca later testified. "And he asked, 'With a knife?' and I didn't answer, I just looked at him like he was an idiot. And after I did that, Amanda started crying."

SEATTLE

A happy person is such an unaccustomed and
holy creature in this sad world!

—*Nathaniel Hawthorne*

THERE IS THE SEATTLE EVERYONE knows: the Space Needle and Pike Place
Market selling organic purple potatoes and line-caught smoked salmon,
where boys with orange Mohawks brew organic free-trade coffee, where
at Danny's Wonder Freeze you can get a tofu hot dog. At the Seattle Art
Museum, you could have attended an exhibit in 2010 celebrating Kurt
Cobain linked with an Andy Warhol retrospective, the whole thing
called "Kurt & Warhol love fear pleasure lust pain glamour death."

Is life hard here? Not by comparison to Darfur or Kandahar, but
there is discontent in some quarters. Boredom. Not enough money in
the world to relieve it. Kids loiter, smoke, and panhandle on downtown
streets in plaid lumberjack jackets, nose rings, and stocking caps, the
uniform of the disaffected white lower-middle-class, young American,
whose life choices on a very bad day may be reduced to two: go gun

like Tim McVeigh and the Columbine boys or go Emo. Kurt, of course, found a way to do both without hurting anyone but himself.

The Pike Place Market. After two-and-a-half years in an Italian prison, convicted of murder and with her once rosy future reduced to a twenty-six-year prison term, Amanda Knox wrote a letter from her Umbrian prison cell remembering the market, the city buses, and her attitude toward smiles:

I have to say I never realized how much it [Seattle] is a part of me, until it was forcibly taken away from me. I think of the public market, which, on good days is buzzing with colors, smells and somewhat chaotic life. I feel like I look at everything that way, as if everything is colorful and interesting and the best things are tucked into nooks that overlap each other, or else are calling out, singing into the street. If anything could be called a "haunt" of mine, it would have to be the public market. I hope you were able to weave through the tunnels, get lost, as I myself have done many times (I have a horrible memory and sense of direction if only because, in looking, I see and then move on to the next thing to see without so much as cataloguing it as being imprinted by its profile and my intuitive feelings about it). Another "haunt" is the public buses. A game I used to like to play was to see if I could make someone smile on the bus. Everyone who rides the bus usually has something on their mind and reflects with such intensity. Sometimes I saw the saddest faces. I would often see someone sitting on their own in their own intense sphere, and I would try to make them smile, either by smiling at them, or by more directly plopping myself right next to them and asking them how they were doing. As weird as that may sound, I've always thought it worth it to see someone smile. I'm in love with smiles. I think they are the most attractive things about a person. I'm drawn to them and I'm drawn towards inviting people to make them.

Pike Place is across a few bridges and highways from the University of Washington. In the so-called U District, streets are festooned with purple-and-white Huskies logo banners silkscreened with pictures of the rainbow-colored student body—Chinese, Africans, white kids—on the soccer fields, goggled up in the labs. Models of health and ambition. Then there's the Piece of Mind head shop on the U District's main drag, shelves lined with elaborate glass bongs of nearly Venetian delicacy and design and a dizzying choice of rolling papers. Next door at Tokyo Garden, the house special is teriyaki corn dog.

A short walk from the U District main drag is Terry Hall, the non-descript five-story concrete bunker of a dorm where Amanda Knox and her white hippie posse first formed out of a group of eighteen-year-olds cut loose for the first time from parents and reduced to anonymity and ID numbers within the massive state school system.

The streets around the U district are packed with yoga studios—they are at least as ubiquitous as Seattle's great gift to the world, Star-bucks, on the streets of other major American cities. In between the yoga studios the spiritually and physically infirm can visit storefront cure clinics run by naturopaths and acupuncturists and reiki and go practitioners. "DON'T BOTOX, DETOX," say the sandwich boards outside the offices where you can get a colon cleanse and a shiatsu treatment, maybe in the same room. On one block, there are East West Bookshop, gluten-free pizza, and cars with bumper stickers that say "ANTIHERO" and "VEGAN" and "MY OTHER CAR IS A BROOM."

A few miles away, in the industrial valley between Seattle and the Sound, under the West Seattle Bridge, at night the lights strung around the giant cement tanks look like Christmastime year round. Backlit white smoke billows dramatically against the night sky. One must cross this hazy, twinkling pit to get to West Seattle, the home of Seattle's true multiculture, working-class whites and Mexicans and blacks and Samoans—lots of Samoans, including the one made famous for hav-ing an affair with his pretty blond schoolteacher Mary Kay Letourneau when he was twelve years old, an affair that produced news and kids and ended in jail terms and then a happily-ever-after marriage.

Brown, black, yellow, and white. In West Seattle this rainbow slice of Americans lives in tiny wood houses, shops at Safeway, and gets quick cash from the Payday Loans outpost across the street from one of the great western nondenominational churches that make newborn Christians out of disaffected downsized divorced and spiritually hungry millennial Americans.

Arbor Heights, the part of West Seattle where Amanda Knox grew up, is not actually at any sort of "height" at all. It is mostly flat and not arboreal, one of those suburban expanses where whatever northwest pines once lined the shores of the Sound and still do in the region's tonier environs have long since been logged to make way for strip malls and blocks of small prefab houses with prefab plastic garages placed at the ends of short driveways to shelter the family car or boat from the salt and rain.

Arbor Heights, not Seattle, more Kurt Cobain than Bill Gates, was where the whole extended broken family lived—the whole Knox "clan," as the Kercher family's stylish Florentine lawyer, Francesco Maresca ("He's the one with the great hair," one American female journalist would sigh), always called them, using the word Italians associate with Mafia families.

The Knox clan is familiar to Americans: a hair on the low side of middle class, aspirational, pursuing their birthright—happiness—on the far edge of the continent, protected from the Pacific by a rim of gorgeous hills and Puget Sound. Huddled together, mixed blood, descendants of white-skinned immigrants. On these far-western shores, the short, doomed love story of Edda Huff and Curt Knox played out.

It was 1986; Robert Palmer's "Addicted to Love" was cranking out of every jukebox and car radio across the United States. "You like to think that you're immune to the stuff, Oh yeah, it's closer to the truth to say you can't get enough." If you were in your midtwenties, *the stuff* was all over and life was one long, hot party. Curt was two years older than she was, tall, built, blond, athletic. A real guy's guy. Into numbers, an accountant. Loved golf, skiing, and football and was proud to tell people that he had read exactly three books in his life so far—including the tax code and *The Swarm,* a novel about killer bees. Edda was a newly minted elementary school teacher, dark-haired, curvaceous, with a small nose, wide dark blue eyes, and a tiny charming overbite, a real beauty. She got pregnant right away, and Curt did the right thing. But before their first daughter was two, and with another baby girl on the way, he met someone else, a blonde named Cassandra with a cascading Farrah Fawcett haircut. Curt and Edda divorced in 1989, and Edda kept custody of toddler Amanda, and their infant second daugher, Deanna.

For Curt and Edda, party animals who came of age in the 1970s who hit the real-life wall much too soon in the 1980s, that was the end. Or, actually, it was the beginning of everything else.

"Both of the girls were unplanned, but you know, that was fine with me. I wanted a family," Edda said with trademark perkiness in 2009, time and fresh disaster having blurred the edges off the early crisis years. When Curt left her, they started fighting in court about money, and the battle was ugly and protracted. Edda turned to her mother, Elizabeth Huff, for domestic help. The Prussian-born Oma, as the grandkids eventually called her, had lost her own mother in an Allied bombing raid when she was only eight. She knew a few things about hard times.

Edda spent the first five years of her daughters' lives overwhelmed. "I was working full-time and getting a master's degree with two kids under five. I have no idea how I did it. I literally don't remember, I was that busy. Every night I would go to school, and my mom was there. She and I were so close. She adored the girls. Out of a year, I spent probably zero nights without her. She doesn't know how to cook for one. We'd hang out, watch TV, and she helped me with the babies."

When the girls were older, Edda relaxed a little and became a soccer mom. By the time Amanda was eight, Edda was behind the wheel of her Jeep, driving to games up and down the West Coast. Mother and daughters lived alone in the tiny house on the quiet corner of 37th Avenue and 99th Street.

Edda taught elementary school math, and for a while she had a laborer named Peter living with them in their tiny first house. When

Amanda was ten, Edda met Chris Mellas in the ultimate "meet-cute," on a Microsoft tech help toll-free line. Mellas, an IT expert, was a quiet Mexican American from Texas a dozen years younger than Edda. The romance worked, and they got married when Amanda was twelve. For years Edda pestered him about whether he might really, down deep, want kids, but he always insisted that he was happy with the two girls she already had and didn't feel the need to leave his genetic imprint on the world. He was a good stand-in for the absent dad, even if he was not Curt. He played guitar and got Amanda into it. He had a boat and fished in the Sound. He helped build out Edda's tiny house, adding a new wing so that by the time the girls were in middle school each had her own room, painted a favorite color. Amanda chose lemon yellow; Deanna, bright orange.

Still, Chris wasn't Curt: Curt who took his fun seriously, who still had read only three books by the time he was fifty. Curt knew that Amanda wanted to spend more time with him, and in the beginning he sometimes took the girls skiing. But things got so bad between him and Edda that even those excursions stopped before the girls were in high school.

IT'S UNUSUAL IN THE mobile West, in rootless America, to find all the relatives in a neighborhood together, still talking to one another, especially with a broken marriage, and for a while, they were not. The strong family bond came from the maternal side of the family, from Oma and her Harley-driving ex–U.S. Army husband, whom the kids called Opa. Oma and her children—Amanda's mom, Edda, and Aunt Christina and Uncle Mickey—all lived within five blocks of one another, each family inside one of the low, small wooden houses on their tiny lots, no sidewalks.

Less than a mile away from them, there was a newer house with slightly nicer landscaping—a saw palmetto to remind the owner of golfing in Palm Springs, some cedar mulch—on a street with fewer cars on the curbs because the garages are bigger. That was the home of

Amanda's dad, Curt; his second wife, Cassandra; and their two daughters, Ashley and Delaney, one paler and blonder than the other. (About the names: Amanda and her sister, Deanna, came first, before Curt had his change of heart about their mom and started his new family, but he purposely chose names beginning with A and D for his next two daughters, too.)

The girl who would become the famous pretty monster shuttled between those two houses, a mile and just the slightest degree of economic class apart, the oldest of two sisters without a dad at home. She and her sister walked across a few acres of concrete—cutting across the Safeway supermarket parking lot and the parking lot for Roxy's Casino (gambling is legal in some places in Seattle, on real estate with Indian rights still attached)—to Explorer West Middle School. Explorer West was where Amanda Knox's thespian inclinations found their first outlet. The blended Knox-Huff-Mellas families, the stepparents, the aunts and uncles, Oma and Opa, when he was alive, all came out and watched her perform.

In summer, they all went swimming in the salty public swimming pool, open late May to September, in breezy Lincoln Park along the Sound. Those summer afternoons, Amanda was always "the loudest" at the pool, recalled one relative. "The one who just had to be noticed." While everyone else was just out there enjoying the sun, "she just needed attention. She was not proud or vain, not like that. She would just . . . sit a certain way, wanting to be noticed. And always, always the loudest!"

Amanda was a thespian from the time she was one year old.

"It was always, 'Look at me, here I am,' she was always running into the room and—ta-da!—twirling and showing off. She loved the limelight."

The light she most loved was the pale blue of Curt Knox's eyes. She desperately wanted her dad's attention, couldn't get enough of it. But Curt had left Edda when he fell for Cassandra, a Macy's buyer, before any of the adults were even thirty years old. By the time his eldest child was ten, Curt had not one but four daughters. He had a lot else on his mind.

Curt could have left the neighborhood altogether, moved away from Arbor Heights, where, from the beach, he could see Vashon Island, where he'd grown up, the eldest and adopted son of a ski-binding engineer and artist. But instead he chose houses within walking distance of Edda and the girls.

Curt grew up in a creative, artistic family, but maybe because he was adopted, he wasn't like them at all. He knew when he was fifteen that he wanted to be an accountant, and he never deviated from that goal. He had no use for the arts; he was a balance-sheet kind of guy. Two colors worked for him: red and black. To save money at the divorce, he told Edda that if she ponied up for her own lawyer (the court was ordering him to pick up the legal tab) she could keep the kids on Christmases. It seemed like a good idea at the time, but Edda really stuck it to him. Edda's German family always celebrated Christmas on Christmas Eve, and there was no changing that, ever.

Because of that Faustian bargain, made in anger, desperation, and financial panic, the holidays were always the most awful days of every year for the four parents. Curt might have wanted to take his girls to Montana, to the mountains, on some of those sparkly Christmas Days, where his new wife's father had a cabin in the snow and snowmobiles and fun. But no way, Edda wasn't going to let those girls away for one single Christmas Eve, and so, if Curt did want to take Amanda and Deanna to Montana, they had to spend almost the entire Christmas *day* in the car, driving, then open presents in a rush and scurry back to West Seattle in time for the custody handoff.

The custody agreement and the money were, as is common in American divorce, legally mandated. Any deviation from the mandate opened gushers of emotion, especially dangerous when judges and money were involved.

Curt bore his cross in resentful silence, and the family seethed and simmered in the glow of the tree.

Amanda tried to be a good daughter. Correction: she tried to be a good son, the son Curt never had. Curt is a guy's guy, never happier than when tailgating a Huskies game or skiing up in the Cascades with his buddies, all of them sliding down the slopes, hooked up to Tuneage inside their helmets, CamelBak backpacks filled with margaritas—"love juice." All four Knox girls had turned out sporty—soccer, competitive diving, softball—requiring military scheduling and endless parental driving to practice and games. But they were also extremely girly girls, squealingly into Backstreet Boys and Jonas Brothers and fancy clothes and applying sticky pink lip gloss and sparkly eye shadow before they could ride bikes—all, that is, expect for the oldest daughter, who couldn't have cared less about clothes or hair. She was an eight-year-old boy in a gorgeous body, her high school friends teased. She was Curt's *boy*, the one who would put on the mitt and play catch with him, and she was his boy in another, even more important, sense, too: Amanda was the sole member of the gaggle of menstruating, jealous, bitchy, angry, loving, needy females around Curt who could keep her emotions in check.

That effort, given the tensions simmering among wife, ex-wife, and Curt, and the competing sisters, came with a price. Only a few people who watched her closely could see it. On the surface she was all smiles and practical jokes; impervious to rejection, disappointment, other people's issues; resistant to the most tempestuous emotional weather. She almost never cried. Even her best friend marveled at her stoicism, her ability to hold it together.

But there was this: "She just couldn't sit still. You could be talking to her, and she would suddenly just get up and play guitar or read or just walk out of the room. Just like that." Some of her relatives thought her fidgetiness came from the fact that "she needed to be the center of attention." When the focus turned away from her, she just scooted right out.

That need was never stronger than when Dad was around. She was always pranking him, always doing mischief, trying to get a laugh out of him, and, if not that, at least an angry glare. She poured extra salt on his food when his back was turned, sneaked up behind him and tapped him on the shoulder, then hid on the other side of him, only to pop into his face like a little jack-in-the-box. Sometimes she yanked the pillows out from behind him when he was on the couch with a beer in one hand and the remote in the other, just to get a reaction.

That was Amanda. She would just "do and deal with it later."

1
PERUGIA

They are polite to foreigners; pleasant, kind and always calm.
Perugians are cheerful during the hours of rest and tireless in their
work, but they are never expansive, nor is their gaiety ever
allowed to exceed certain limits.

—*Margaret Symonds Vaughan,* nineteenth-century British visitor,
author (at age twenty) of the first guidebook to Italy in English

AMERICANS HOLD DEAR A NUMBER of fantasies about Italy. There is the
foodie fantasy, involving extra-virgin olive oil and buffalo mozzarella
and Norcina sausage and fried zucchini flowers and Sicilian pastries,
washed down with Prosecco. There is the house-proud Tuscan villa fantasy. There is the art history fantasy, the fashionista fantasy, the George
Clooney at Lake Como fantasy, the Dolce Vita Nouvelle Vague 1963
Rome on a Vespa and in Ray-Bans fantasy, the find-an-Italian-lover-to-
cure-my-blues *Eat Pray Love* fantasy. There is the Mafia, Sopranos, Godfa-
ther, red sauce and checked tablecloth, guns and Guidos fantasy. There's

the big, all-American, cashing in the blue chips, divorce alimony fantasy embodied by Frances Mayes in her renovated Tuscan farmhouse, eating roasted figs "drizzled with cream" on pale blue plates laid on an old farmhouse table painted a shade of yellow found only in sunshine, a bottle of Pinot Grigio sweating in a bucket nearby.

Italy is indeed a beautiful, fantastic land, peopled by a race with a long and august history, packed with more art and culture than any other country in the Western world. Americans associate Italy with music and sculpture, wine and love, not gruesome murder. Americans know even less about the underside of Italian culture, the tense web between Mafia and government, the secret politics of the Vatican, the low-grade but bloody civil war between terrorists on the right and left that dominated the Cold War decades, and the Italian judiciary's liberal use of wiretapping, all of which lead the Italian public to practice "dietrology," literally, looking behind, and assuming that conspiracies are behind all crimes.

On the sunny side, the nation's undeniable charms have seduced northern Europeans for centuries. The British especially have fallen under its glorious spell. Whole swathes of Tuscan countryside, conquered by the pound sterling in recent decades and inhabited by British expats, are dubbed "Chiantishire." Traditionally, the stiff upper lip drools here, the reserve melts. The poet Lord Byron lost his sense of discrimination in Italy, falling in love with every woman he saw in Venice before he perished. The naval hero Horatio Nelson, a staunch man of duty, came to Italy, and fell in love with another woman, not his wife.

Italy, wrote the native culture chronicler Luigi Barzini in the 1950s, gives outsiders of a certain age and ilk, "middle-aged and resigned people, the sensation of being, if not young again, at least daring and pleasing to others, and the illusion that they could still bite the fruits of life with their false teeth." Italy has changed since Barzini, but that aspect remains. Contemporary expats living in Rome, some who would cover Amanda Knox's trial, still wax rhapsodic over the possibilities of complicated middle-age love lives, of assignations with *amanti* in the shadows of classical antiquity and long, lazy lunchtime hours spent lolling in bed with illicit lovers.

American tourists come to Italy without time for stolen afternoons with lovers, rarely encountering the pale-blue-linens Italy. The Italians they meet are like them, a little tired, tense, and hot, jostling children into line at gelaterias in summer. These Italians live on the average national income of 1,000 euros a month and maybe bunked with their parents until age forty. These Italians are the chief consumers of the *cronache nere,* and they are the Italians who would, ultimately, come to know and judge Amanda Knox.

In the fall of 2007, Italians watched the dark blond Amanda Knox on TV, kissing her boyfriend as her roommate lay dead in a crime scene just yards away. The video clip looped on national television for months. So did video of the Knox family arriving on Italian soil. Fleeing the cameras, Curt Knox, with his stiff walk and gritted teeth, resembled George W. Bush with his peacock strut and gunslinger jaw. Italians saw a pale-skinned family honking American English out their noses. Italians train their dogs in English and German because the languages sound more forceful.

Of the nations around the Mediterranean, Italy may actually be the country with the most natural affinity for the United States. Italians share Americans' distrust of government, if for different reasons. And the lowbrow cultural phenomenon of state television in Silvio Berlusconi's Italy, shamelessly glorifying celebrity over substance, is only the clarified essence of American pop culture.

Italians do like Americans, but it's not unconditional love. The good karma Americans earned by liberating Europe from the Nazis expired a generation ago, rekindled briefly after 9/11, and then was snuffed out like a Marlboro under a Gucci boot when W bombed Afghanistan and invaded Iraq.

Italians in the fall of 2007 had reason to be even more disgusted with official, warlike, imperial America than the rest of Europe. In 1998, America's marine flyboys, flying dangerously low as part of a daredevil game they sometimes played, sliced the cables of two gondolas carrying skiers on a ski lift in the Dolomites in the middle of ski season. Twenty skiers died, and the United States invoked a NATO rule to keep the Italians from prosecuting the responsible marines, who were acquitted of involuntary manslaughter in the United States. Left-leaning Italians had long resented U.S. bases on Italian soil. The disaster, which Italians call the *strage del Cermis*—the Slaughter of Cermis, after the mountaintop where it happened—made the American bases even less popular.

In 2005, American soldiers "friendly-fired" on a car in Baghdad carrying a Secret Service agent and an Italian journalist who had been held hostage for months by Iraqi Islamists. The agent—already a hero in Italy—died on the spot. The journalist was wounded but survived. Again, no one was punished.

Italians are compassionate people who love children and care for their poor and infirm. They watched the televised drowning of New Orleans in the fall of 2005 with horror and disgust. Most Europeans already have strong notions of American racism, implanted by years of televised imagery of police brutality, dogs set on civil rights marchers, the assassination of Martin Luther King, Jr., and the ugly fact of slavery at the nation's core. As they watched the waters rise around the Louisiana Superdome, Italians' native compassion was offended by the United States' disregard for its poorest.

In April 2010, the *Newsweek* travel writer Seth Stevenson penned an article advising Americans how to be more discreet about their nationality, which he deemed a useful skill for Terror War–era global travelers:

> So how do you avoid coming off American? In general, you should shun corporate logos, stick to blandly neutral colors, and—I can't emphasize this enough—don't ever wear white tube socks. In particular, don't wear them with knee-length shorts and a pair of overdesigned running shoes. That outfit is a dead giveaway that you hail from the land of the free and the home of the brave. (Also known as the land of the baseball cap and the home of the baggy khaki trousers. Better ditch those, too.)

The American stereotype is problematic enough for seasoned travelers, let alone a twenty-year-old girl in jail and a provincial family coming over to get her out. The stereotype is even more complicated for American women. Italians had no trouble believing that Amanda Knox shared the druggy recklessness that distinguished young American womanhood in the eyes of Europe in 2007, exemplified not by Jean Seberg in *Breathless* but by Paris Hilton, Britney Spears, Lindsay Lohan.

Most Italian girls don't engage in sports. Soccer—*calcio*—is taken seriously and played by men, not schoolgirls. If women go to the gym, what happens there stays there. They wouldn't think of breaking a sweat in public. In Seattle, Amanda Knox was habituated to breaking into a downward dog wherever the urge to have a stretch overtook her—on the street, in a restaurant, at a party. When she did cartwheels and yoga stretches in the police station, Italians could only compare her moves to the provocative poses struck by the television *veline*—jiggly showgirls, a hallmark of Berlusconi-era television, who didn't speak but giggled and danced in G-strings during breaks in programming to keep viewers from changing the channel.

Amanda and the Knox "clan" had no pale blue linens in their dining rooms back in Seattle. In Italy, they were among the *agriturismo* Americans, in Italy on the cheap. They encountered the cypress-shrouded lawns and gardens of the Chiantishire villas only if they took a wrong turn in their rented Fiat Panda, and later, the used Ford Fiesta they were given by German relatives when it looked as though they'd have to stay in Umbria for an extended and indefinite period of time.

IT'S A LANDLOCKED MOUNTAIN town, a medieval fastness deep in the heart of Umbria, about equidistant from Rome and Florence, midway between the two seas. Its streets are so steep and its many stairways so pitched and crooked that nonnatives are perpetually out of breath and off balance. Pig is and has been for centuries the main source of protein, consumed dried, baked, cubed, sausaged, roasted, eaten almost daily;

fresh fish is a rarity. The city has been on its hillside for two millennia at least, a staunch construction of ancient brick and rock, walled in, built originally by the Etruscans, overrun by the Romans, lorded over by feudal powers, and brutalized by popes when it was one of the rebellious Papal States before and after the Renaissance.

Perugia was an Umbrian settlement, first recorded in 309 B.C. as one of the twelve confederate cities of Etruria. The people that built and named it, the Etruscans, were probably a mixture of Mediterranean peoples from Babylon and Greece who had immigrated to Italy and who thrived before ancient Rome, but their language and culture died after the Roman conquest. Historians believe that the Etruscans gave ancient Rome whatever it possessed of a soul. The Romans vanquished the Etruscans but retained aspects of their more ancient religion. Etruscan priests and augurers were early Roman spiritual leaders.

Some Umbrians today still claim Etruscan bloodlines, and sometimes one can see the resemblance between certain faces on the street and the large-eyed visages with level brows and flattish noses that decorate the frescoed tombs, cinerary urns, and vases in local museums. But their culture is long gone. All that's left of them now are the great stone blocks that form the bases of some of the oldest buildings in the city. The greatest of those, the Etruscan arch marking the entrance to the via Ulisse Rocchi, across from the University for Foreigners, is less than a hundred yards from 7 via della Pergola.

The ancient city's remains lie mostly below ground, in great tombs and tunnels. The archaeological museum at Perugia is piled with Etruscan white stone cinerary urns, many engraved with the same mythological scene: the sacrifice of Iphigenia, the daughter of Agamemnon, offered to appease the forest/fertility goddess Artemis win sea battles. In some tellings of the myth, Artemis switches in a deer for Iphigenia at the last minute, saving her life and making her a temple priestess. Archaeologists who study the Etruscans have no idea why that particular myth was so important to them. Possibly it had something to do with maternal mortality. Iphigenia was the subject of one of antiquity's greatest "heroine" cults, and one of the most worshipped female figures in ancient Greece.

Perugia's spires and sunset colors—ocher, rust, terra-cotta—date to the Middle Ages and have inspired painters and writers for centuries. Its churches contain museum-quality art from the early Renaissance, when one of the era's greatest painters, Pietro Vannucci, known as Perugino, lived there. Creative people who find themselves there today complain that the city retains a feudal mind-set that resists creativity and change. Even Italians working in the local government, university, and hospital systems don't stand a chance of advancement within the system if they are not Perugian-born.

In 1766, the French astronomer Joseph Jérôme de Lalande published the first description of Perugia by a foreigner, in *Voyage en Italie*. He noted that the inhabitants were "still a little savage" nursing medieval blood feuds and hatreds. There was an upside for him, though, one that remains a consolation for the similarly disposed male visitor to Perugia today. "I have been assured," Lalande wrote in 1766, "that in recent years the brothels or meeting places where ladies go each night, have served to mitigate local customs and to render the society more open and tolerable, and the young more amiable. As for myself, I cannot be less than satisfied with the courtesy I have received."

Modern Perugia is a university town with forty thousand students who annually come from all over Italy and the world. The natives and the *stranieri*—the Italian word for "foreigners" is also the word for "strangers"—don't mingle much in Perugia, except in the matter of paying for room, board, and entertainment.

When Americans come to Perugia, after laboring uphill from parking lots lower on the mountain, they reach a broad, windy hilltop street, Corso Vannucci, named after the painter. The corso is a long, mostly car-free plaza, a stone expanse linking the thirteenth-century duomo at one end and, at the opposite end, the luxury Hotel Brufani Palace and a small green park with a fountain and a graceful marble balustrade overlooking the flats to the east and the industrial suburbs, framed by mountains. Assisi, Perugia's traditional enemy and moral opposite, the city of Saint Francis, is a white settlement on the sloping side of bald Mount Subasio, about twenty miles away.

Perugia is an exotic side trip for tourists, not on the standard Italy tour, and visited mainly by the more intrepid or moneyed or sophisticated. It has always been white-stoned Assisi's rival, and even today, more tourists visit the city of Saint Francis. Those who do make the trip from Assisi to Perugia find a stark contrast in its stone doorways engraved with pentacles and mysterious symbols that once represented the alchemists' dream of turning lead into gold.

Visitors to Perugia inevitably experience the elegant, art-filled city as disorienting and mysterious. That most unromantic of Americans, Henry James, advised travelers to "set haste aside and calmly wander through the city streets, giving an esoteric meaning to almost everything he might happen upon."

It is drenched in the layered mysteries of the Etruscans, the medieval monastic orders, the alchemists, and the Freemasons. Pagan traditions lasted here well into the Christian era, possibly because of the city's strong Etruscan roots. The sacred coexists easily with the profane. The blackened steps of via delle Streghe, the Street of Witches, twist downhill to a lawn where junkies nod on the grass in front of the pale green and flesh pink sixteenth-century chapel dedicated to San Francesco. Nearby, another steep path winds around an ancient fig tree, tangled with berry vines, knotted together with a walnut tree, all three annually shedding the biblical fruits of plenty.

Besides the characteristics of a pagan and Catholic past, Perugia is filled with relics of medieval sorcery, with many dark nooks, dead-end lanes, shadows, and streets named after the witch, the moon, the cross, the thorn. A historical interaction with the macabre is commingled with the mortar between its bricks.

Perugia reveres three main patron saints, each martyred in a fantastically grisly way. The chief local saint, Ercolano, was a Perugian bishop, never a Catholic saint. His name comes from the pagan god Hercules, and the origins of his legend lie in the lost years of the Dark Ages, when rampaging Goths besieged Perugia for weeks. The city was utterly exhausted, and Bishop Ercolano had the idea of feeding an ox the remains of the city's wheat and, throwing it over the city walls, to fool the Goths into believing the siege was failing and supplies were still abundant. But a small boy—dressed for some mysterious reason as a deacon—peered over the city walls and revealed to the besiegers the true level of misery and starvation within.

The Goths renewed their siege and captured Ercolano, skinned and decapitated him, and threw his body over the walls, along with that of a dead child. Forty days later, survivors returned to find the child's body decomposed but the bishop's corpse intact, neither skinned nor decapitated. Perugians venerated Ercolano so fervently that one eighteenth-century Italian writer said, "They believe more in Saint Ercolano than in Christ; they think he is above even the most saintly of all Heaven's saints." Perugians still celebrate Saint Ercolano on March 1, always a cold, windy, and otherwise hopeless day on which, historically, prisoners were set free but that now is marked by solemn candlelit processions through the *centro*.

The city's other patron saint, Lorenzo, was one of the earliest Christian martyrs, roasted on a grill by the Romans. His uncomfortable final hour is commemorated in the stained glass of his namesake duomo. San Lorenzo is the patron saint of actors because, while being cooked, he retained the sangfroid to remark to his torturers, "Turn me over, that's not my best side." He is also the patron saint of cooks, for obvious reasons. And Lorenzo is associated with the pagan god of fire, Vulcan, the remains of whose temple are believed to be underneath the Perugia duomo.

The third patron saint is Bishop Costanzo, martyred in the third century near Foligno. Annually, on and around his day, January 29, Perugians consume a ring-shaped sweet bread called "torcolo di San Costanzo"—from the Italian word for twisting or wringing a neck—commemorating Costanzo's decapitation.

Perugia may be a central Italian provincial town, but it is unlike any backwater in America. Its natives, born and raised among priceless art and sophisticated ancient stonework, are steeped in religious and cultural history rife with decapitations, roastings, and skinnings; worship in jewel boxes of medieval and Renaissance churches; live and work in the Quattrocento artists' landscape of rolling hills and clear pale light. They tend olive groves whose trees produce some of the world's finest oil and vineyards that yield limited quantities of specialty wines and vinegars. The best of human civilization is on display everywhere one looks.

It is also isolated.

When the autostrada was built, Perugia lobbied to have it pass nearby, but it veered west to Arezzo instead. Driving from Perugia to Rome or Florence involves forty-five minutes on a rutted, perilous regional road whose soaring accident death rate is chronicled in lurid headlines in the daily paper.

A rusty regional train leaves Perugia every few hours, chugging like a pre–World War I steam locomotive at a snail's pace for half an hour or more, allowing ample time for contemplation of gorgeous scenery before finally linking up with a faster train that connects travelers to one of the major cities.

For tourists from within and outside Italy, Perugia's biggest draw is a relatively recent tradition, the Umbria Jazz festival, an annual two-week midsummer event begun in the 1960s, which has attracted American jazz greats such as McCoy Tyner and Herbie Hancock and has left in its wake a fine tradition of jazz music schooling. Tourists also flock to Perugia in October for the newer Eurochocolate festival, when thousands pack into the hilltop piazzas and pay top dollar for chunks of high-end chocolate and Styrofoam cups of thick, rich *cioccolato caldo* topped with a glop of *panna*—full-fat whipped cream.

The Corso Vannucci is lined with medieval buildings housing glass-fronted shops—Sisley, Intimissimi, Timberland—selling designer clothing at astronomical prices. Perugians take their clothes seriously. Cheap clothes are relegated to the weekend flea markets. There are no vintage clothing stores in Italy. Used clothes that would fetch a nice price in the Seattle thrift stores Amanda Knox frequented are preserved for the grandchildren or chucked into the trash.

As genteel as those shops seem, Anglophones venturing into their perfumed confines are always startled to hear uncensored American rap music on the speakers, a stream of jarring *shits*, *fucks*, *bitches*, and *whores* that eerily never shocked proper Italian mothers with children in tow.

Perugians call their city *tranquilla*—the Italian word for calm. To them, the *caso Meredeet*—the Meredith case—was an atypical event that the media seized upon, blighting the city's reputation. A gruff old bartender at the Piazza Grimana, located less than a hundred yards from the murder house, was so fed up with people asking about the crime two years after it happened that he started shouting in Italian, "Murders happen every day! You'd think this girl was Jesus Christ!"

Perugia is home to the University of Perugia, founded in 1308 and educating about thirty thousand students annually, mostly from south and central Italy, and the University for Foreigners, with another ten thousand foreign students studying the Italian language and culture. The student population gives the city a vitality that its large, sedate neighbors—Assisi, Foligno—lack.

The University for Foreigners was founded in 1921 as part of a Fascist effort to promote Italian culture, but the student body in more recent years has distinguished itself for more scandalous reasons. Besides Amanda Knox, other infamous alumni include Mehmet Ali Ağca, the attempted assassin of Pope John Paul II, and an unknown number of other Middle Eastern citizens who used the student visas as entry cards to join up with a militant Islamic group that was, until recent years, operating out of a mosque below the city. Albanian criminal gangs have also posed as students to get into Italy. The university has since restricted applicants to individuals who have been cleared through the government first.

Perugians have a love-hate relationship with the students. They like the income they bring in but not the "foreign" element that comes along with the transient population. Many have fled the *centro* because at night their town center is not as *tranquillo* as it appears at *mezzogiorno*—midday. In warmer weather, Albanian and Moroccan gangs have knife fights over turf in the alleys. Junkies flock from Rome for the cheaper heroin on sale near the train station and loll on the duomo steps. Foreign college kids high on hash stumble around, wandering from café table to table, muttering *"Hai una sigaretta?"*

According to the local criminologists and magistrates, Perugia in recent decades has increasingly become central Italy's criminal trading post, appealing to international organized criminals because it is a less policed region halfway between Rome and the Adriatic Sea through which both women and drugs can be transported. Drugs, petty crime, break-ins, and prostitution are increasingly common. A few years back, the city was at the mercy of gangs of former Serbian mercenaries trained to scale walls, who robbed buildings by breaking through the upper windows. The police and press dubbed them *ladri acrobati*—acrobat thieves.

Though the drug sellers ply their trade openly on the duomo steps and in the shadows of the medieval lanes, the transvestites and female prostitutes almost never enter the *centro*. They stroll the streets on the flats below the city at night and rent rooms in the dingy, dirt-colored, earthquake-vulnerable box apartment buildings near the train station.

Tourists who don't read Italian pass the green wooden Perugia news kiosks with their sandwich boards advertising the day's headlines, oblivious to news of weird crimes involving blackmail and transsexuals, mothers who kill, murdered prostitutes, Mafia arrests, Mafia bombings, Mafia prosecutions, open-air killings somewhere down south, and ongoing updates from the war between the national kleptocracy and the judiciary trying to assert control.

The headlines provide a glimpse of mayhem at odds with the beauty of the city center. During the summer of the Kercher murder trial, a typical headline read, *"Prostituta Nigeriana rapita e ferita"* (Nigerian prostitute kidnapped and wounded). Prisoners burned beds and rioted at the overcrowded jail (where Amanda Knox was residing) five miles away. Mug shots of *altamente pericolosi* (highly dangerous) Albanians accompany stories about how they are being sought by authorities or deported for *droghe* (drugs). Screamer headlines keep count of the almost daily traffic deaths involving motorcyclists and drunk drivers on the surrounding country roads.

The headlines seem like fiction when perused over a coffee and brioche at the elegant outdoor tables around the Corso Vannucci in the clean, crisp mountain breeze. All of it happens out of sight of the *centro*—at least during the day.

PIAZZA

PART TWO

5
AMERICAN GIRL

Well she was an American girl
Raised on promises
She couldn't help thinkin'
That there was a little more to life somewhere else

—*Tom Petty, "American Girl"*

BESIDES THE MONEYED, VILLA-COLLECTING, ART and foodie, film-buff fantasy of Italy, there is the college exchange student fantasy, and that's the one Amanda Knox, University of Washington junior, Italian and creative writing major, had in mind when she left Washington in July 2007, just after her twentieth birthday.

Before she signed up as an independent student at the University for Foreigners in Perugia, an adventure she was paying for with her own money, Amanda had been a barista, an art gallery receptionist, a rock climber, and a self-described hippie, into hiking, theater, yoga, a little partying, and tea. She was scholarship-smart. Jesuit-educated. Dean's list.

And a writer.

From the age of eight, Amanda had been a compulsive journal keeper. She filled hundreds of pages in neat, rounded penmanship decorated with bunnies, smiley faces, and peace signs, leaving no margins. In her first month in prison, she filled seventy-eight pages of a diary and wrote countless letters before the authorities took her notebook away and put it into the investigative record.

"Graphomaniac," concluded one Italian criminal lawyer who met her in the early days. He'd never seen anything like it and advised a psychological analysis. Other defense lawyers disagreed, fearing a stint in an Italian madhouse would be worse for the girl than a provincial trial.

"She is a writer, and she will write her own book about this," Curt Knox always insisted. During his daughter's early months in prison, Italian authorities taped him telling Amanda that "a major editor" in New York was prepared to buy her book.

She has a natural knack for languages. She studied Japanese for a while and spent a few weeks in Japan while in high school. Growing up, she got a smattering of German from her Oma. She studied it in college. Then, in her sophomore year, she fell in love with Italian.

To get to Italy, Amanda worked several jobs—including one at a coffee bar and another as a receptionist in a U District art gallery where the items for sale included the owner-artist's book *365 Happy Meditations,* which featured "Only a cloud feels like a cloud," and "Happy are they that do not lose a childlike heart." She got her passport in order, bought her ticket, and signed up for school in Italy outside the auspices of the University of Washington exchange program. Amanda arranged her Perugia study scheme on her own. She explained her choice in a peace symbol–decorated letter to me in 2010, after she'd been convicted of murder.

Perugia I picked because it was a sister-city with Seattle, had a very specific language school, was right in the middle of Italy and was small enough that I felt I would be able to mingle with the Italian culture and

people. I chose it over Rome or Florence or Venis [sic] because I was ad-
vised that in larger cities it's too easy to stay within a group of Ameri-
cans, for instance, and it's harder to integrate. A small town forces you
to. Granted, I hadn't counted on Perugia to be so full of students, many
of whom wanted to practice their English with me. I had the same expe-
rience in Japan actually, while living with a Japanese family. I tried to
speak Japanese to them and they tried to speak to me in English.

She was ready to go in July.

FOR MOST OF HER life, Amanda explained herself to herself in her scribbled pages. She didn't spend much time looking for answers in front
of the mirror. After November 6, 2007, her written words, the aimless
scribbles, the doodles from the soul, the habit of trying to sort out her
thoughts on paper, became clues to back up the theory that the pretty
girl only *looked* naive, trusting, and innocent. The Miss Sunshine pod
concealed a psychopath who had waited until All Souls' Day to emerge.

In Seattle, it was easy enough to find people who remembered only
Amanda's lack of guile, the total absence of a dark side. Early on, British reporters with wads of cash to soften up sources scoured the town
looking for anyone who could share the real goods on the pretty psychopath. The best they got was a police report about a wild party at a small
house she had shared in the U District. Everyone in her hometown just
remembered the *I'm in love with smiles* Amanda.

Brett Lither knew Amanda Knox as well as anyone in Seattle. Born
a few months apart, growing up within walking distance of each other
in West Seattle, they joined the same soccer team when they were eight
years old and became best friends. On the field and off. Amanda played
stopper, Brett played sweeper. Their team was so good, the parents
drove the girls to competitions miles up and down the West Coast. On
seventeen-hour drives south to Sacramento, they passed the hours listening to the Back Street Boys. Amanda wasn't a fan of the boy bands;

she preferred older bands that her parents liked—one of her weird quirks, in Brett's opinion. But she knew sign language, and she could sign the words to an entire Destiny's Child song. That helped pass the time in the backseat.

Before they were teenagers, Amanda and Brett played "Jungle Barbie," a private joke they made up. The idea of their big-breasted girly dolls on rough adventures cracked them up. Brett thought Amanda was kind of a tomboy. She loved nature and wouldn't even kill a big spider.

"Amanda and I, I hope it doesn't sound offensive, we were truly little white suburban girls from West Seattle." Before Amanda left for Italy, "the only travel we had done really was travel for soccer, which wasn't travel. That was driving to a field, do our job, and go home. And eat at Subway. Amanda and I, just very middle-class suburban girls. We were very naive. Trusting. Very, very, very trusting. Amanda was unconventional. She was weird, but in a truly harmless sense. Goofy. Even more naive and trusting than you could imagine. *Über*-nice. Like, she would walk down a street, and if she had money in her pocket she'd take it out and count it in public. She wouldn't be aware of the fact that maybe you shouldn't count your three hundred dollars in a trashy alley. She could be very oblivious."

Amanda, Brett thought, wouldn't get angry even when she should have. Amanda's dad, Curt, would do things to get back at Edda, like take his two older daughters on lavish shopping trips. They'd be thrilled, Brett recalled, because they thought he was rich, and he'd let them buy whatever they wanted.

Edda was a teacher, and before she met her second husband, she struggled to support herself. They were just "super dirty poor," Brett thought. The difference between her mom and dad's two houses and lifestyles was stark, but Amanda never blamed Curt. She never said, "I hate my dad," even when he and Edda were at each other's throats.

"Amanda was just unbelievably resilient and forgiving," her friend said. "She never said, 'My dad's so vain and really messed up, and I'm not going to talk to him,' but she would be, like, 'He's my dad. I'm going to go play catch with him now.' And I don't know if maybe she was just oblivious at the end of the day to it or what.

"There were these weird things that happened throughout her life, but she'd never really sit down and wallow. She was always so happy-go-lucky. So forgiving. I didn't talk to her once for three months because I went through a really weird phase or whatever, and afterwards, she was, like, 'Where were you?' I said, 'Don't know, just being weird.' She was, like, 'Okay.' She was very forgiving."

In front of her friends, Amanda "didn't spend time exuding negative energy." Brett saw her cry only a few times. Maybe because Amanda was so rarely sad, Brett never forgot it. "One of the times it happened, it had to do with her sister. Her sister and she had been fighting and fighting and fighting. And Amanda just broke down. She just wasn't of sound mind then. Who is when they completely break down? And she would just . . . I can't really fully articulate or explain it. She just wouldn't—she'd just sit and cry in this way that I didn't think anyone could cry that hard. She'd just cry and cry and cry. I'd never seen her like this before. She must have been like ten. I saw her break down like that a few other times. So I can just understand how maybe in the interrogation room she was trusting, really trusting in the beginning, and then when people started pushing and pushing and dropping threats. I can see how she'd probably just crumble. Just kind of went into hysterics, crying. Maybe just say whatever she needed to say to get out of there. She was seemingly a strong person, but I don't think she is."

BOTH GIRLS WERE ACCEPTED to Seattle Prep, an expensive, highly rated Jesuit high school. Amanda got a scholarship. Most kids at Seattle Prep had parents who were doctors or lawyers or tech millionaires, and they lived in rambling, flower-shrouded Victorians with magical views over Seattle all the way to the Sound. They didn't have a clue about life across the twinkling industrial pit, about growing up in an eight-hundred-square-foot prefab in West Seattle. Amanda didn't even try to fit in with them. She found her niche among the geeks and theater kids. She sang in the choir and belted out songs on stage in *The Sound of Music*. She was not easily embarrassed. She didn't care about clothes. She even pulled off a passable British accent for hours at a time in a production of *Honk*.

She wasn't a looker in high school, but she wasn't without boy admirers. She just didn't have much use for them—yet. "There were tons of boys in that high school that were stalker-y in love with her," her friend Brett Lither said. "And she was just not into it. None of these were boys who were, you know, good dating material, but she was still so nice. She was so *dumb*! Like, she didn't understand that you couldn't just be nice to everyone. She'd still be nice to people, even if they were creepy." She was not a girly-girl. Schoolmates at Seattle Prep thought she might be a lesbian. On her Myspace page she named her mother as her hero. From her jail cell in spring 2008, she wrote Brett when Barack Obama beat Hillary Clinton in the Democratic primary, "Does this mean America is more sexist than racist?"

Brett, who always liked to curl her hair and wear lip gloss, had to instruct her friend in the ways of teen style. "We were preparing for our first day of high school together, and I fought with her to do her hair, to dress up. I begged her, I said, 'We're gonna be cool. She wouldn't have any of it. She was very natural. Not into makeup. If you wanted to put hair spray in her hair, you'd have to chase her down. And I hated her because she was naturally beautiful. She had perfectly clear skin until, I want to say, the end of middle school and high school, then both of us started getting acne but did Accutane. And her skin cleared up in high school, but she didn't have any boyfriends. Guys liked her, but she wouldn't really get it. She was much more into playing soccer, writing and reading and drama class. She was not boy crazy."

AMANDA'S HIGH SCHOOL ENGLISH teacher, Kris Johnson, found her student sensitive and "longing to undo" evil and sorrow. "I make everybody do a poetry project," Johnson told a Seattle monthly. "Students choose a poet and analyze their work. Amanda was drawn to the poetry of Sylvia Plath, whose biography affected her greatly. The suicide"— Plath stuck her head in a kitchen oven and died of carbon monoxide poisoning—"and the fact that she left behind two young kids really bothered Amanda. She came to my office to wade through these issues. Plath was a very real person to her, and Amanda was longing to undo things that had been done."

Amanda and Brett continued playing soccer on the Seattle Prep team, enduring four bleak, losing seasons. Teenage girls were nastier on the field, too. "When you get old enough, girls will say things to you," Brett said. "I remember this girl said the most profane thing ever to Amanda on the field. And she'd get really fired up and play really well, but she'd never respond physically. She was really the most nonviolent person ever."

To get across the geographical and class divide between West Seattle and Seattle Prep, Amanda rode the bus to school, or Chris or Edda or Brett's parents drove. She wasn't much of a driver herself. She never caught on to the finer points of parallel parking, and she had a lead foot on the gas pedal and kept getting pulled over for speeding. By default, her transportation means were bike or bus.

When she graduated from high school in 2005, Amanda's adviser was a little surprised that she didn't choose to apply to some of the more prestigious East and West Coast schools, like the rest of the smart kids at Seattle Prep. It wasn't a choice; it had to do with money, most likely. She had to earn it herself. When she was arrested in Perugia, she had $4,457 in her bank account, which would have to last her for a while. She knew how to be frugal.

She could have taken a soccer scholarship to Washington State— "Wazoo"—the party school in Pullman, on the other side of the Cascades range. She opted for the more sober and sophisticated University of Washington in Seattle instead, just a long bicycle ride away from her mom's and dad's houses.

In the narrative of the girl monster, all that pent-up class rage was another motivation to murder the sophisticated British girl. If so, she never let her friends in on it. All those years, so many reasons to be furious, and she never got angry. Not even when she should have.

Agreeable to a fault.

Freshman year at "U-dub," right away, she began defining herself as a hippie—as opposed to a preppy, a sorority girl, a jock, a science geek, or any of the other myriad categories that the massive student body was breaking into. She also had sex for the first time with a guy named Kyle. It was traumatic, though, because Kyle ended up being a cad. "They had sex, and then Kyle left her. She was devastated because then he started dating her roommate. I was angry, and I tried to convince her to be angry. She was just hurt. I was like, 'You shouldn't be hurt. You should be pissed.' Vengeful? Never."

She did smoke pot, maybe starting in the second half of her senior year at Seattle Prep, when her English teacher noticed a subtle decline in classroom enthusiasm, or maybe the summer before college, when her family began hearing rumors of wild parties. But before she left for Italy, she had by all accounts not approached the level of drug use associated with the common American college pothead.

"I'll be honest about the pot smoking," said one close friend. "If anything, I think her smoking should be proof that she wasn't involved at all. Because high people don't go on sex-crazed killing sprees. They sit on the couch and stare into space. Amanda did not have an addictive personality in any way. The only thing she was addicted to was the hiking and being in nature. Being healthy. She always wanted me to eat more. She was, like, 'You're too thin.' She was just very into being healthy, in the sense of healthy, not looking skinny or superhot.

"I was completely opposed to pot smoking when she first did it, in college, I think. But then I tried smoking for the first time, and she wouldn't do it with me. She tried it. Did it a couple of times here, didn't really like it. I guess she had tried it and drank and ended up throwing up. And she was, like, 'Oh, I never want to smoke again.' She never smoked it a lot, but if her friends were doing it I think she would. If her housemates were having a party, maybe she'd smoke a little pot. But she got to a point before she left for Italy where people offered her pot—even me—and she wouldn't do it. And then when she went to Italy, well, you're in Italy. Do what every American girl does there: get fucked up. Even if she did drink or smoke, after that one time where she ended up throwing up, she never would do it in excess, she never would get superhammered, never would get superhigh. They had a stupid YouTube video of her saying something like 'I'm hammered off a shot and a half.' She literally would get hammered off a shot and a half." That video is still on the Internet.

In college, Amanda made new friends and became very close to a redhead from Colorado, Madison Paxton, a fallen-away Mormon interested in photography and women's studies. After Amanda was arrested, Madison became one of two college friends deputized by the family to speak to the media. She came off as serious and levelheaded, and after the verdict she decided to move to Perugia, where Rocco Girlanda got her a job at the local newspaper. She conceded that her friend had what pop psychology calls boundary issues.

To Madison, Amanda was simultaneously "too blunt" and "extremely naive"—an odd combination of a tough hide on a gentle spirit. "She isn't easily offended, so she doesn't understand that she offends other people," Madison said after Amanda had been in jail three years and counting. "It's hard to explain the contradictory personality. She can be loud and offensive, yet she is nonconfrontational. Her boundaries are 'out here,' and she doesn't understand that other people's are 'in here.'"

Before she left for Perugia, Amanda added a major in creative writing to her college plan. Creative writing as a field of study doesn't exist in Italian schools. It wouldn't occur to Italian educators to nurture the spilling of dreams, thoughts, whimsical fragments, fantasies, and perversions that in the United States may be regarded as the juvenilia of the next Great American Novelist. Italian first graders are taught to perfect their cursive letters before they can read printed text, and they are graded not on comprehension but on the neatness of their script. American first graders are taught to write anything they want to without paying attention to spelling, grammar, or backward letters. The two systems veer further apart as children grow. Italian grammar school children who have learned cursive soon begin copying out passages from Dante and Saint Francis, word for word. In the United States, children who can write are encouraged to tell stories about what they did over the weekend or to make up stories about dragons, elves, baseball, and video games—whatever strikes their fancy. The different methods have different outcomes, not always favorable to the Yankee side of the Atlantic. Most Italian high schoolers can recite Dante. The convicted murderer and high school dropout Rudy Guede even cited a few lines of the Italian bard in his prison writings. American teens would be hard pressed to spout a single Shakespearean couplet.

Teachers had encouraged Amanda Knox from a young age to continue to write, write, write, and to regard every word as precious. Edda had a special shelf for the dozens of diaries and journals. Amanda thought of herself, by the time she was twenty, as a writer. She was proud enough of her efforts that she posted two of her short story exercises on her Myspace page in 2007 before leaving for Italy.

Those two short stories, out of the reams of pages Amanda had filled in her years as a scribbler, provided the world a glimpse into the inner working, maybe the subconscious, of the sunny girl. It was not at all as pretty as she was. Like everything else she posted, no one knows why she chose those stories. They deal with rapes, self-cutting, voyeurism, and domestic violence, but their most striking aspect is an intense, detailed description of the physical sensation of suppressed rage.

One of the stories, titled "Baby Brother," features a rapist villain named Kyle—perhaps not coincidentally also the name of the college boy who took the author's virginity and then dumped her for a roommate. The narrator, Kyle's older brother, Edgar, seethes with suppressed rage. He picks at hidden scabs under his arms, where he's been self-cutting since grade school. Confronting his brother about the rape, his "burning rage pulsated in his forehead, chest and throat." Later, he "felt the tightness of his brow ease and he swallowed a large, slippery gulp of the aching, burning rage . . ."

In one section, Edgar confronted his brother about a rape. Kyle responds, "A thing you have to know about chicks is that they don't know what they want."

In the second short story, titled "The Model," a young girl named Aislinn (possibly named after a soccer-playing Aislinn one year older than Amanda at Seattle Prep) is part of a triangle with her mother, the story's narrator, and the mother's ex-boyfriend, a creep who stalks them and secretly snaps pictures of them while they are asleep and who may have raped Aislinn.

Again, Amanda wrote line after line trying to describe the physical manifestation of hidden rage: "Feelings that left me hollow in my chest like my insides had been poured out of my mouth" and a feeling "hard and strange, almost like a wounded animal, which had been clawing at your insides, had finally found its way out, and the empty feeling of the space it had left bubbled up inside, and then disintegrated." The story is packed with disturbing mechanical and insect images: "I was a machine," she wrote, and the narrator's hands worked the keyboard "like crafty spider legs," and other people moved "like ants."

To the press, the stories' sinister images and themes confirmed the presence of a Mr. Hyde buried inside the smiling girl who never got angry and who, even after her arrest, kept a prison diary filled with pop-song platitudes, doodles of peace signs, random lists of things such as "My Values" (Friendship, Compassion, Ambition, Intelligence, Workmanship, Love), schoolgirl ruminations on faith versus atheism, and plans for a coming-home party in Seattle.

Curt had no idea where his oldest daughter got her literary bent, only that it certainly was not from him. He reckoned it was her way of coping. "Amanda, since she was this high"—Curt gestured to his thigh—"she wouldn't say she was angry. She doesn't confront. She writes down her emotions. She wants to be nice. Helpful."

Curt's own attitude toward life was never too introspective, although that changed a bit after his daughter became a world-famous accused and then convicted murderess. Hard times hit him from every side. While Amanda was on trial, he was downsized out of his Macy's job, and headhunters in Seattle wouldn't touch him with a ten-foot pole once they'd Googled his name. Still, he had a second chance to emotionally support Amanda—which he did by mortgaging his house and traveling to Italy regularly, toting over suitcases full of Manwich sloppy Joe sauce and Hamburger Helper so he wouldn't have to eat Italian food. In Italy, he learned at least one important fact about himself, he said: "I hate old." Old included Renaissance art, churches, medieval buildings, and the Latin-based language itself, which neither he nor any member of the family besides Amanda tried to learn.

In Italy, when he was not visiting his daughter or the lawyers, Curt was on the couch in the tiny *agriturismo* apartment twenty miles from the prison, navigating the remote to American sports channels on the satellite television, trying to catch a pro football or baseball game. Back in West Seattle, he made sure he had his younger girls covered. He surreptitiously installed GPS tracking on their phones. It wasn't that he distrusted his daughters, he just didn't trust their dates. "Boys," he said with a rueful smirk, "are bad for girls."

IN COLLEGE, ALMOST OVERNIGHT, the chubby theater geek turned into a curvaceous beauty. She still dressed like a hippie, but she was now becoming aware of her effect. For the first time in her life, she held the male gaze. It was simultaneously exhilarating, intoxicating, and confusing, like smoke.

In the months before she left the United States, the girl the Italian press would call the *ragazza americana* crafted her own "Foxy Knoxy" Myspace page. Her family and friends would say the name was a totally innocent joke, based on a childhood soccer club nickname, referring to the way she ran on the field, low and fast. But the twenty-year-old Amanda couldn't have been oblivious to the "adult" connotations attached to the old nickname when she crafted her web page. Wink.

Blogging in the summer of 2007, she portrayed herself as a girl answering the call of the wild Italian style. By October 15, she had posted a picture of a naked Italian man identified only as "Federico" she'd met on a train, had written about "smoking up" with her sister, and was extolling the delights of the three-hour Italian lunch break. "I love it. I wish we had that in America. I think Americans work too much and don't live. Having that time in the middle of the day reminds you that life really isn't all about going to work and making money. It's about who you are and what you choose to do and who you choose to spend your time with."

From the website, an early journal of her travels in Italy:

plane was chill, and the train wasn't hard. in fact, met a guy named frederico [sic] on the train to florence from milan, and we ended up hanging out together in florence, where he bought both deanna and i dinner and then, when deanna went to bed, we smoked up together, my first time in italy. . . . took pictures early the next day of neptune's fountain and naked david, conveniently located right next to each other. then the train the next day to perugia, wasnt bad. had a little adventure trying to find our hotel though. carrying everything on our back, deanna and i buy a map and discover that the hotel booked for us is actually as far on the edge of the map as it can get on some random little road that doesnt list it's whole name. 2 hours of hiking up and down perugia's hills, we were lost. deanna was drowning in her own sweat, and i was pissed to say the least. or at least hot. i just wanted to find this place, but it was ridiculous. then some 40-something italian guy pulls over and looks at our map. he offeres us a ride when he explains that it's another 20 minutes away by CAR and there is no bus to it. alright, ill risk my life to get to my hotel. so deanna and i pile in and we do indeed get to our hotel alive, the only awkward

part is when i have to try to explain to our driver in broken italian that
we aren't interested to going out with his 40-something year old self this
evening.

Wandering around sweating in the September sun, puffing up and down the steep, cobbled lanes with her more fragile, ghostly pale, ash-blond sister in dripping mascara, Amanda was already on her way to cutting a memorable swath through the late-summer haze, attracting forty-year-old men. She smiled. They smiled back.

The sisters sauntered through a hillside arpeggio of pink- and red-tiled roofs on brick and stone buildings. The palette complemented the pink and white Umbrian stone, cut in floral shapes or arranged like cake icing on the fronts of the perfectly preserved churches, some dating back to the twelfth and thirteenth centuries. The girls passed beneath interlinked stone arches of Etruscan, Roman, and medieval vintage, up and down narrow brick and cobblestone lanes, past walls plastered with posters for student parties at the disco called Domus and for the PDL, the Berlusconi party, Il Popolo della Libertà. Finally they clambered up onto Corso Vannucci and encountered the scene on the duomo steps: young men and women in hobnail boots sporting dreadlocks, facial piercings, and fading tattoos, accompanied by half-feral dogs, itching for a fix beneath the massive bronze statue of Pope Julius III on a pedestal, holding up his hand in blessing.

For nine months out of the year, weather permitting, the San Lorenzo duomo steps are an Italian Amsterdam, with young people sunning themselves and drinking beer from plastic cups and smoking *spinelli*—joints filled with hash. Did the hash sellers on the steps eye the two pretty blond Americans with mercantile or lupine interest? Most likely both. And did Amanda regard the scene on the steps with an inner riff of glee? Getting some smoke and having some fun wasn't going to be hard in Perugia.

Inside the duomo, a stone wall's width away from the party scene outside, lies the town's most precious relic, the Virgin Mary's wedding

ring, a circle of green onyx that pilgrims and knights supposedly res-
cued from Jerusalem in the fifteenth century through great peril. The
ring is secreted in a locked silver reliquary, tucked high in the wall behind red velvet curtains, accessible only by a ladder and pulley system.
It has been displayed only once a year for the last five hundred years.
The reliquary can be opened only with fourteen different keys, held by
fourteen different prominent Perugians. It is situated just beneath the
stained-glass window depicting the martyrdom of San Lorenzo.

6
ROOMMATES

We really were very good together. We all had our part in the house.
I looked up to Laura. She is a very opinionated and strong woman
who plays guitar and listens to music. Filomena, she is definitely the
most loved I think because she sings and is very funny. She gives
advice to everyone and is always happy.

—*Amanda Knox, in Il Mio Diario del Prigione,* November 8, 2007,
two days after her arrest for murder

When women kiss, it always reminds one of
prizefighters shaking hands.

—*H. L. Mencken*

FILOMENA ROMANELLI AND HER BEST friend, Laura Mezzetti, were twenty-
six years old when they found the stone cottage at the edge of the *centro*
and decided to rent the four-bedroom upstairs apartment. The two girls
had studied law together at the University of Perugia and were work-

ing in Perugia law firms as assistants. They knew the city well, and the house seemed ideal. It was located far enough out of the *centro* to avoid the din and filth of the nightly drunken party scene but close enough to walk to the action when they wanted it, and with a great view, too. The Italian girls both had boyfriends, cars, and income, but the rent was steep, and it seemed sensible to rent the other two bedrooms to female foreign students, with the columned entrance to the Università per Stranieri practically within sight of the house. They found their first roommate while Laura was tacking up the rental notice on a board at the university.

Filomena later recalled her first impression of the girl who would become her American roommate. "We got the house at the end of August for four people, from Tecnocasa [a Perugia agency]. We were looking for two more students. It was an expensive house. Amanda came first to see the house, and she loved it right away. She was with her sister, Deanna. She came with her sister, gave a look, and said 'fantastic' and kept repeating 'Fantastic. Perfect, perfect, I want it.'"

In her Myspace blog, Amanda swooned over the house and the Italian girls:

> we run into a very skinny girl who looks a little older than me putting up a page with her number on the outer wall of the unviersity. i chat it up with her, she speaks english really well, and we go immediately to her place, literally 2 minutes walk from my university. it's a cute house that is right in the middle of this random garden in the middle of perugia. . . . i put down a down payment. im feeling sky high. these girls are awesome. really sweet, really down to earth, funny as hell.

"We explained everything, the pay, the deposit—in English because we wanted her to understand what she was doing," Filomena recalled. "Six hundred euros in advance and three hundred for the rent. We explained everything. Then she said, 'Perfect. I want the house." She told the Italians she planned to stay until December or January, but when the girls insisted that would be too short for a real contract, she said she would stay until June.

Laura and Filomena had one more room to fill and soon a young British woman named Meredith Kercher called to inquire, in what Filomena would later describe as "good Italian," about the rental. "She spoke Italian better than Amanda, but still we talked English at the beginning. We always communicated in English. She called me from an English number. She came, she saw the house, and around the same time another girl had called us, from Avellino. And Laura and I had to decide who to have. We picked Meredith because she seemed to be the kind of person we liked more—she was beautiful, polite, and very nice to us. She said it wasn't a problem, the monthly rent. And for us it was a good thing to have two English girls. They could learn Italian, and at the same time we could learn English."

LIKE MANY ITALIANS—AND especially those in smaller cities—Laura and Filomena were monolingual. Italians study English in their public schools, but few become fluent in the language they are told is so important. Unless they plan to leave their country for an extended period or interact with foreigners in hotels or banking, they have no strong incentive to learn it. Even the university professors and civic and business leaders in Perugia—unless they work with tourists or international business—don't know more than the most rudimentary English words.

Laura and Filomena, with their freshly minted degrees in law, couldn't communicate well in English, but they wanted to improve, and they were pleased with their young Anglophone roommates. They even thought they had achieved an Italian friend-finder success story by introducing the two young women.

"Laura and I are the same age and have been friends for a long time. The other two girls were the same age, both spoke English, both had to stay in Perugia for a shorter time," Filomena later told police. "We were kind of divided. We got along all together, but Laura and I were closer to each other, and the other two got closer."

Filomena watched the two English speakers together their first few fall days in Perugia and felt they seemed to really hit it off. To Filomena, it seemed natural and right that two girls, both pretty and young, would go off together into the streets. "Meredith had been in Perugia for a few days, going to the University for Foreigners, and already had met some friends, and she would tell Amanda, 'You have to meet somebody, I will introduce you to my friends.'"

BEAUTIFUL, TINY, AND SIMULTANEOUSLY outgoing and reserved, Meredith Kercher, nicknamed "Mez," had some surface similarities with Amanda Knox. Both were pretty, both in their early twenties, both children of divorce, and both very far away from parents for the first time in their lives. Kercher came from a binational family and grew up the youngest of four children in the leafy suburban neighborhood of Coulsdon, Surrey, near London. Her mother, Arline, is Pakistani, and her father, John Kercher, has the long, bearded, melancholy face of an aging Merovingian king.

The Kerchers had four children—two boys and two girls—before separating. John Kercher was a freelance journalist who'd made a living writing for British tabloids such as the *Daily Mail* and *The Daily Mirror*, interviewing entertainers, and penning books about celebrities such as Madonna, Guns N' Roses, and Wham!

Meredith, the youngest Kercher, was popular, smart, pretty, and witty, something of a perfectionist. At twenty-one, she was sophisticated and worldly, had worked as a bartender, and had even snagged a silent cameo in a British music video.

She was in her third year at Leeds University, studying modern history, political theory, and Italian. Leeds, a massive state-run school in Yorkshire with thirty thousand students, is reputed to be a party school, but Meredith had high grades and was dedicated enough to her books that she won a spot in the competitive Erasmus Program. In her set, she was the fun but levelheaded girl who practiced moderation and made sure her bingeing friends got home safe.

The Erasmus Program, named after the Dutch Renaissance humanist and philosopher Erasmus of Rotterdam, was created in 1987 as one element of the European Union effort to forge a pan-European person to go along with the coming pan-European currency. Erasmus offers young Europeans the opportunity to live in a foreign country and has a sexy frisson. The scene has been covered in movies such as *L'Auberge Espagnole,* a French film about college students hooking up and coming of age in the lovely multilingual setting of a Spanish university town.

The Erasmus experience combines learning and socializing—perhaps, say many graduates, more the latter than the former. "Erasmus parties" are notorious in university cities across Europe for being raucous multilingual events. Erasmus student experiences vary enormously from country to country. In some countries, they complain of the high workload in a foreign language. In others, they complain that schools treat the exchange program as an extended holiday and give no deadlines or grades.

Erasmus Program students often study politics or international relations—Meredith Kercher's field. According to the British press, Erasmus is seen as a great opportunity to study abroad without the expense of studying outside the European Union. Erasmus grants are not available to students who leave the EU.

In Europe, having "Erasmus" on one's résumé is useful. That one word signifies not just the experience of studying abroad but the manifestation of a unified Europe. Like the euro currency, Erasmus Program graduates are expected to become a powerful bonding force in creating a new European identity. "Give [Erasmus] 15, 20 or 25 years, and Europe will be run by leaders with a completely different socialization from those of today," said the political scientist Stefan Wolff, referring to the so-called Erasmus generation.

. . .

MEREDITH KERCHER SET OFF on her Italian adventure with this laudable goal. She was deeply committed to learning and her studies. According to the *Daily Telegraph,* her professors at Leeds University initially told her she wouldn't be able to defer her final year in order to take the Erasmus grant, but she resisted and eventually won them over. "She fought so hard to get out there. There were quite a few setbacks, but she was determined to go and kept persisting and eventually got what she wanted," John Kercher told British reporters.

"She had the choice of going to Milan, Rome, or Perugia. But everyone told her to go to Perugia because it is smaller and quieter and, we thought, safer." Kercher also told reporters that Meredith chose Perugia because of its annual chocolate festival. Not long before she was murdered, she told her family she would be coming home with "a suitcase full of chocolate."

In one of their few comments about Meredith, the Kercher family described how she was "excited at the prospect of spending the year studying there to improve her language skills, make new friends, and immerse herself in the culture. She was pursuing her dream."

Having grown up in the suburban sprawl of Coulsdon in Surrey, and having worked at Gatwick Airport to pay for her year abroad, Meredith couldn't believe her luck when she found a room in an authentic Umbrian cottage with stunning views of the countryside.

WHAT APPEARED A DREAM cottage to the American and British girls, accustomed as they were to postcard, travel-magazine Italy, was, in fact, not what Italians would consider the best housing for young women newly launched in the world alone. The cottage looked large from outside, but inside it was cramped and charmless. A three-hundred-year-old farmhouse, its once airy, solid, open stone rooms had been Sheetrocked in to contain modern plumbing and electricity and—crucially in a college town—cheap walls to make a warren of rooms for the greatest possible number of rent-paying students. The front door opened into a narrow hallway, barely wide enough for two people abreast, along which were four doors. The hallway led into a kitchen/living room with a couch and a table, some chairs, a television.

In fall 2007, the real problem at the cottage wasn't the ugly rehab job. It was the deficient blinds and a malfunctioning door lock.

Shutters are an important aspect of Italian life, an ancient and efficient way to repel winter cold, block blazing summer sun, and deter unwanted intruders. In the quiet back alleys of Italian towns, one can mark time by the sound of them clattering open with the sun and banging shut again at dusk. Perugia is a damp, windy place, and the shutters at the cottage, perched on the edge of a ravine and exposed to the raw winds more than most houses in town, were even more essential.

The high-strung Filomena Romanelli later told police she had already been worried about her security, and her shutters, in September. As the weather cooled, Filomena noticed that her window and shutter were almost impossible to keep closed. A nervous young woman at the best of times, this bothered her deeply. "The window was old and wouldn't close," Filomena later said at the trial. "I would have liked them replaced, also the shutters, maybe change the window or put bars on it like in Laura's room. It was used, old . . . warped. It gave me the sense of not being secure. Sometimes I thought even the wind could have opened the window, it didn't give me the feeling of being secure. I didn't feel it would stay closed, and I didn't like it."

The malfunctioning front door to the girls' apartment didn't close unless it was locked with a key from the inside. "We had decided to talk about it as soon as possible with the owner," Filomena recalled.

The cottage's location was deceptive, too. It had a great view of the *campagna,* but it was situated beside a very urban, seedy piazza known as a drug market. One evening, Meredith thought she saw someone in the garden after dark. She told friends she'd found needles in the garden.

Another night, one of the male visitors to the house saw a shadow lurking. If they grew worried, though, no one did anything about it.

British reporters later ferreted out a former occupant of the cottage named Valentina who described dubious characters lurking outside the house. "There were always junkies and drug dealers around, especially in the garden and in our car park," Valentina said. "We would come out and find syringes everywhere. I never felt safe there."

The police and prosecutors knew that Valentina had good reason to worry. Umbria is second only to Lazio, the region that includes Rome, in terms of drug-related deaths in Italy. It is also a national locus of the Mafia-run sex trade.

Six years before Meredith and Amanda moved into the cottage on the edge of town, at least eight young women—possibly more—disappeared in the region, believed to have been murdered by gang members who had brought them to Perugia for prostitution "training." The hammer-battered body of a twenty-year-old Russian girl named Tania in a field outside the city provoked Italian authorities to launch a sting called Operation Girasole—Sunflower. The sting netted a hundred Albanians and Italians who worked as a criminal network trafficking in both human beings and drugs.

"The operation . . . reveals the ugly underbelly of Perugia, one of Italy's most prosperous and well-administered cultural cities," reported the British newspaper *The Independent*. While traffic in women is hardly new, Operation Sunflower also brought home a hideous truth about the sex trade: many of the women who rebelled were killed. And in true Mafia tradition, so as not to attract unnecessary attention, their corpses simply disappeared.

"The women, mainly from Eastern Europe but also North Africa and Colombia, were brought to Italy with promises of jobs as waitresses and au pairs," *The Telegraph* reported. "Before they got here, they were systematically raped and tortured to break down their resistance. 'It's difficult to prove but there are at least eight cases in which women may have met this end,' said Antonella Duchini, the anti-Mafia magistrate heading the inquiry."

Prostitutes told police the girls were present one day and gone the next. A dedicated "antislave" line installed after the operation was receiving an average of four thousand calls per month within months after the sting.

A Perugia journalist, Vanna Ugolini, with the national daily Il Messaggero, wrote a book about the brutal local flesh trade, starting with Tania's murder. Ugolini determined that the mafiosi running the prostitutes launder the money through the local building trade. Anyone who wants to build even a small house in Umbria needs to first bribe a variety of powerful contacts. The larger the project, the more corrupt the process. The clans have no problem doing business there.

The "impresarios" training the Perugia prostitutes were as business-like as they were brutal. They procured the girls from Eastern Europe with promises of jobs or by kidnapping. Like sales reps, each impresario had his territory—Moldova, Ukraine, Kosovo—and they earned off the prostitutes for the rest of the girls' working lives.

Though the student world and the hooker world rarely intersected, they were geographically close: Corriere dell'Umbria reported that the local late-night clubs, such as Discoteca Gradisca and RedZone, "were a sort of training school for prostitutes." Once the sex workers had grasped the fundamentals of entertaining men and were earning well, they were sold on to Albanian gangs and put to work in much tougher conditions on the streets in larger cities.

For residents of Perugia, Operation Sunflower emphasized some ugly truths. Their lovely city is tranquilla for them, not so for many stranieri. And Perugians only have to drive around the city's modern outskirts late at night to see hundreds of women lined up in skinny minis and thigh-high boots along the streets. The presence of so many sex workers in and around such a relatively small town means that they have customers, or they wouldn't be training there.

• • •

UNBEKNOWN TO THEM, THE "fantastic" house Amanda Knox and Meredith Kercher fell in love with had its own strange history. The current owner is the widow of a man who bought it more than four decades ago from the family of a well-preserved Roman heiress named Marisa Orlandi.

In the 1940s, the Orlandis—two parents and two children—had a lot of money and at least three houses in and around Perugia. They called the little cottage on the hill their *poderetto*—country cottage.

The *poderetto* was painted pink then and set on five pleasant mountainside acres planted with figs, peaches, and apples. No parking lot, no busy road, just terraced land spilling down the hill, crosshatched with gravelly walking paths.

One of those paths led down the steep incline to an ancient, vegetation-shrouded stone basin, opening into ancient black tunnels built by the Etruscans. Marisa Orlandi's mother fell into the basin once, and the fire department was called to see where these tunnels went. They walked in about a hundred meters but were repelled by the darkness and the many twists, turns, and forks in the underground complex. "They turned back," Marisa remembers, "in fear of getting lost." Speleologists have still not mapped the warren of tunnels beneath Perugia leading to that basin.

Marisa Orlandi lived in Rome when the murder happened. She had bright blue eyes and dyed russet hair, and in her seventies, she still remembered much about when she, her brother, and her parents lived in the *poderetto* in the 1930s and 1940s. They moved into the cottage just after the Second World War, and she attended a nearby elementary school that at night was transformed into a dance hall for American soldiers stationed in Perugia. She could hear boogie-woogie and swing coming from the school's open doors on warm nights.

During the war, the carabinieri asked the Orlandis to leave their garden gates open so people fleeing bombardment in the city could escape across their land. The years immediately after the war were a time of desperation in defeated Italy, and Perugia was no better off. People sold their property in order to eat, raggle-taggle bands of refugees foraged, food was scarce, thieves roamed. The Orlandis were among the lucky few who had retained money and property through the chaos.

Signore Orlandi decided to buy an old convent building with a blackened brick wall that bordered the *poderetto* garden's northern boundary. Cloistered nuns had lived in it for four hundred years before the sect abandoned it, leaving a tangle of vines and unpruned trees shrouding its blackened walls.

Marisa, eight years old, tagged along on the first exploratory visit to the interior. Holding her father's hand, she went from cell to cell, peering into the tiny rooms. At the top floor, they arrived at a small attic room with a wall of dusty closed cabinets. Marisa's father began opening them and made a disturbing discovery.

"Dollies!" the little girl cried out at first sight of the tiny skulls and skeletons. Marisa, now in her seventies, still gets goose flesh recalling the sight of the bones stacked in the cabinets. Her father called a man, who came with wooden boxes and gave the infants a proper burial. Apparently, the corpses were those of illegitimate infants and aborted fetuses delivered over the centuries by or of the nuns.

A few more events convinced the Orlandis that the *poderetto* was haunted. A deranged man showed up at the door one day, inexplicably took out a knife, and cut the very beautiful and very wealthy Signora Orlandi, Marisa's mother, on the forehead and arm. Soon after that, the family woke up in the middle of the night to the sound of their front door vibrating, as though someone was trying to kick it in. "We weren't scared, we were terrified," Marisa recalled.

The Orlandis sold the little stone house immediately after that and moved down the hill to their country villa, protected by dogs and gates.

Signor Tattanelli, a man with a Singer sewing machine shop in the *centro,* bought the *poderetto* as an investment. In the 1950s and '60s, he

rented the little cottage to a farmer who worked the small hillside or-
chard. Later, he ceded the garden so the city could build the parking lot
across from the front door.

In the 1980s, Tattanelli replaced the farmer with a revolving cast of
rent-paying students, and let the carefully terraced acres on the hill go
to seed. Tattanelli divided the house into two separate units, upstairs
and downstairs, with four bedrooms in each, which brought in a nice
income for his widow. By 2007, a housing agency collected the rent. The
widow Tattanelli never laid eyes on the tenants.

WHEN IT CAME TIME to explain why Amanda had killed Meredith, the
police and Public Minister Mignini decided on the theory that the
American had grown to hate her roommate Meredith Kercher with
such an intensity during the approximately five weeks they had lived
together that she finally cracked and drove a large kitchen knife into
her neck.

The fervor of female roommate dislike and envy is nothing to be
trifled with. Most women can attest to this from personal experience.
Every woman who has ever been to college or simply moved in with
a group of women in their twenties can recall the visceral tension of
loathing at least one sloppy, fastidious, passive-aggressive, mean, envi-
ous, boyfriend-seducing, hypercompetitive, fill-in-the-blank obnoxious
dorm mate or sorority sister. Or being loathed and envied herself. The
nature of the college experience, the beauty of it supposedly, is that students meet people who are utterly unlike them and are then forced to
negotiate and compromise their way toward civil behavior, practice for
real life. But for young women on their own for the first time, these
experiences test a particularly female way of dealing with conflict, and
it can be traumatic.

Nancy Friday, in her book *Jealousy,* explored many aspects of female envy, including the complex, veiled ways in which young women
compete:

When young girls first get out of the house . . . there is no female equiv-
alent of the boy gang, no spirit of camaraderie in which sexuality is
explored, separation and independence encouraged. Sameness and uni-
formity are the rule. The prettiest girl—born with extra power no one
can control—must especially watch her step. She can have nothing more
because she already has so much. Very early, beautiful women learn not
to flaunt their beauty. It arouses too much envy.

To outsiders, and even to participants, it can be very difficult to
discern corrosive veiled competition from forced pleasantry and surface
camaraderie.

The older Italian roommates thought the English-speaking girls
got along nicely. They watched Amanda and Meredith go off to school
in the morning together. They knew the girls went to events like the
Eurochocolate festival together, they knew they went out for pizza together, they knew they occasionally smoked hash together.

Meredith had moved in first and already had a set of British girlfriends. Her routine mixed focused studying with hard partying. She
would rise early, leave the house at eight, and return at one for lunch
with some of the Italian newspapers, with their screaming headlines
about local crimes and car accidents, picked up at the kiosk in the Piazza
Grimana.

"She would study newspapers to learn the language better, and
sometimes she would write down words and ask me to help her," Filomena recalled. "She was very studious. She read a lot of newspapers, novels in English. And then she would go out with the friends, she would go
out to the bars and parties around ten thirty or eleven at night."

The American girl also had a set of habits, a routine. She rose early,
did yoga, drew, played Laura's guitar. She arrived punctually for her
9 A.M. Italian class at the University for Foreigners. Her instructor, Antonella Negri, called Knox "a model pupil, diligent and active in class."
She always sat in the front row. Afterward, she too would return to the
cottage for the one o'clock lunch.

"At the beginning, they were together a lot," Filomena recalled for police in December, a month after the murder and Knox's arrest. "When Amanda arrived, Meredith had been in Perugia for a few days and already met some friends, and she would tell Amanda, 'You have to meet somebody, I will introduce you to my friends.'"

The investigators prodded Filomena to describe how the friendship between the English speakers had cooled at some point. "I would leave in the morning and come back at night," she recalled. "But to me personally, I thought that around halfway through October, Meredith was a bit—"

Magistrate Mignini interrupted her. "Had put some distance."

"Yes. And I and Laura had noticed this, and I said, 'I think Meredith is annoyed with Amanda and has had enough.' She was not evil but a little bit too outgoing. Laura and I thought it was a bit because of her age. Laura was a bit too indulgent toward Amanda; sometimes I would get more disturbed with her. I didn't like her way of being so outgoing. Laura would say, 'She's only twenty, don't be such a nag.'"

After she was arrested, Amanda became known as the girl who "brought strange men home" regularly. But Filomena could recall only two, and one was Juve, a man Amanda eventually worked with. In any case, none of the roommates had to travel far to find men, strange or otherwise. The downstairs apartment was full of them.

LIVING OUT A COMFORTABLE widowhood in Rome, Signora Tattanelli let the Perugia rental agency handle the tenant vetting, so she also never met the boys who rented the lower half of her Perugia house and whose money made up half of the 3,000 euros she earned monthly on the property. She might have been told that they were simple, good Italian boys from Marche, the region to the east of Umbria.

Marco, Stefano, Riccardo, and Giacomo were indeed four country boys, some of them the first in their families to go to university, and they had reinstituted the agricultural spirit that had once animated the farm cottage. Their five healthy pot plants were thriving by the sunny southern window. Growing pot in Perugia shocks few. The Mysticanza emporium at the base of via dei Priori—across from a tiny chapel with a priceless Madonna inside, built and conserved by the Knights of Malta—sells everything an entrepreneurial home pot farmer needs, including lights, hydroponic kits, and seed catalogs.

The boys downstairs had already been renting the apartment for a few years when the girls moved in. They liked to party and they liked girls, and they were thrilled to discover that as of August 2007, the renters upstairs would be four very pretty girls, including two English speakers, one American and one British—a sure sign, according to Italian male lore, that someone would get laid.

It was a typical college-boy house. Besides the pot plants, there were the LSD poster, the mold-crusted shower stall, and two cats, one stray and one tame and all black, that stayed inside.

The boys may have been officially students, but in Perugia that designation doesn't always involve studies, books, or attendance at class.

Unlike American universities, Italian colleges don't have a set deadline for graduation or even for finishing a class. The decision about when to finish school lies with the students alone. They take an array of classes, moving toward a major, and decide when they want to sit for their final exams in each class. Sometimes a student will finish a class but not take a final exam for years afterward, necessitating months of grueling refresher studies.

Perugia student life is therefore leisurely, and those so inclined can take their time and party. The party scene appalls many Perugia professors, who, if they have morning classes, reel at the odor of alcohol exhaled by their students. Graduation, when it happens, can occur on almost any day of the year, with the exception of the major holidays. Year round in Perugia, gowned students wearing crowns of green laurels can be found trooping through the streets trailing a gaggle of beaming family and friends, all embarked upon the bacchanalia that marks every baccalaurate.

On the first floor of 7 via della Pergola, young people calling themselves students came and went, bearing hash, beer, and wine. The boys didn't always know the names of their visitors. Later, after the murder, they would strain to remember who had been inside their house.

"Sometimes I would smoke joints with my housemates, but I don't use other drugs," recalled Stefano Bonassi, one of the four when police interrogated him in the hours after the murder as "a person informed about the facts." "And yes, I have hanging in my room an article on LSD, just because I found it interesting and written by a famous scientist."

Of the four boys, one of them—Riccardo—was the nerdy house director who made cleaning schedules, collected the rent, and generally made a pill of himself. "Riccardo is neat and organized," recalled Stefano. "The living room is mostly used by Riccardo. I usually sit in my room when my girlfriend comes to visit me. Riccardo is weird, none of us got along with him. He is very egotistic. When he wasn't there, we pissed in his room from the window."

The downstairs scene was a never-ending party. Full names were the hardest part of the reconstruction. "The people who came to our house . . . ," Stefano recounted in the police station a day after the murder, when all the police had to go on was a dead girl and some bloody sneaker prints.

Then he really had to think.

"Pepe, a friend of Marco Marzan, from university. He is large, comes from the South. Comes frequently.

"Then there was another guy that came in. They called him 'the Baron.' He is a little shorter than me. He is South African. One night I found this guy in my house when I came back. He was with my friends, and he was very drunk and he ended up sleeping on my toilet. This boy was physically attracted by Amanda."

HASHISH IS AN ARABIC word that means "grass." It is Euro-pot. It's made from resin extracted from the flowers and tops of marijuana plants

grown on the green, lower slopes of the Himalayas, in Nepal and Afghanistan, or in the dry soil of Morocco and Lebanon. By the time it
gets to the European consumer, it's packaged in sticky green, yellow,
black, brown, or red chunks, depending on its origin, and wrapped in
foil. Users can smoke it or put it into food, much like marijuana. It can
be stronger than pot, but the effects are similar: a sense of euphoria, disorientation, loss of coordination and memory, and, in some individuals,
paranoia, lasting up to three hours. The active ingredient is the same
as that of pot: delta-9-tetrahydrocannabinol, or THC. THC isn't associated with violent behavior, although researchers have found that the
drug can provoke individuals predisposed to "psychotic thinking" to
become psychotic. Some hash is cut with PCP (angel dust) or crack, in
which case the effects are stronger and unpredictable, and can include
psychosis.

It didn't take long for Amanda Knox to start peeling back the onion
layers of Perugia's party scene. She had no shortage of guides and consi-
glieres in this effort. First and foremost, there was her English-speaking
roommate, Meredith, who had already been in town for several weeks.
Then there was Laura, with the hypnotic aquamarine eyes and multiple
piercings, who played guitar and knew where to get hash. And there
were the Italian boys downstairs, cool customers who also knew where
to pay 10 euros for a gram of hash, out of which they could roll four
joints.

The boys hosted dinners downstairs, with bottles of red wine, followed by group outings to the bars. Most of the Perugia bars are cave-
like, restored medieval grottoes. Students drinking rum and pear juice
today are standing where medieval butchers or tanners once worked.

The girls quickly came to know a few of the bars and their manag-
ers quite well. The favorite was Merlin Pub, two quick turns off the
Corso Vannucci, with an entrance next to a barred-off stone dungeon
whose original purpose has long since faded into oblivion along with
the medieval jailer who once guarded it. It exuded the unmistakable
odor of college bar—stale booze, cheap cleaning product, hair gel, tang

of vomit—but with the additional undertone of crumbly medieval brick-work. A tall, amiable, fortyish Italian, Pasquale Alessi, who goes by the single name of Pisco, presided over Merlin's nightly festivities. Pisco's gigantic, lumpy square brow and deep-set eyes give him a Frankenstein-ian look. A gentle giant, he was the master of ceremonies of the nightly foreign-student boozefest. He came to know some of his clients pretty well, and Meredith had him on speed dial by the time she was killed.

Men in their thirties and forties operate most of the Perugia student bars. They came to Perugia to study, drifted into the scene, and never left. "It's like a family," said a Perugia writer and gadfly who goes by the name Frank Sfarzo, one of the men who let twenty years of his adult life slide away in the clubland of Perugia. Reflecting on his lotus-eater's existence, he said, "You start doing these things, organizing parties, and then you get used to it. It's a life."

During warmer weather, the street party on the duomo steps spon-taneously spills onto the piazza. Tiny coffee and pizza bars sell drinks in take-out plastic cups, and as the sun sets, thousands of young peo-ple congregate in the sulfurous lights affixed to the priory and duomo, under the shadows of the griffons and Pope Julian III. Sipping beer from plastic cups, smoking cigarettes and hash, scampering from group to group, they hook up in a half-dozen languages. One night some Span-ish Erasmus students carried a couch up from one of their flats and out onto the street, the better to pass out on after drinking straight rum from the bottle. Men use the dark corners of the streets angling steeply down from the corso to relieve themselves. After especially convivial evenings, rivers of urine course down the cracked stone alleys and past the doorsteps of bakeries and regional produce shops, jewelry stores and bookshops on the side streets.

The dawn light reveals the duomo steps littered with plastic cups, cigarette butts, vomit, the stray passed-out partier. The carabinieri gen-erally stay away, but as the sun comes up, the city's little green sanita-tion trucks pull up and men in coveralls alight to sweep away the mess.

7

THE BARON

Surveys show that among Europeans, Italians are the most suspicious about immigrants. A majority believes immigrants have too many rights and that many of them should be deported, and that immigration has brought only crime. Talk of an immigrant "invasion" is widespread.

—*Sylvia Poggioli*, NPR, January 2009

PRESSED TO REMEMBER HIS NAME, the boys downstairs recalled the young man they believed was South African either as "Body Roga" (after the Serbian basketball star Dejan Bodiroga) or "the Baron" (a nickname he chose that Italians mispronounced—meant to be "Byron"—for NBA star Byron Scott). The Baron was a sinewy, lanky, sleepy-eyed guy who shot hoops at the scruffy Piazza Grimana basketball court across the street from the via della Pergola house. None of the boys knew his real name or would ever admit to being the one who had first invited the Baron inside their house. He was just there one night several weeks before the murder, another drifter among the revolving partiers.

"I was woken by noises," Stefano told police, describing one night. "I looked out and saw everybody in the kitchen." He saw Meredith and Amanda and the guy called the Baron. Stefano didn't know if Amanda and Meredith had brought him in or if one of his other roommates or one of the Italian girls from upstairs had.

During the trial, prosecutors prodded Stefano to give Amanda credit for bringing the Baron home, but he couldn't do it. No one remembered how the Baron had arrived that first night. The police would ask and ask again. It made perfect sense that it be Amanda, because the Baron, who was actually an African Italian named Rudy Guede, really liked Americans. Sometimes he pretended to be one himself, one named Kevin Wade, when he wasn't pretending to be South African. Sometimes if a girl he was talking to didn't know English very well, she fell for Kevin Wade, a cool American boy. Amanda would later say she had known Rudy only "vaguely."

"Someone rang the door, I don't know if it was Meredith or Amanda, who got into our apartment after that," Stefano told lawyers, adding, "Amanda and Meredith, they looked very much alike."

Stefano did remember that eventually on that night in early October, the Baron stumbled out of sight into the bathroom, and the boys found him there later, door open, sleeping perched on an unflushed toilet full of feces. Stefano tried to prod him out of the house, but the Baron was too drunk or high to leave. He spent the night passed out on the living room couch. The boys didn't know it, but the Baron didn't like to sleep in his own house alone by then. Bad things happened to him after dark. He would show up at the downstairs apartment at 7 via della Pergola once more, uninvited, a week later, to watch a Formula One race on television.

His eyes were half shut, his trademark look, but to the other people in the room, he seemed to be awake.

ITALY IS A HOMOGENEOUS nation. Tuscany, the Veneto, Puglia, Emilia-Romagna, and Calabria are historically separate regions with dialects that mystify outsiders, but Italians share a common culture and theirs is an insular society in which jobs, opportunities, and social class are very much based on family ties. Birth determines all.

Italy once exported emigrants to the United States by the millions, back when Italian life was nasty and brutish, when few had electricity, when there wasn't enough food, employment, or education to go around. But in the last half century, the old country, like other Western European nations, has prospered. Now the world's poor and hungry arrive by the millions, piled onto flimsy vessels in Libya and Somalia, floating over the Mediterranean, or speeding across the Adriatic in little boats from the Balkans. By 2010, Italy had an estimated four to five million immigrants, about 7 percent of the population. And more were clamoring to get in every day.

Italians didn't much like it. Racial violence has become so prevalent that Italian media in 2009 dubbed the situation "a racism emergency." Italian society and the national political structure had not caught up with the new demographics. No services eased the new brown and black arrivals into Italy, no welcome wagon taught them Italian ways. Newcomers had little protection or legal recourse. The European Network Against Racism called Italian police the second largest group— after ordinary citizens—committing racist crimes in Italy. Amnesty International accused Italian politicians of legitimizing the use of racist language.

As of 2010, there was exactly one black in Italy's Parliament.

As in America, the newcomers took the dirty, backbreaking jobs that Italians didn't want or need to take. They laid bricks, cleaned houses, worked fields, broke stones. In the South, African laborers became virtual chain gangs for the Mafia, working in fields and factories for subsistence wages, and were beaten or killed if they asked for more.

Italy's powerful anti-immigrant party, Lega Nord, originating in the northern town of Bergamo, had eighty-six seats in Parliament in 2011. Lega Nord's platform vows to protect Italian life and culture from the perceived disease and chaos of immigration. The party has pushed to make illegal immigration punishable by up to four years in prison, to require doctors to report to police any patients in Italy illegally, and to create separate classrooms for Italian and immigrant children.

Lega Nord thrives on fears of invasion. During campaigns, the party has offered free self-defense classes for women. One of its logos showed a Native American above the words "They let immigrants in, and now they're living on reservations."

A northern Italian town called Cittadella (the Citadel) was the first to take extreme measures. Cittadella is surrounded by walls and a moat, but they were not high or deep enough to deter foreigners looking for work. In 2009, Mayor Massimo Bitonci imposed an ordinance with strict restrictions for immigrants wanting to live in the city. As of 2010, immigrants could reside in Cittadella only if they produced a regular work contract (virtually impossible, as immigrants are generally hired as off-the-books, temporary labor), had a minimum annual income of 5,000 euros per family member, and rented or bought a dwelling of a size per family that is too expensive for most immigrants.

"We're very frightened by what we see around us," Bitonci explained to reporters. "We write the rules here, we want to safeguard our culture. Yes, we're raising the drawbridge, and we're on the battlements to defend ourselves from external attacks."

Other villages and cities soon copied the Cittadella ordinance. In Tuscany, a small town called Lucca decided that Italian food was under siege and barred new ethnic restaurants from opening in the historic *centro*. Lucca officials explained that the measure was needed to protect local specialties from the rising popularity of "different" cuisines.

Rudy Guede was a black Italian, or rather an Italian black. He arrived in Italy from Ivory Coast when he was five years old—before that he had few memories—and he was more Italian than African. He spoke Italian with a Perugian, not an African, accent. He dressed in fine Italian sweaters and stylish jeans. He had a First Communion in the Catholic church. But Guede was not and never will be Italian. Before he was arrested and sentenced to prison, he had to present himself at the Perugia police station regularly to be photographed and fingerprinted in exchange for a residency card.

Rudy grew up an immigrant's son in a nation with one of the West's most restrictive citizenship laws. Immigrants cannot apply to become citizens until they have lived in Italy for ten years. Their children, even if born in Italy, are not guaranteed citizenship when they turn eighteen. All his life, Rudy was only a guest in his country, *permitted* residency, like a traveler at a hotel.

Rudy Hermann Guede was born in Agou, Ivory Coast, on Christmas Eve in 1985. According to one of the legends of Neapolitan witchcraft, men born around Christmas are cursed as werewolves. "The malady seizes them at night; they run on all fours at night, trying to bite," according to an English accounting of the folk beliefs of Italians written a hundred years ago. "But they retain human form." Their madness can be stopped only if they are wounded so as to lose blood.

Ivorians have their own superstitions, but Christmastide werewolves are not among them. Rudy Guede's birth was an unremarkable event in a poor village in a poor country. Agou is in cocoa plantation territory forty miles outside of Abidjan, the capital of Ivory Coast. A few citizens have wealth and own some of the farms, but most are poverty-level laborers or civil servants. There is electricity in Agou, but only the main street is blacktopped. Most of the houses have sheet-metal roofs. Still, Agou is one of the more developed areas in Ivory Coast. The road from Agou to Abidjan is paved. People can take buses from the village to Abidjan on Saturdays to shop and dance.

Guédé is a Bete name, from a Christian tribe in the western part of Ivory Coast. Former Ivory Coast president Laurent Gbagbo was a Bete and Christian. Ivorian Christians, proselytized by Western missionaries hundreds of years ago, retain the converts' zeal: one former president erected what is still the largest Christian church in the world in Abidjan. The other half of the nation is Muslim, and the two groups are at constant odds.

Ivory Coast is a former French colony, and the citizens speak French.

But in recent decades visas have tightened up, and more of those who leave emigrate to the United Kingdon or Italy than to France.

In the 1960s and '70s, Rudy's grandfather was based in Agou as a member of the military police. He had seven children, two of whom died in childhood. Roger, Rudy's father and one of the surviving sons, went to university in Abidjan.

Rudy's mother, Agnes, was just one of Roger's girlfriends. The Bete practice polygamy, and when Agnes was pregnant with Rudy, another girlfriend of Roger's also became pregnant and gave birth to another son, almost the same age as Rudy. That son—Rudy's half brother—has never left Ivory Coast, where he lives with his mother. While Agnes was pregnant with Rudy, she moved in with Roger's sister Georgette, who took over the care of little Rudy when he was a baby.

Roger was good at mathematics and studied physics for three years at the university in Abidjan. He had some dreams. Then his father died and his education concluded abruptly. No more money. He stuck around for a while, working seasonal jobs in the cocoa fields, and then heard there were better jobs and educational opportunities in Russia. But he couldn't get a visa to Russia from Abidjan. Russians at the consulate advised him to go to Italy and try to get a visa from there.

Roger arrived in the *bel paese* in November 1987 by plane. It quickly became clear that the Russian bureaucracy would never respond to his pleas for a visa from Italy either, and thus Roger became an accidental Italian. He learned to speak Italian with a French accent and went to masonry school on the advice of an Ivorian friend. The work was always plentiful, but long hours and physical exhaustion took their toll, and he soon looked older than his years. For the next two decades, Roger worked throughout Umbria and in more distant regions, shoring up antique Italian farmhouses, turning them into villas for the British, and tuck-pointing the great churches. Sometimes his jobs took him away from his apartment for weeks at a stretch.

In fall 2009, with his son convicted of murder and facing a thirty-year sentence, Roger was working as a bricklayer and living with his common-law wife in Bastia, on the plains halfway between Perugia and Assisi. He was completely estranged from Rudy, who had instructed his jailers and lawyers that he didn't want his father to visit him in jail or show up at the trial. Roger agreed to meet me in the Perugia train station. He chose it because of an African specialty grocery store across the street, where he could buy produce rare in Italy—papaya, avocado, mango—that reminded him of home.

He is a small, very dark, compactly built man and was dressed neatly in acid-washed jean jacket and jeans. When we talked, the whites of his eyes were bright red, as though he was very tired or had cried for many days. His eyes filled with tears when he talked about giving up his university studies in physics all those years ago. He could not understand, he said, why Rudy wanted nothing to do with him anymore. He had done his best with the boy.

Roger brought Rudy to Italy when his son was five years old. Up until that point, Rudy would tell Italian friends, he had never even met his father. He saw his mother, Agnes, only once or twice after that. A boy with one parent is not unusual in Agou. At least half of the kids in Ivory Coast are born out of wedlock. What is unusual is for a man to take a child so far from his mother, but Agnes either couldn't or didn't want to take care of her baby alone. She never married, nor did she have any more children after Rudy. She was still living in Abidjan, eking out a living selling trinkets at the Saturday market, when Rudy was on trial.

In Italy, Roger remained technically a polygamist. He kept a wife in Italy in addition to a wife and family back in Abidjan. One son back home in Africa is exactly Rudy's age. Roger remained close to that family and bought them a house with his Italian earnings. He tried to visit once every year or so.

Roger's sister Georgette, Rudy's aunt, soon followed her brother and nephew to Italy and was sometimes around to help keep track of the boy. They all tried to keep in touch with Agnes. "In the beginning we would call home very often, and he would talk to his mother," Roger said. But time and distance frayed the maternal bond. By the time the boy was a teen, what existed of it had withered. Rudy went back to see his mother only once in 1997, when he was twelve. After that, Roger said, he didn't want to go to Ivory Coast anymore.

Roger, on the other hand, was growing more attached to his homeland. He returned to Africa every year starting in 2000. He bought two houses there and enough land on which to grow some coffee. He installed his second family and other son in one of the houses. He planned to return permanently in 2012.

In summer 2004, when Rudy was sixteen years old, Roger left Umbria on his annual visit to Abidjan, planning to stay for a few weeks. He lost his passport, though, just as a vicious civil war was raging. The fighting was random and ferocious, and a man needed to keep his head down to stay alive. That summer, UN human rights watchers logged numerous atrocities in Ivory Coast. Sixty prisoners were left to die of suffocation in a crammed transport container. A team discovered three mass graves containing the bodies of at least ninety-nine people—some of whom had been beheaded—in the northern, rebel-held town of Korhogo. And that was just in June.

In the chaos, the French never gave Roger a replacement passport. The one-month trip became a four-month confinement. Whereas Westerners viewed the civil war as a battle between competing Christian and Muslim clans, Roger and his educated friends knew the war was really about money, between factions supporting France, which wanted to control the oil that the Canadians and Chinese had discovered, and factions supporting the Canadians and Chinese. As usual, the generals and politicians were just puppets of the colonizers. There was nothing anyone could do but wait, lie low, and avoid the machete, the bullet.

Roger had left Rudy back in Bastia, in the care of his common-law wife. The teen was supposed to be attending Alberghiero high school in Assisi, a vocational high school for young people planning careers in the hotel or restaurant industry. But Rudy didn't like Roger's woman, who had young kids of her own to look after. He stopped going to school, and he stopped going home at night. The school would call and say they couldn't find him. The wife would call Roger. Roger would call Rudy, who simply turned off his cell phone. The boy was lost to him after that.

EVERYTHING ABOUT IVANA TIBERI and her home perched on a hill on the edge of Perugia is decent and good. She could be the Italian poster mother, the tranquil, infinitely generous center that creates and binds the extended family with her unconditional love. She sits outside at sunset, golden light bathing her and her great pots of flowers and herbs—thyme, peppers, giant bushes of basil—and citrus trees. She has a green thumb, but literally everything she touches seems blessed. Grandchildren gambol happily at her feet, and her own snowy-haired hundred-year-old mother nods off in a chair beside her, a spotless white linen towel draped under her chin. Her husband, an artist, is in the back somewhere, making sculpture.

Hers is a simple house but rich in art, flowers, love.

Mrs. Tiberi was Rudy's first teacher in Italy. She gave him the closest thing to real mothering he ever knew.

When Rudy first came to Ponte San Giovanni, he was the only little black boy in the school. Now Mrs. Tiberi's classroom is filled with brown, black, and yellow children, in Italy speaking only Arabic, or Tagalog, or African French. She reckons that families from 130 countries have attended the school in recent years, and she is their lifeline to the new land and its customs.

"I have an Indian student now who didn't want to come to school because the family couldn't find the right shade of red for her dot. I told her it was okay, that here nobody cares. People are coming here from all over the world now, and we take care of them in the cultural and physical sense. We are now specialized in integration."

Things were not so when Rudy first arrived.

"We were neighbors first. The thing I was most surprised about was that this little boy was alone most of the day. It was just *padre* and Rudy. No mamma, no *donna*." Mrs. Tiberi's maternal heart broke when she saw the skinny black boy coming to school in winter clad only in a T-shirt. She knew the boy's life was hard. Sometimes Roger would call the school, asking if they had seen his son. Sometimes she would find Rudy wandering the streets and learn that his father had locked him out and left for the day. She decided to intervene.

"He was six. He had already gone to the first year of school in Ivory Coast, but when he came here, he started again the first grade. And we started asking him, what do you eat, where do you stay? He would say that his father cooked a pasta or something and that he would heat it up himself and eat it alone at the house. He would also go out by himself. We saw him alone in the street. We [teachers] started talking to the other mothers and families, and we decided that each day of the week, he'd go to a different family to eat and spend the day after school. There he would do his homework, eat properly, and then we would send him home when his father came home. The father was very young, disoriented, and not prepared to take care of his child."

Mrs. Tiberi became his chief surrogate mother and enlisted some of the class parents to help. They all took turns feeding him pasta lunches, watched his health, gave him a proper Italian upbringing. Mrs. Tiberi collected money to buy him a suit for his First Communion in the Catholic Church. He grew close to the local priest, Padre Annibale, after that ceremony, and he and other men—coaches, teachers—became surrogate fathers.

"We learned that sometimes to punish him—if he got home too late or did something wrong—his father would close him out for the night, so Rudy would sleep upstairs in the attic, or even on the streets, when he was little, when he was young," Mrs. Tiberi said. "Rudy wouldn't tell us. He never told us the real reason why he was sleeping outside. I just came to understand there was no communication between the two. I would ask, where does your father work, where does your mother work? And Rudy knew nothing."

•   •   •

MRS. TIBERI'S ELDEST SON, Gabriele Mancini, ten years older than the boy, became like a big brother to Rudy. "Lots of people loved him," Gabriele said. "He had more friends than I do. People would come and ask after him. He's polite. He never showed anger. He would stay quiet if he was upset, he was melancholic, not violent."

As the boy grew taller, Mrs. Tiberi and the local priest introduced Rudy to the coach at Perugia Basket, the local semipro basketball team. For a while, basketball focused the boy, and the gym, located on the bus route at the base of the Perugia hill, offered him another sort of home and family.

While Roger was trapped in war-ravaged Ivory Coast and Rudy was skipping school, Mrs. Tiberi stepped in again. Rudy had long since graduated from elementary school and left her direct care, but she still felt responsible for the boy. She and some of his other former teachers realized he was now officially parentless and called in social services. And for a while, Rudy got a family of dreams.

IF MRS. TIBERI WAS infinite simplicity, Ilaria Caporali was infinite nobility, entitled and perfectly unconscious of it. For about three years, the doe-eyed, delicate, soft-spoken girl was Rudy Guede's adopted sister. At twenty-seven, when Rudy was sentenced for murder, she was almost painfully well bred and soigné. The silver on her pale caramel-colored wrists was heavy and real. It matched the gray suede of her ballet flats. Her shiny brown hair was effortlessly smooth. She was one of the richest young women in Perugia, one of three children of Paolo Caporali, the owner of the Liomatic vending company, which in turn owned the town basketball team and its gym, and employed its coaches.

"He was a friend of my brother," she explained in fluent English. "They played basket together. When his father left the country, my brother spoke to our sister and then to me, and we decided to ask our father, together, if Rudy could stay with us. And my father asked us if we really wanted him with us, and we said yes, so he came and stayed. And then they worked it out with the state so that my father would adopt him for a year and take care of him until he turned eighteen."

The Caporali family took Rudy into their home without premeditation, the way people do when their children find homeless pets. Working with social services, the family agreed to formally adopt him until he came of age. When the richest man in town adopts the poorest boy in town, the reader is entering Charles Dickens territory, but in real life, not fiction, Rudy Guede, rejected in the Third World by his mother as an infant, abandoned by his father as a teen, suddenly found himself at age sixteen with his own apartment in a palatial gated villa in the heart of Perugia. The Caporalis installed him in their late grandfather's suite. He had his own TV, and he ate breakfast, lunch, and dinner with his new parents and brother and sisters. He worshipped God beside them in the family pew at the Church of San Filippo Neri on via San Francesco, a gorgeous, art-filled pile of fifteenth-century white marble that Caporali money was renovating.

He summered on the island of Sardinia. During winters he skied in the Dolomites. "We laughed," Ilaria recalled of that in a tinkly, soft voice. "He was this little black dot in the white of the mountains."

Rudy was "sweet," "shy with girls," and "afraid of the dark." He loved the family's two huge dogs. He loved nature, he was always affectionate. He was absent-minded, always losing his jacket. He wouldn't hurt anyone.

He didn't say much about his life before, but the Caporalis came to understand that it had been difficult, brutal, maybe traumatic. Rudy told his new family that his father used to leave for the day and lock him in the bathroom to keep him inside the house. In his own writing later, Rudy alluded to a childhood incident where someone he referred to as his "father"—in his own quotation marks—broke a stick over his head, causing him to bleed "like a fountain." He told them that an aunt had brought him to Italy because his mother in Abidjan couldn't take care of him. If he knew anything more about this mother and that seminal event in his childhood, he never told them.

The Caporalis enrolled the boy in a prestigious math school. A chauffeur ferried him to and from the gates.

Then, as abruptly as the fairy tale had started, things went wrong and the dream ended. In his second year with the Caporalis, Rudy was falling seriously behind in the prestigious school, but rather than ask for help, he started lying about it. Caporali had hired a special tutor to meet with Rudy twice a week. After two months, the tutor called to say that Rudy wasn't showing up, even though the boy had told the family that that's where he was going in the afternoons. He was now flunking all his exams—and had been lying about his whereabouts every day.

"We got angry. We had trusted him," Ilaria said. "My father told him, you don't have to finish school, but you have to go back to work, because now you are nineteen."

The family gave him a job at their villa outside Perugia, a stone mansion behind a graceful wall of swaying cypress. He was supposed to work in the garden, but he kept showing up late, saying that his alarm clock hadn't gone off or he was sick. "Now we didn't trust him anymore," Ilaria said. "He was a good guy, but he lied. He didn't know the difference between good and bad. He didn't have values. He was a like a baby that can't understand right and wrong."

Fed up with this amoral rescue baby, his adoptive father, Caporali, tossed him out of the house and out of the family. In his sole public statement after Rudy was arrested, Caporali told local Italian reporters, "We gave him an opportunity, even though we knew he was a liar and had been in trouble, but we wanted to give him a chance. We took him in as a son, but he was more interested in other things than studying and work. . . . In the end we asked him to leave our home because we just couldn't cope any longer." Caporali added that the family had had no contact with Rudy for a year before his arrest.

RUDY'S AUNT GEORGETTE LIVED in Lecco, in the northern lake country, not far from Lake Como, the actor George Clooney's paradisal lair. The

Alps shimmered on the horizon. The seventeenth-century Italian writer Alessandro Manzoni opened the first Italian novel, *I Promessi Sposi,* or *The Betrothed,* with a reference to Lecco, and every Italian schoolchild is made to learn those lines by heart. Lecco is in the Italian soul.

Georgette walked with a waddle, having gained a lot of weight since she left Abidjan more than twenty years before. She had made a good life for herself in northern Italy. She worked as a home care nurse. Her husband, Vincent, had once been pretty close to Rudy, the father figure that Roger couldn't or wouldn't be. Rudy, he said, could talk to him about anything, even girls.

After the Caporalis kicked Rudy out of their villa and out of their family, Rudy moved up north and stayed with Georgette and Vincent in the winter and spring of 2007. He got a job at a café. They loaned him money for the white shirt and pants he needed for the job, and he was very proud of the uniform, Georgette recalled. For a while, he seemed to be focused and self-reliant. He had a girlfriend, a white Italian girl in Milan. He told them he was playing basketball again, also in Milan. And he was cutting a swath through the Milan club scene, even getting his picture taken with designer Giorgio Armani. Then abruptly he lost his job and started sliding off the grid. He said the bar had closed down. He drifted back to Perugia sometime in the late spring of 2007. That's the last time Georgette and Vincent saw him outside his prison cell.

The thing Georgette and Vincent wanted the world to know about Rudy was that he couldn't possibly have killed that girl, because he couldn't bear the sight of blood. When he was twelve, his dad had brought a live bunny home for dinner and lopped off its head in front of the boy.

Rudy had fainted.

RUDY GUEDE'S OWN MEMORIES weave into and out of this story like loose threads, holding it together tenuously, not easy to pull out. In each of his tales, there is an element of truth.

In a letter from prison that became part of the public record, Rudy described his encounters with Amanda Knox, beginning, he said, when he laid eyes on her at Le Chic pub. She was smiling.

"I remember very well that she approached me with a smile stamped on her face," he wrote during his first days in prison. "After that I ran into her many times, but it was always 'Hi' and 'Bye,' each going our own way. I didn't strike up a relationship with her."

He played pickup basketball games with the boys downstairs on the grimy court at Piazza Grimana, next to their house. Rudy says he ran into some of them outside the Irish-style Shamrock Pub. Amanda was with them. They all walked back to the via della Pergola house together. Amanda went upstairs, and the boys stayed below.

"We all began to critique Amanda," Rudy wrote. "Some more, some less, in the sense that she was a pretty girl. Some imagined doing it with her, etc. etc. . . . stuff that all guys do, some more, some less. That evening I don't remember exactly what I said, but to go to bed with her, yes, all of us guys ended up with that as the goal."

Someone lit a joint and passed it around, and the smoke only heightened the group arousal. "We imagined ourselves, each one of us, with Amanda in bed. We were guys at home, what were we supposed to be thinking if not of this? Then I heard a knock at the door, and who was it? Amanda. We all looked at one another and laughed.

"Amanda sat down, and she too began to smoke. Then and there I knew she smoked a lot because the guys told me so, and I saw it with my own eyes. For the entire evening she had a joint in her mouth, and she was smoking and smoking. I, in comparison, was a real novice, which I am with regard to smoking, because I know little.

"That evening my glance and Amanda's glance kept meeting a lot, and she exchanged with me a smile of the type . . ."

Sometime in the cannabinoid haze of that after-midnight session—probably the same night Stefano Bonassi woke up and saw the Baron and the girls upstairs in his kitchen—Rudy said he heard another knock on the door and saw another English-speaking beauty drift into his sights. Unbelievable. This one was Meredith.

"Damn, she was beautiful," Rudy wrote. "I looked at the two girls and saw that she was very pretty, but that was the end of it."

Eventually, the two girls left the apartment. Nothing had happened. The fantasies remained zipped up inside the pants. It was frustrating. Rudy wrote, "We guys were left 'high and dry,' as they say."

As for that mysterious smile from Amanda, the one so full of promise that Rudy could only end his memory of it with an ellipsis when recalling it from prison for his friends? Only the girl who craved the limelight, especially the flickering light of her dad's distracted eyes, and who in her first month in Perugia was the center of so much male attention, surrounded by appraising eyes, could say for sure what that smile meant. Perhaps she was testing the edge where a smile becomes an invitation. Maybe the smile meant nothing more than that she was high and happy and basking in the lazy, appreciative gaze of all the stoned men in the room.

8
THE VORTEX

It is said that in Etruria wild boars and stags are caught with nets and dogs in the usual manner but that hunters are even more successful when they use music. Nets are stretched out, and all kinds of traps are set in position in a circle. A skilled flutist then plays the sweetest tunes the double flute can produce, avoiding the shriller notes. The quiet and the stillness carry the sounds, and the music floats up into all the lairs and resting places of the animals. At first the animals are terrified. But later they are irresistibly overcome by the enjoyment of the music. Spellbound, they are gradually attracted by the powerful music and, forgetting their young and their homes, they draw near, bewitched by the sounds, until they fall, overpowered by the melody, into the snares.

—*Aelian,* a Roman writing about the Etruscans, third century B.C.

Madre, sorella, povera bella,
Suora, putana, bellissima befana . . .

[Mother, sister, poor pretty girl,
Nun, whore, beautiful witch . . .]

—*refrain of a popular Italian song*

THE MUSIC IS SO LOUD, they can't hear one another without shouting. The arched ceilings and windowless stone walls are elements that stylish clubs in New York and London might pay architects millions to replicate. The foreign college girls begin arriving in small clusters around 11 P.M. They have spent a significant amount of time primping. Lips are glossed, eyelashes freshly clotted with mascara. They have applied this makeup with care and carefully selected special shoes that no one will notice in the dark. They've blown out and curled their hair.

They are twenty years old, and this is their junior year abroad. Few have ever been this far away from home before, and they are thrilled with their independence and afraid of it at the same time. They cling together nervously and start tossing back mixed drinks.

Certain Perugia bars aggressively court the foreign female clientele, offering free drinks, two-for-one deals, special "English" nights. Italian men who like foreign girls make it their business to know when these are, because they think those venues offer the best odds in the nightly sexual lottery. Within a half hour, as though alerted by some scent—the fruity odor of recently washed and sprayed hair—the boys and men start arriving, in groups of two, not more. Once in a while, a slightly older guy, alone, pulls up with the same hungry look in his eye. All appraise the girls, so young, barely not children anymore, and catch snatches of conversation in the girls' nervous children's voices, giggling, in their nasal English.

"I really wanna dance."

"He said, like—"

"I couldn't find my hotel."

"They didn't spell my name right."

The boys buy drinks and circle in closer, until the bravest one, the one with *molto coraggio*, leans over and starts talking. *"Ciao, come stai?"* It comes out with exaggerated slowness, "Cha-oooh, comay sty?" His friends laugh, and the girls giggle and brush back their hair and sip long sips through tiny cocktail straws. And sip some more.

In an hour or two, the girls will have consumed enough rum and pear juice to forget how nervous they are, to forget the shoes they so carefully selected. The self-consciousness dissipates, faces flush, a red that rises from the neck and covers the skin of the long-haired blondes, obliterating the effects of the foundation makeup, revealing excitement.

Eventually the Italian boys, emboldened by the growing disorientation of the English-speaking girls and their desire to learn Italian, rub up against girls in the dark, grinding against them, grinning the whole time and talking of other things. Stunned, flattered, and titillated, there is nothing to do but submit.

Then there are gales of laughter and, maybe, a dance, a kiss, a walk home . . . not much different from any bar scene in any college town in America, except that the couples don't speak the same language.

The DJ plays a blend of American music, rock classics, and Italian tunes. When American rap songs spray the room with thumping rhymes celebrating total female submission, the American girls brighten up, make gang symbols at one another, united by this memento of home. The British girls are a little more reticent at first, but they drink more and soon catch up.

BLOND, WITH LONG SILKEN hair flying, they moved together as a perfumed, impeccably tailored, well-bred pack. As in high school, it takes only one clique like this to change a girl's life. The press took to calling them the "British girls." They were a tribe of six young women, Meredith's party buddies from the U.K., all in Perugia on the Erasmus Program: Amy Frost, Sophie Purton, Natalie Hayworth, Jade Bidwell, Samantha

Rodenhurst, and Robyn Butterworth. Three of them had shared what came to be referred to as "Meredith's last supper," a final meal of pizza and apple crumble.

The British Consulate whisked the British girls out of Perugia within days of the murder and resettled them in the northern Italian town of Bergamo to finish their studies. At least one went back to the U.K. Before they left, shocked, grieving, and horrified, they huddled at the police station, the questura, together with Amanda on the first night and answered questions about Meredith's last days, her boyfriends, and her habits. They said very little about the American roommate in those interviews.

Three months later, on February 8, 2008, Perugia policewomen traveled to Bergamo and interviewed the British girls again. That time they talked only about Amanda Knox, who had been arrested for murder three months prior. Now the British girls remembered many things they had failed to think about in the days right after Meredith's death. They remembered that Amanda Knox was loud, rather boorish, and strange. She played the same guitar chord over and over and burst into song spontaneously when people were talking. She had the unfortunate American ignorance about European toilets, which are designed differently from American toilets, with less standing water inside them, and must be scrubbed out with a toilet brush after use. Amanda never cleaned up after herself, and Meredith agonized over the propriety of telling the American, asking her friends how to handle something so intimate.

"The first time I met Amanda it was in the Pizzeria Il Bacio, halfway through October," Amy Frost said. "I was a bit perplexed because she was speaking very loudly, and I remember that more or less our table had been split into three people on one side and three on the other, and Amanda wasn't talking with any group in particular. She was kind of like an outsider. At one point, without talking to one group or the other, she started singing, and everybody was perplexed."

"Tell us," encouraged the police.

"Meredith said a lot of things when Amanda arrived in the house. She said she was very weird."

For example, Amanda kept a bunny vibrator and condoms in plain view in the bathroom the two girls shared. She had a suitcase, and instead of keeping clothes in it, she had a teapot in it and different kinds of teas. "Meredith told me also that Amanda cared a lot about keeping Filomena's friendship and Laura's friendship," Amy went on. "Laura had five or six or seven earrings on one ear, and the next day Amanda had six or seven earrings in her ear."

"Did Meredith ever tell you if Amanda had proposed to have sexual parties?"

"No," Amy replied. "But I remember Amanda told Meredith she didn't have problems with nudity, with showing herself naked; she said she talked on the phone with her boyfriend completely naked. She said that back in America she even talked to a friend's boyfriend while naked. Meredith also told me that Amanda told her she had an erotic dream and wrote it in a letter to send to her boyfriend in America.

"When we met her the first time, she told me she had a boyfriend in America who was about to leave for China. She told me they had agreed to be very free, that she was open and could have other relationships. She also told us her boyfriend told her he had met a girl in China, and she had told him, 'Wonderful! Describe her to me.' And I thought this was strange."

IN LATE SEPTEMBER, MEREDITH Kercher had already been in town for several weeks and knew where to go with her English posse. They knew that even if they stayed at Merlin Pub until closing time at 2 A.M., they could still board buses to take them outside the *centro* and down to the bigger discos that stayed open until five or six in the morning.

The British girls stuck together. They shared the universal collegiate party goal: to drink without losing consciousness, flirt without becoming too entangled, laugh until the sun came up.

A Moroccan immigrant, Hicham Khiri, joined their entourage for a few weeks. Slight, dark, and intense, Hicham, who also went by the name "Shaky," made up for what he lacked in machismo with his passable English. Arabic was his first language, English his second, Italian his third. As an immigrant, he was a Perugia success story: he worked two jobs, making pizzas from four until midnight and, in the morning, running his own hip-hop clothing store from a tiny storefront on the street a few dozen yards from the Etruscan arch. He called his shop "Street Dream."

Shaky had acquired one other critical and tangible sign of success: a car, which aided greatly in the pursuit of women. The British girls cared more for his wheels than his personality.

"We were at the Gradisca bar," he told police a few days after Meredith's body was discovered, when he was summoned as "a person informed about the facts." The Gradisca was a massive after-hours party warehouse with seven bars a half hour away from the *centro*. Perugia pubs provide buses to ferry students to it after midnight. "It was Saturday, and I was with a friend called Abdel. I could see that all the staff from the Merlin were inside and lots of foreign women students. As we were leaving the car park at the end of the evening, we met Meredith and Sophie—Sophie was drunk—with another woman I don't know. Meredith asked me if we could take them home, given the state Sophie was in."

Shaky drove the girls home, and later, in a fit of drunken appreciation, Sophie "loaned" him a silver ring he admired. She would spend the next few weeks trying to recover it, while Shaky held on to it as bait to keep the pretty English girl coming back.

Later she told police he had stolen it, but that was not his story.

AMANDA HAD NO PREEXISTING set of friends from home, cultural companions like Meredith and the British girls. In the fall of 2007, she was isolated in her nationality. Most of the foreign students in Perugia were

Polish, Chinese, or Spanish. Amanda's isolation was partly self-imposed. There was a group of young Americans in Perugia at the Umbra Institute, a tiny private school for Americans just up the hill from her cottage. But Amanda avoided them. She said she wanted to avoid speaking English, to immerse herself in Italian.

Umbra Institute founder Daniel J. Tartaglia never met Amanda. He is a rotund Italian American from New Jersey who has founded schools for Americans in Rome and Florence as well as Perugia. In those larger cities, which annually host hordes of upper-middle-class American kids traveling internationally and alone for the first time, students regularly wash up in hospitals on weekends with alcohol poisoning or careen into the Arno or Tiber River or Trevi Fountain and get arrested. Tartaglia carefully steered his students away from what he called "the vortex" of Perugia party life. He brought in police officers or other local authorities to explain local laws and had students sign documents indicating that they understood and respected Italian customs. He aimed, he said, to ensure that his students avoided the fate of Amanda Knox—a girl he reckoned was probably guilty of participating in murder.

The Università per Stranieri, Amanda's school, offered no such training. Administrators there took what might be considered a more European attitude toward college-age students. They were expected to understand how to behave responsibly and respect local rules.

Amanda liked to party, but she wasn't into hard drinking as the British girls were. Her choice of intoxicant was, apparently, "smoke." Besides her more moderate drinking habits, she contrasted with the British girls stylewise. Meredith got full Brazilians and varnished her nails, advanced feminine grooming habits that had never occurred to Amanda, who strummed guitar in a sweatshirt and and went for a natural look. No mascara and no lip gloss. She did, though, get the extra ear piercings and, in some accounts, had begun lightening her dark blond hair.

The American was a lone wolf, alone with her English language, alone with her rudimentary Italian, alone with male admirers she collected at every bend in the medieval alleys. On her own, Amanda wandered the city, picking up mostly male friends. She started socializing with a young Greek who ran an Internet café near the house. Spyros Gatsios, a longtime Perugia resident, later said of her only that she was a sweet girl who liked Raffaele because "he was timid." Meredith and the British girls gave Spyros a nickname—"Internet Man." Amanda also brought home another guy, an Algerian nonstudent her roommate Laura had introduced her to, with the cumbersome name Louerguioui Juba. He went by the nickname Juve after one of Italy's soccer teams. Juve had a job handing out flyers for a pub called Le Chic, and eventually he introduced Amanda to his boss so she, too, could get a job.

Diya "Patrick" Lumumba was one of lily white Perugia's few long-time black residents. Born in Congo to well-off parents who earned a living in import-export, Lumumba was distantly related to the Congolese independence movement leader Patrice Lumumba, the first legally elected prime minister of Congo, who was assassinated by the CIA in the 1960s. Patrick Lumumba arrived in Perugia to study Italian and political science in the 1980s and stayed. He played bongo drums, organized classical and contemporary musical concerts at the Università per Stranieri—his alma mater—and lived with a Polish woman with whom he was raising a son. With his roly-poly brown face and nubbly short-dreads hairdo, he looked about as sinister as a teddy bear. He was something of a multicultural town mascot.

Lumumba had opened Le Chic only two months before Juve brought Amanda around. "Juve told me she needed money, and I gave her a job for five euros an hour," Lumumba said.

The pretty American girl turned out to be both a boon and a problem. She was pretty enough to attract customers, but Lumumba felt she spent most of her work time responding to come-ons from male admirers, and she almost never wiped the tabletops clean without being reminded.

Lumumba said he had grown disappointed in her work habits. But the young American kept tables of men around buying drinks. "As soon as people get up, you clean up so other people can sit down, and she didn't think of that. The men come in, and when they see a pretty girl, they start talking and try to chat and stuff, and she would stop and talk to them instead of working."

He talked to her about it a few times. Amanda would apologize profusely and then still not clean the tables. Amanda later insisted that she was deflecting the advances by being agreeable. "I went out of my way NOT to flirt," she wrote in her prison diary.

It might have been a matter of perspective. Sexual innuendo and harassment are a fact of life for young women. Navigating it is a matter of style and experience, and Amanda's hallmark was agreeability. *I'm in love with smiles. I think they are the most attractive things about a person. I'm drawn to them and I'm drawn towards inviting people to make them.*

Lumumba recalled a girl who was simultaneously confident and transparently desperate to fit in. "If she walked into the bar now, within half an hour she'd be talking with people. And with guys, because she was pretty and sometimes she maybe didn't realize, maybe she was too accessible. And she'd socialize too much. There's open people and talkative people—and people who have problems talking to others.

"She was very sure of herself. For example, if there's a famous person in the place, some people will say, 'Oh I don't want to bother her' . . . but Amanda would have just gone right up. And she would change her personality based on making people happy. Not that she was an actress. She'd change things and make them hers, based on what the people she liked liked. Let's say I dye my hair red and you ask me why and I say, 'Oh, because I love my hair red,' when actually it's not true, it's because someone she admires has red hair. She would interpret roles based on the situation. Like in a movie, if the film requests it, the actor has to change for the role."

Lumumba thought his winsome barmaid had fewer girlfriends than boyfriends. "In court I saw the friends, but I didn't meet many friends. She attracted more men than women."

She didn't have to try hard, either. "She dressed like a student.

Maybe she was even a little more classic than other students can be. Never saw her stomach."

THE BAR GIRL JOB brought in money and the male fans provided diversion, but Amanda often had little reason to wander far from 7 via della Pergola for amusement. Most nights there was some kind of party happening downstairs. The scene wasn't much different from what had gone on in the UW dorms, but smoking up with Italians who spoke barely a word of English was infinitely more exotic.

To Amanda and Meredith, the boys downstairs were cool Italian hipsters, not just four unsophisticated country boys from the wilderness east of Perugia. Marche is where Hannibal met his fate with the Romans, but besides that fact, there isn't much of interest in the area for non-Italians. It's a rural backwater.

To the girls, the coolest boy downstairs was Giacomo Silenzi, a long-haired, soft-spoken boy with something infinitely desirable in the eyes of both women: he played guitar in a rock band.

ONE SATURDAY NIGHT IN early October, the residents of 7 via della Pergola ventured out together to a now-shuttered disco called RedZone that attracted hard-core after-hours partiers from all over central Italy. Loosened up by drink, blaring music, and flashing colored lights, Meredith and Giacomo started making out. Amanda cuddled with a boy from Rome named Daniele who was visiting Perugia for the weekend, a cousin of her housemate Stefano Bonassi. Eventually the foursome piled into one of the boys' cars and headed back to 7 via della Pergola, where they paired off into bedrooms and had drunken sex.

After the murder, the press and authorities portrayed the romance between Giacomo and Meredith as a true-love affair. The Italians, uncomfortable with the terminology—if not the facts—of "hooking up" familiar to young people in the United States and United Kingdom, euphemistically call all young people who have sex *fidanzati*—literally, "engaged."

Giacomo and Meredith had slept together for only about two weeks before Meredith was murdered. The language barrier between them was so strong that they rarely spoke on the phone, and they never went on dates in public. Giacomo was shy or embarassed about Meredith. "I think Giacomo was more into it than she was," said Giacomo's roommate Marco Marzan. Pressed for all the intimate details, Marco told police that Giacomo had boasted of having had anal and oral sex with Meredith.

In the early days, long before the trial, before he understood what was at stake, Giacomo revealed more to reporters than he did to the prosecutor about the casual nature of his relationship with Meredith Kercher, the girl the prosecutor and press insisted on calling his *fidanzata,* his betrothed, even though he'd known her for less than a month. "I really liked her," Giacomo said to an Italian reporter, "but I didn't feel at all jealous about her." In fact, he had kept a public distance: when he saw her on the corso or unexpectedly ran into her anywhere outside the house they shared, he pretended not to know her.

Eventually the British girls remembered something else they'd failed to think about at the questura, and they told Mignini about that too: Meredith, they said, thought Amanda was competing with her for Giacomo. Amanda played guitar with Giacomo; they had that in common, even if they couldn't speak to each other. Meredith came to suspect that even after she and Giacomo were "together," Amanda would sneak downstairs and play guitar with her boyfriend. When Giacomo went for Meredith instead of Amanda, Amy Frost told police, Amanda said to Meredith, "I like Giacomo too, but you can have him." According to Frost, the remark "upset" Meredith.

.   .   .

AT JUST BEFORE SEVEN in the evening on October 25, 2007, students trooped into the Aula Magna, the "great room," on the second floor of the baroque-styled, eighteenth-century Università per Stranieri main building. The art on the walls—murals of bricklayers, bridges, horses, men and women at work—was painted by the Italian futurist Gerardo Dottori. Hard-backed chairs upholstered with blue velvet were lined up in rows before a grand piano. White plaster busts of Virgil and Dante protruded from the front wall, and the Quintetto Bottesini was setting up. The five musicians—on viola, violin, cello, double bass, and piano—would play music by the eighteenth- and nineteenth-century composers Franz Schubert, Ferdinand Ries, Franz Limmer, Ralph Vaughan Williams, and Wolfgang Amadeus Mozart and contemporary pieces by Astor Piazzolla and modern Italian composers.

As the musicians tuned up, Amanda and Meredith slipped into the room and took a pair of seats. Amanda scanned the room and noticed a pale boy with wire-rimmed glasses, a hank of light brown hair, sharp cheekbones, nice mouth. The boy was more pretty than handsome, more Aryan than Italian. Her luck had been excellent with men in this town so far, and there was no reason to exercise restraint or caution now. She stared boldly into his eyes and didn't look away. Smiled.

Italian girls rarely, if ever, approached Raffaele Sollecito, twenty-three, quite so brazenly. A computer major and rich doctor's youngest child and only son from a southern seaside town, in Perugia, Raffaele was like a rich kid from Miami at a small-town school in the Midwest. Not as hip as a kid from New York but still noticeably a cut above. Young sophisticates from Milan or Turin or Rome rarely washed up in Umbria.

Raffaele's mother had recently died, and the young man had a melancholy streak, a hash-smoking habit, and an expensive car and was two weeks away from getting his computer engineering degree. But he didn't have the savvy self-confidence, hairy chest, or five o'clock shadow masculine looks that girls his age went for. In fact, he had apparently given up hope of having actual sex, although he was no stranger to the virtual delights of porn. He was a virgin and pothead, and he had ventured down to the concert to take a break from writing his engineering thesis, not expecting to meet the girl of his dreams.

In the popular narrative of the crime, Raffaele played the supporting role of the weak, sexually besotted male, the coddled boy with hidden perversions that Amanda unlocked. The truth was both more and less complicated.

The boy did grow up with money, in the small, ancient Adriatic town of Giovinazzo, supposedly founded by Perseus, a son of Zeus, with a fortress dating back to Trajan, just north of the port of Bari. In the ubiquitous Christmas plays and crèches performed in his church-dominated childhood community, Raffaele was always picked to play an angel because of his yellow hair and green eyes. His life was not blessed, though, nor was he particularly angelic.

The doctor's youngest son was the apple of his mother's eye, but the marriage was troubled and the family dynamic highly unusual. His six-years-older sister was a tomboy who grew up to become a ranking carabiniere, even organizing security for a Bush visit to Rome. But after Raffaele was arrested, her perceived efforts to help him got her into trouble, and she was fired. At the time of the trial, Vanessa, a short, muscular blonde, was making a living as a personal trainer in Rome.

School friends remembered Raffaele as a quiet, reserved, even melancholy child. In a picture of the boy at five years old in his father's living room, his face has a hauntingly sad expression. "We called him the Little Lord," said one, "because he walked and dressed like English nobility." He was a dreamy, imaginative boy, somewhat solitary, not aggressive, although he took up kickboxing in high school. He played with dolls, too. "I liked to play with toys, with videogames, with computers, and also fight my big doll," he wrote to me from prison in good but far from perfect English, trying to describe his childhood. "I liked to mix heterogeneous toys to imagine apocalyptical stories with war and love. I also played with my sister's dolls, combing their hair and dressing them."

As a teenager, besides kickboxing, he collected manga comics. He also got into the habit of wearing a small knife on his jeans, which his friends insist was an affectation the boys shared. He hung out with a large group of fifteen kids calling themselves the *giovanezzi*. Timid around girls, he also held females in unusually high regard, at least by local standards. His friends scoffed at the notion that he would participate in a sex game with a third man. "Normally if he saw one girl that he liked, nobody else existed until he got that girl," said one boyhood pal, who was in China when he heard his old friend had been arrested. "When we saw them on TV saying that Raffaele was a sex freak, we all knew that when he set eyes on one girl, that was the one he wanted to marry. It was totally out of the question for him to go to rave parties or look at any other girl apart from his girlfriend. Once he got the girl-friend, he couldn't believe he'd gotten one, so he was careful not to lose her, and he put the blinkers on. If he liked a girl, she was, to him, the best girl around."

When Raffaele was a young teen, his father left his wife for another woman, and Raffaele remained in Giovinazzo with his mother. Vanessa was already out of the family house and training to be a carabiniere.

At eighteen, Raffaele left his mother's house and moved three hundred miles north into Perugia's ONAOSI building, a marble-floored, three-story luxury hotel of sorts with a huge park, its own church, a library, a gym, a palatial lobby, and a reception desk, housing six hundred boys and young men between the ages of ten and twenty-five. The dorm had strict rules (no flip-flops or shorts, no piercings, early curfew, no girls at night) and luxury (Sky TV in every room, sheets changed daily by the staff, a hair salon, and tennis courts).

Among the many privileges afforded to children of doctors in Italy is luxury housing created for the orphaned children of doctors, called Fondazione Opera Nazionale Assistenza Orfani Sanitari Italiani, or

ONAOSI. These fancy dormitories are also available to the children of living doctors, offering a supervised halfway point between the family nest and apartments at colleges, which generally do not offer dormitories.

"I chose Perugia because I wanted to find my way away from home," Raffaele wrote to me in 2010, "and in Perugia they had ONAOSI." His father also had some say in the decision. The doctor felt the setting would provide a secure transition to independence for his shy, sightly wayward son.

The ONAOSI system offered parents like Dott. Sollecito a sense of security, but for the boy residents, the place was part monk's cloister and part boarding school dorm, with the worst aspects of both, including hazing and bullying, among the hazards. "There is a bad feeling in there," said one former resident. "Lots of envy. It is clean, you eat very well, you can study, but it's just boys and very repressed. There is violence inside, stories of abuse, and the bathrooms are in common. If you stay there too long, you can get crazy. There are a lot of strange people inside, it's very closed, and you get into weird habits. You do the same things every day. Spying is a big part of what they do."

Before Raffaele, previous sensational ONAOSI misfits included a young graduate who killed several children in the 1990s, becoming known as the Monster of Foligno. Another young resident simply disappeared off the face of the earth, rumored to have been the victim of a satanic cult.

At ONAOSI, Raffaele was certainly watched if not actually warped. After his arrest, prosecutors ferreted out some former dorm mates who described the boy as withdrawn but also into hard-core "violent" or animal porn. For the shy young man who had played with dolls in his mother's house, the transition into a rooming house with other young men was traumatic.

When Raffaele was nineteen, during his second year at ONAOSI, tragedy crashed down on him: his beloved mother died. According to the family, she died of a sudden heart condition. The rumor among the boys in the dorm was that she had committed suicide because Dott. Sollecito was about to remarry. In any case, Raffaele felt both bereaved and guilty because he was not home when she died. Yet for months, his sister remembered, he couldn't cry about it.

Her death also made Raffaele and his sister rich: they inherited her real estate. If the civil suits against the convicted students reap anything for the Kerchers, the money will come from his assets.

"My mother was very calm and devoted to her family, especially to sons (daughter)," he wrote to me. She was not at all like Vanessa, he added: "She was more womanly than my sister."

After his mother died, Raffaele went to Munich with the Erasmus Program and there, for the first time in his life, apparently felt free. When he returned to Perugia, he moved into an apartment of his own. He wrote about living abroad in his blog in October 2006. In one entry that would come back to haunt him a year later, he described how well his grandmother was doing and his needing to take care of her, and how weird and depressed everyone was at the ONAOSI dorm, how happy he had been to live abroad. "Erasmus is just a dream, pure lightheartedness, you only have to worry to live and not how to live, it feels like an ideal society that can't work in reality." The experience had changed him, he wrote, and "I can only hope to find stronger emotions that can surprise you [sic] again."

Judges, police, and reporters would take the "stronger emotions" phrase as the words of a young man capable of a twisted sex murder.

LIKE ALL ITALIAN PARENTS, whose child coddling is legendary, Dott. Sollecito kept a tight grip on his boy in Perugia from a distance—calling him several times daily and eventually sharing the young man's personal blog password, apparently so he could monitor and clean up any embarrassing indiscretions. He would live to rue the day he did not take down a picture Raffaele had posted of himself dressed as a surgeon wielding a meat cleaver. Even with paternal oversight, on his own in

Perugia, Raffaele maintained a regular hash habit and managed to post what would be seen as incriminating statements and pictures on his blog. Like most of the college boys in Perugia, Raffaele had maintained some adolescent habits well into his twenties. He had never given up his thirteen-year-old affectation of clipping a penknife to his belt, and he still treasured his boyhood sword collection. He actually had a drug record: he'd been picked up in Giovinazzo holding two grams of hash but released without charge. He eventually told Amanda—according to one of her scribbled notes to self at the police station after they had been arrested—that he had suffered from depression, had felt guilty about his mother's death, had once dyed his hair yellow, and had tried acid and cocaine.

His hash habit had perhaps slowed but not derailed his studies. By October 2007, he had summoned enough focus to be just two weeks away from graduation at age twenty-three—not a terribly overdue graduation age by University of Perugia standards. His professional plan incorporated his adolescent passions: after getting his secondary degree in visual computing at Milan, he wanted to go to the United States or Cambridge and study virtual reality computing.

That same week, in a posh seaside apartment complex near Bari, his stepmother was consumed with the details of planning a huge party for him in two weeks. She had already mailed out the party invitations for his graduation, along with little cards that read "Dott. Raffaele Sollecito."

The last thing he expected to find while writing his graduation thesis on genetic programming was love. He later wrote to his father, "My first impression was that this was an interesting girl, she looked at me over and over again and seemed to be searching for something in my eyes, like a particular interest. Then I sat near her to talk, and I noticed that her opinions on the music were odd because she didn't concentrate on the emotions it provoked but on only the rhythm—slow, fast, slow."

When Amanda met him at the concert, Raffaele had reached a number of young-adult milestones. He had lost a parent. He was living on his own in the maid-serviced apartment of a medieval building on Corso Garibaldi. He had his own car, a dark-colored Audi parked on the street below. But he was still deep into video games and manga comics and hash. His dad still checked up on him every day.

And he was a virgin.

His favorite song, according to his blog, was the catchy 1980s ballad "Sweet Dreams" by the Eurhythmics, in which Annie Lennox tells of having traveled "the world and the seven seas" only to find out "everybody's looking for something. Some of them want to use you, . . . some of them want to abuse you, some of them want to be abused." Besides having sex for the first time in October 2007, Raffaele thought he had found something else in Amanda in the two weeks they spent together: a soul mate.

"It was love at first sight. I was attracted to her curious disposition and, of course, to her beautiful teen appeal," he wrote in one letter from jail. Amanda had Raffaele at *"Ciao."*

MEREDITH LEFT AT INTERMISSION, and Raffaele took her seat. After the music stopped, they stepped outside together under a nearly full moon. Amanda went to work at Le Chic, and Raffaele followed her. When her shift was finished, they walked together to Raffaele's maid-serviced apartment on Corso Garibaldi, a five-minute walk from Amanda's.

Corso Garibaldi is a very old street, lined with convents and social clubs and door mantels carved with religious and alchemical symbols. Tiny lanes lead off into dark courtyards and down steep staircases with names like via Scura, via Spada, and via Gentile (shadowy, sword, nice). Amanda told Raffaele he looked like Harry Potter. He rolled a joint, cutting the hash with the pocket knife he always carried.

They spent that night together in Raffaele's bed. The boy woke up the next morning no longer a virgin, with an American girl next to him. Later that morning, Amanda brought her new admirer home for lunch. They'd known each other less than twenty-four hours, and the young

Italian was in thrall. To Filomena, reflecting on it after the arrests, their intense "PDA" behavior was bizarre.

"He was really attached to her," Filomena told police. "Physically attached. She would stand up to wash the dishes, and he would get up and hug her; she would play the guitar, and he would follow her. She said she had just met him."

After she hooked up with Raffaele, Amanda never slept another night at the via della Pergola cottage. "You could tell she wasn't at home, and then she came back in the morning. I would see her at one in the afternoon," Filomena told police. "She told me and Laura that because she had a boyfriend in America, she was feeling guilty, but she said she was happy with Raffaele because he treated her well. We asked if she had told her boyfriend in America about him, and she said, 'Yes, he doesn't care.'" Amanda had the attention—the complete, puppylike devotion—of a wealthy Italian doctor's son. By American man-hunting standards, Amanda was the winner of the college boyfriend competition hands down. It is possible that to the hippie-chick Amanda, money and status were less important than rock-boy style, and Raffaele was too shy and conventional to seem like a great prize. Thus, in theory, Meredith's relationship with Giacomo remained a jealous thorn in her side, even when Raffaele entered the picture.

From jail, in the early days of his incarceration, Raffaele wrote his dad about Amanda: "During that time when we were together, she was elusive. I thought that she was out of this world. She lived her life like a dream, she was detached from reality, she could not distinguish dream from reality. Her life seemed to be pure pleasure. . . . I try to understand what Amanda's role was in this event. The Amanda I know . . . lives a carefree life. Her only thought is the pursuit of pleasure. . . . But even the thought that she could be a killer is impossible for me."

Later he wrote to me from his prison cell at Terni, after he and Amanda had both been sentenced for murder, "I think that what we have in common is the love for fantasy, dreams and imagination."

9

VENDEMMIA

What can I say of the games we won and lost together? It was great
when we went to the away games in the Mitico minibus. There was
laughter on board with Segoloni, who called me "Little Chocolate."
God. What beautiful moments. . . . I remember also, from that time,
that I knew that little, all-black dog that you found abandoned and
took to your house and that often I took him for a walk. . . . What
can I say, Paolo? It would be a lot to remember, but these pages
wouldn't be enough. . . . I thank you, Paolo, your Wife, your Son . . .
Your Son Francesco (THE BROTHER I WOULD HAVE WANTED
TO HAVE). And that little black dog.

—*Rudy Guede,* letter from prison to his childhood teacher and
basketball coach, Paolo Barbini

BY AUGUST 2007, AS THE days began to shorten even as the oppressive
summer heat still pressed northward across the Mediterranean from
the Sahara, Rudy Guede was back in Perugia, a lost man seeking direction, though he knew not how to find it. He had lost the care and good

graces of the Caporalis, and his bartending job in the North was a thing of the past, as was his Milan basketball team standing. He had no income and no prospects. But he was still a basket prodigy and a proper Perugino. Thanks to the three years with the Caporalis, he could walk the walk and talk the talk of the aristocracy. He had forfeited the trust of the *padrone,* but Mrs. Caporali still had a soft spot in her heart for the poor abandoned boy, and she gave him a crucial character reference enabling him to get his own first apartment right in the *centro.* Without any known savings or a job but with that letter, he persuaded a Perugia property owner to rent him—for 360 euros a month—a studio apartment in a little building at the end of a narrow lane called via Canerino, the Street of the Little Canary, just off Corso Garibaldi and mere yards away from Raffaele's place. Rudy's apartment, big enough only for a bed and a stove, was in a medieval three-story structure, honeycombed like the rest of the Perugia housing stock with Sheetrock cubicles to contain as many rent-paying students as possible. Upstairs were some hot Spanish girls; downstairs, some fun-loving Italian guys.

In the summer of 2007, Rudy befriended a tall blond American from Seattle named Victor Oleinikov. Victor was a University of Washington film student in his junior year, studying Italian in Perugia to fulfill his language requirement. Although he shared an Italian professor with her, Victor had never met or heard of Amanda Knox. In fact, he left Perugia at the end of September, just as she was settling into the via della Pergola cottage, and their paths never crossed.

Nineteen-year-old Victor (tall, very white, orthodontically corrected, blue eyed, gawky, parent-supported, and American) and Rudy (tall, black, broke, and parentless) got along nicely. Victor had spent the previous year studying Italian in Seattle, and he had acquired some vocabulary and a decent accent, but he was still pretty embarrassed to road test it. To Victor, Rudy was a nonjudgmental Italian with a real admiration for Americans, even if he was "kind of an eccentric and kind of a weird guy."

Victor doesn't remember exactly how he met Rudy. When he arrived in early summer, all the Italian kids were already home on vacation, leaving a core of transient international students in town on brief summer programs, partying into the hot nights and moving into and out of the city every week. Victor bounced around, staying at different times in three different student apartments, hanging with Spaniards, Brits, Greeks, Central Asians, generally having a good time. The students regularly bought hash—not very good hash, Victor noted; the high lasted only fifteen minutes—from dealers who stored their stash in little metal utility boxes on the side streets off Corso Vannucci.

For a while Victor was partying with a Tajik guy who introduced him to some wild Moroccans, and through them, he thinks, he maybe first encountered Rudy out on Corso Vannucci during Umbria Jazz. They met again at Merlin or Domus, and Rudy invited them back to his apartment and cooked them pasta with pancetta, which they ate sitting on his bed. After that, Victor says, "me and Rudy started kickin', I guess."

The tall young men played basketball together at the Piazza Grimana court, and Rudy told Victor he had stopped playing with a league because he'd had surgery on his leg. He showed off a vertical scar to prove it, which Victor thought looked like Achilles' tendon surgery, down near his ankle. "He was pretty good at basketball. He was, like, really athletic, six foot one or two. He was long, and he could jump." In late August, Rudy started working out with the Perugia team again and was gone most of the day. Then, Victor thought, he looked as though he was in even better shape than before.

Victor never wondered how his friend supported himself because Rudy told him his dad was a computer programmer in Florence and every other Wednesday Rudy took the two-hour train ride up into Tuscany to visit him and get his allowance. Once Victor and Rudy went to Bologna and Parma on the train and just bummed around for a weekend. Rudy never asked Victor for money.

At night Rudy would cook pasta at his tiny apartment, and then the buddies would disco until dawn. Domus opened at 1 A.M. Once the club bouncer inexplicably barred Rudy at the door, and Rudy got angry and claimed it was racism. He even complained to a nearby cop, who ignored him.

Rudy was a good dancer, and girls really liked dancing with him, was how Victor saw it. Rudy "wasn't really a creepy dude," he was just a fun-loving guy with a few quirks. For instance, he really did listen to his iPod in the bathroom.

The two friends got close enough in a few weeks that Rudy started sleeping over at the students' pad instead of at his own place. That's when Victor realized just how eccentric his quiet friend was. His version of a night spent with Rudy reads almost like one of Amanda Knox's bizarre "dark" short stories.

"He'd be, like, 'I'll just crash on your floor.' Okay, cool. We had two beds, and we put down blankets in the middle on the floor for him. And he'd fall asleep, but at some random point he'd get up and you could interact with him when he was in this weird stage. His eyes were semi-open. It was obvious he'd still be sleeping. It was weird. He was acting out these weird things. At one point I remember he was acting like he was a teacher. He'd ask us questions like a quiz or something like that. He was up and standing by what he thought was a board, which was actually a dresser, and giving us this lecture thing in Italian and English, mixed. And then he went to sleep and he started, like, he had a dream that he was a dog, so he started crawling around barking and shit. It was weird."

Next morning, the students asked Rudy what was up with that. "We were, like, 'Dude, you've got this problem, man. You were up all night.' And he was, like, 'Yeah, I know.' Apparently when he was in his apartment, he had to hide his keys because he claimed that he'd left the apartment before and walked for miles somewhere and woken up somewhere random."

While Victor and Rudy's other party buddies chalked up his behavior to just being "a weird dude," he was actually showing symptoms of a clinical condition. According to the sleep disorder expert and psychiatrist Mark Mahowald of the University of Minnesota, psychiatrists call such behavior a psychogenic dissociative state, or fugue state, and it often afflicts survivors of childhood abuse or other trauma. Dissociative fugue involves unplanned travel or wandering, sometimes accompanied by the establishment of a new identity. Fugues may be preceded by stressful events and can last for hours, days, or even months. Psychogenic dissociation is associated with multiple-personality disorder and is always related to childhood physical or sexual abuse, Mahowald says.

Rudy wasn't a big drug user or seller. When they first met, Victor saw Rudy go to the duomo steps and buy some coke, and then they all went to a club. But later in the summer, Rudy "got really weird"—practically phobic—about not wanting to go near the drug sellers and the duomo steps.

"We'd be hanging out on the steps, like prefunking, going to the bar, and just hanging out, and he would want to leave. Like, 'Dude, I don't like the steps, there's all these drug dealers up there' and stuff like that. And he'd never want to go back—after that one time. We smoked a little hash too, I think once, and he didn't join us. He was, like, very antidrug after that one episode."

It's possible, Victor thinks, that Rudy owed someone on the steps some money. "That's the only plausible explanation for him all of a sudden not wanting to go and be around them. Because another reason why he'd wanted to sleep over at our place was he didn't want to walk back home alone. He'd say, 'It's late, there's a lot of drug dealers and robbers around.' And we were, like, 'Dude, it's not that bad!' But, that's another reason he'd cite for wanting to stay at our house.

"Another day, Rudy came over, it was later in September, and told us a story about something that had happened the night before. He said, 'I got into some weird shit last night, I saw this guy follow this girl home, and I went into her house and had to fight him off.' It was like one of those 'what happened last night' stories. And it sounded serious."

It wasn't easy for a young man of no means to keep up with the parent-funded students, who, like him, had no visible means of support but who, unlike him, didn't have the wolf at the door. He never asked Victor for money, but he was seriously short on cash: two days before the murder of Meredith Kercher, he tried to borrow 10 euros from an Italian student acquaintance.

By the end of October 2007, Rudy's secret life as a young man teetering on the edge of poverty was like antimatter, a thing that threatened to annihilate every story he told his student friends. There was no dad in Florence with money and computer skills, there was just Roger, an African bricklayer down on the flats, with several children by different mothers, a family Rudy wanted nothing to do with anymore. Rudy now stood at the windows of the warmly lit houses of proper Italian lives, desperate for any kind of home.

As summer turned into fall, his two lives were running closer together, especially at night, when Rudy let down his guard, smoked hash, had a drink, tried to sleep, and helplessly found himself *transformed*. He had to stay alert, but he couldn't. He started falling asleep on toilets with his iPod clamped on his ears.

Ivana Tiberi and her son Gabriele last saw Rudy in October 2007. They knew he didn't have a job, and they were worried about him, but he didn't seem too concerned about it. On the contrary, "He seemed very calm, he wasn't panicking or anything," Gabriele, a sad-eyed, sincere man in his thirties, recalled. "He told us he had saved money and he had these little jobs. He always said that he was lucky because he had a lot of families when he was small. He didn't have a true, a blood family, but he had a lot of families. Sometimes when he had down moments, when his childhood things came back and made him sad, I would tell him, 'Look you've been very lucky in your misfortune. Your bad experiences.' With his personality, the way he was, a lot of people loved him."

But Rudy wasn't finding another welcoming family or much unconditional love on the streets of Perugia in late summer 2007. Weeks before Victor left Perugia for the United States at the end of September, the American got fed up with Rudy's sleepwalking episodes, and he and his roommate told Rudy to sleep at his own house.

Meanwhile, Rudy's old friends from Ponte San Giovanni were worried about him. One of them, interviewed by prosecutor Miginini after the murder, recounted Rudy's final months before the murder as a period when the young man seemed to have "lost his bearings" and was depressed. "He liked being with people and he loved meeting different people, breaking down barriers, and if they were foreigners, he always had this ability to get to know everybody. I think it was the only way he had to get out of his situation. I think he was very down, in a bad situation, and was starting to not have money." The friend described Rudy's life in September and October as "this unstable situation . . ." and said the friends Rudy was making in the Perugia *centro* were false friends. "The real friends were us, the ones from Ponte San Giovanni. The others weren't all friendships."

Unbeknown to his Perugia student buddies or his more downscale Ponte San Giovanni friends, Rudy had been caught in one home invasion attempt in early fall 2007. By the time he was convicted for the murder of Meredith Kercher, police knew he'd been involved in three break-ins before the killing, one in Milan and two in Perugia.

On the night of September 27, between 1 and 4 A.M., the bartender Christian Tramontano woke up in his loft bed beside his girlfriend and heard someone in the room down below. He jumped down and saw a young black man "rummaging through our personal things," he later told police officer Monica Napoleoni. Tramontano shouted at the man, who "smelled like wine and spoke perfect Italian." The intruder responded by brandishing a chair like a lion tamer to keep him at bay. "Then he pulled out a pocketknife, which scared me, and then he ran away." Tramontano called the police emergency number, but he never filed a report at the questura because whenever Tramontano went— three times, he claimed—the line of immigrants seeking official papers was too long and he didn't feel like waiting.

Tramontano later recognized Rudy at the Domus disco. When he saw Rudy in Merlin after that, Pisco kicked Rudy out. Tramontano went to the police in January 2008 after pictures of Rudy, now a Kercher murder suspect, appeared in the newspaper, and finally told his story to the police.

A week after the Tramontano incident, hundreds of miles to the north, on a busy commercial street in Milan, the nursery school owner Maria Antonietta Salvadori Del Prato entered her school on Monday morning, October 8. The private English nursery school served fifty children between the ages of one and five and was located on a court-yard behind a massive wooden door that slides open to allow cars to enter and park. The door was usually closed and had to be buzzed open or opened with a code. The entrance to the school itself was across the courtyard and up some steps, through a locked glass door. To find it, one actually needed to know it was there. There was no sign, and it was impossible to stumble upon from the street.

Mrs. Del Prato walked in that morning and immediately sensed that something was amiss. The kitchen was a mess: over the weekend, some-one had cooked pounds of pasta and frozen spinach and left heaps of food in the sink. A small bowl of pasta with a spoon beside it lay on the floor near one of the tiny cots the preschoolers napped on.

The closet door in her office was open, and she quickly realized that 2,000 euros—cash from parents who had paid her on Friday in ad-vance for the coming month—was missing from a small cash box. She called police, who came, took her report, and left. The nursery school had never been robbed before, and Mrs. Del Prato found herself in the uncomfortable position of wondering if she should distrust any of the young girls who worked there as aides. One, an English girl, frequented the Milan clubs a little too often, in Mrs. Del Prato's opinion. "She was very moody, and I think she was doing drugs," Mrs. Del Prato recalled. "I always wondered if she had something to do with it, if she let some-one in." Not long afterward, the young woman resigned.

The following weekend, on the night between Saturday, October 13, and Sunday morning, someone broke a second-floor window to enter and rob the law offices of Paolo Brocchi on via del Roscetti in Perugia. The intruder or intruders entered from the unlit back of the building on via del Lupo—the ominously named Street of the Wolf—using the metal grate over a first-floor window as a sort of ladder by which to reach the small terrace of the second-story window. The intruder disabled the burglar alarm, then smashed the window and entered.

When Brocchi came to work the following Monday, he found the office stiflingly hot—whoever had broken in had turned up the heat, consumed a Fanta from the refrigerator, thrown coats on the floor, and moved objects around the office in mystifying ways—a pile of utensils and a screwdriver were neatly lined up on a lawyer's briefcase. Bits of glass had been moved from where the window had been broken and arranged in a neat little pile in another room. There was evidence of random rummaging everywhere: a medical kit had been rifled. Brocchi's cell phone, laptop, several USB sticks, and a portable printer were also missing.

Ten days later, on October 23, Rudy Guede's immediate next-door neighbor on via Canerino, Mara Madu Diaz, was at a friend's farm in Gualdo Tadino, about an hour's drive from Perugia, participating in the *vendemmia*—the annual grape harvest. She knew Rudy, as she often saw him in front of her house on his phone—he had to stand outside his own house to get cell service. She saw him almost daily, when she walked her dog in the morning and evening. He always said hello and often leaned down and petted her dog. That day, police interrupted her grape harvesting with bad news. Her little medieval house in Perugia—narrow, three floors high, with a single room on each floor—had been badly damaged in a fire.

She raced home to find her cat dead and her house nearly destroyed. Firemen and police told her a thief or thieves had entered through a lower window and that the fire had started on the third floor, in her bedroom, where someone had thrown a scarf over a lamp. Whoever had done the crime had first cooked a meal in the first-floor kitchen, pulling foodstuffs out of the pantry and refrigerator, scattering them on the floor, and leaving the stove on and refrigerator door open. "The firemen told me these exact words, '*Loro hanno gozzovigliato*' [they feasted here]," she recalled. "They had seen signs of eating, drinking, feasting. It was such a great mess when the firemen left."

Her cat strangled on the smoke, because whoever had feasted in the kitchen had left the pantry door open, blocking the animal's escape route. When Mrs. Madu Diaz finally assessed the damage, she found that the thief had cleaned out her jewel box, including a gold watch of her mother's.

She didn't see Rudy again after the fire. When she learned he had been arrested and had a habit of breaking into homes, she wondered if he'd had something to do with her disaster. But the police never charged anyone. Her insurance paid for repairs, and the little house became habitable again after three years of work.

Four days after the Perugia house fire, on Saturday morning, October 27, back up in Milan, Mrs. Del Prato needed to let a plumbing repairman and his assistant into her nursery school. It was around 9 A.M. She arrived with the workmen, unlocked the door, and walked past the children's "cubbies" with their taped-up names and large alphabet and teddy pictures, into her office. There she encountered a young man sitting in her office chair, looking mildly surprised to see her. "He was pulling the cable out of my computer," she recalled. "I think he was getting ready to hook up his laptop." She could see on the screen saver a picture of the stranger and the designer Giorgio Armani.

She was outraged, but the young man was cool and apologetic. "He was mellow, relaxed." He made no move to leave, but the plumbers blocked the exit stairs with the ladder anyway while Mrs. Del Prato dialed the police. "He kept saying, 'Oh, don't worry, I didn't take anything.' And then he sat there and waited."

The police arrived and asked the young man—Rudy Guede, it turned out—to open his backpack. Inside, they found a large knife. Mrs. Del Prato identified it as a kitchen knife from the nursery kitchen. "He didn't explain it," she recalled. "He didn't seem worried at all. He was, like, so what? Almost as if he had a right to be there. He told police, 'I'm a student from Perugia, and I got here last night and somebody told me for fifty euros, I could come here and sleep.'"

He told police he was South American. And since he was clean and polite, police didn't cuff him when they led him out of the nursery school and drove him to the police station. There they inspected his backpack and found a bunch of keys, a laptop, a cell phone, a small hammer of the type used to break bus windows in emergencies, and a woman's small gold watch. The laptop and cell phone were soon identified as belonging to Perugia lawyer Paolo Brocchi. Neither Perugia nor Milan police has ever revealed the ownership or fate of the women's gold watch.

The Milan police held Rudy for four hours, during which he sat in a chair and refused to answer questions. The Milan prosecutor, after a call to the Perugia police, released Rudy that afternoon. The Milan police didn't want to let him go, according to the officers involved, but they had no choice. Detention is up to the prosecutor on duty, and on that October Saturday morning, the prosecutor had many more serious cases to sort through than to keep this minor, nonviolent, potential burglar on their roster. Rudy was Perugia's problem, not Milan's. According to some accounts, the prosecutor actually called the Perugia police, who instructed him to send Rudy home. He confiscated the backpack with the laptop, cell phone, and watch and directed the young man to the train station. If they tried, the Milan police were never able to coax anything more out of Rudy about how he had happened to find the nursery school or whether he had been there before. The Milan authorities also made no connection between the stolen 2,000 euros at the nursery school and the Saturday break-in two weeks later. The first robbery remains unsolved.

On Monday, Rudy was back in Perugia and apparently concerned about his image. He showed up in the Brocchi law office in warm-up clothes, bobbling a basketball in one hand. Standing in the hallway, he earnestly explained to the office director that he'd bought the lawyers' cell phone and laptop from a guy in the Milan train station.

Mrs. Madu Diaz never saw the gold watch that had been in Rudy's backpack to know if it was her mother's. The Perugia police eventually gave the laptop back to the law firm.

Three weeks later, the robbed Perugia lawyers, Mrs. Del Prato, Mrs. Madu Diaz, Christian Tramontano, and the Milan police officers all recognized Rudy's picture on TV and in the national newspapers, when he was being sought for Meredith Kercher's murder. Other than Tramontano, who approached the Perugia police himself in January 2008, none of them was called in by authorities in connection with Amanda and Raffaele's case. Defense lawyers subpoenaed Mrs. Del Prato, who testified. Their subpoena to the Milan arresting police arrived "too late," according to the police, and they did not appear at the trial.

HALLOWTIDE

Returning from the nocturnal assemblies, we stopped in the cellars
to drink the best wine, then we shat into the barrels.

—*Mountaineers of Valais,* tried for witchcraft in 1428

NOVEMBER, THE NINTH MONTH IN ancient Rome. From the Latin *novem,* meaning "nine." Nine in the Bible is the number of finality, conclusion, judgment.

Across Europe over many cultures and eras, these are the Days of the Dead. The ancient Celts believed the dead mingled with the living at this time. The northern pagans called the period Samhain, and they wore costumes and lit bonfires to ward off ghosts. By order of the Catholic Church in the eighth century, the first day of November was reserved for veneration of saints, and the second day for remembering the mortal dead, whose souls return to their homes on that night, requiring candles to light their way. In English, October thirty-first through November second are called Hallowtide.

In America, the solemnity of these days has been trivialized, sweetened with chocolate bars and candy corn, celebrated as Halloween, with latex masks and plastic glow-in-the-dark skeletons commemorating the origins of the holiday. In Italy, the Days of the Dead are more somber, marked by family reunions, church visits, and feasting. The living turn their minds toward the dead. Children who have moved out of their parents' homes make their way back for this annual ritual. Italians dress up in their Sunday clothes and stroll to graveyards to lay piles of gold chrysanthemums on tombstones, in respect and in memoriam. The bakeries sell pale, almond-flavored cookies called *fave dei morti*, literally "beans of the dead." The annual family pilgrimage to the graveyards is only slightly less important than Christmas and Easter.

BY HALLOWEEN 2007, ALL the cliques and friendships, secret resentments and envies, flirtations, romances, crushes, and hookups were in place at 7 via della Pergola. Amanda Knox had spent the preceding six days and nights symbiotically joined with Raffaele Sollecito, an Italian rich kid with a secure future but possibly a computer geek by comparison with the guitar-strumming Giacomo downstairs. Raffaele had come to the cottage a few times to help cook the ever-important one o'clock lunch. Mostly they were sleeping at his maid-serviced apartment on Corso Garibaldi.

Meredith was spending some nights with Giacomo, but, as Giacomo would later testify, they didn't spend a lot of time outside the house on what would be called dates, nor did they make plans to meet on their cell phones, because they couldn't understand each other's speech very well.

Meredith and the British girls were on first-name, cell phone speed-dial basis with some of the Italian pub owners who catered to foreign students. They had figured out exactly who they needed to know to get free drink tickets and bus rides to the discos below the medieval city.

Everyone was looking for a costume.

Halloween isn't celebrated in Europe as enthusiastically as it is in the United States, but there were enough American and British students in Perugia to make a decently wild party of it. The British girls got their "fancy dress"—British for costumes—together. Meredith decided to go out as a vampire in a black cape with a high collar, a long bloody drip coming out of the side of her mouth, blood red lipstick. She and the girlfriends planned to wade out together into the party scene. Amanda Knox, on the other hand, would dress as a cat and go out alone. Raffaele would decorate her face before she left, drawing on whiskers and a nose.

On the streets of Perugia on Halloween night 2007, the moon was a few days into waning but still round. In the *centro*, a national feminist organization held a commemoration ceremony in honor of what it called "the Female Holocaust"—the burning of nine million women as witches during the Inquisition. If the English-speaking girls from the via della Pergola cottage—one of whom would be murdered in twenty-four hours in a supposedly satanic rite, the other convicted in what her lawyers and friends would call a witch trial—knew of or attended this commemoration a few hundred yards uphill from their cottage, there is no record of it.

The prayers for dead witches were concluded by the time partying students across the city poured out of their apartments and into the bars and the Corso Vannucci at the customary party hour of 10 P.M. Dozens of men in Edvard Munch *Scream* and Jason hockey goalie masks filled the streets. Hundreds of sickly ghouls, ax murderers, and vampires like Meredith Kercher pressed into the maelstrom of Merlin Pub, shrieking with laughter at one another's costumes, fidgeting in their own, downing copious alcohol to encourage the hilarity. They posed for endless pictures—snap, snap, snap went the digital cameras, recording Meredith Kercher and her girlfriends with dozens of different people.

Amanda was not in any of their pictures. Where was the American girl on that night of high holy partying? According to Raffaele, she left him around eight or nine after he painted her cat face on. She went to her workplace, Le Chic, alone. When prosecutor Mignini interrogated her in December 2007, after she'd been in jail for more than a month, she said she'd gone to Le Chic because she "knew everyone there."

"I went by myself, I knew everyone there, I know Patrick, I knew classmates, I knew there were people who would go to have fun there, like the girls from Kazakhstan, who were always together."

In his first statement to police, Raffaele Sollecito said that after he helped Amanda paint her face as a cat on Halloween, she tripped off into the dark alone without him. That perplexed both Mignini and the police. Why was the pretty, eye-catching American girl dressed in a cat outfit barhopping alone on Halloween? Where were her friends?

The police could only conclude that she must have felt lonely and rejected. Happy young women don't go out alone. Eventually the police read all of Amanda's phone messages and found a Halloween Day SMS exchange with Meredith in which Amanda asked what she was doing. Meredith had replied that she was going out with her friends, full stop. No invitation. The young women ended their SMS with "xxx"—kisses. Of course, those little *baci* could mean nothing at all or even their very opposite.

According to Amanda, she stayed at Le Chic until one in the morning, then strolled over to Merlin Pub, where she knew the English would be found. She went to meet Spyros, "Internet Man." Eventually they drifted back out into the *centro,* where she finally rejoined Raffaele at the duomo steps at two in the morning. Together they walked back to his place and made their way directly into his bed.

Lumumba, when a British tabloid paid him 70,000 euros for an interview in 2008 (and again after getting 20,000 euros from an Italian television show), said that Amanda had swanned into his pub alone on Halloween, started downing his free red wine, and cozied up in a back corner with not one but two men he didn't recognize. He also told them he had let Amanda know, before the murder, that he was going to fire her. When he later spoke with me, Lumumba dialed it back, barely remembering seeing Amanda out on Halloween night and denying numerous other critical statements he'd made in the paid interview, including that his wife had distrusted Amanda on first sight and that Amanda was "jealous" of Meredith. He also admitted that, contrary to what the British tabloids had printed, he hadn't fired Amanda before the murder, but that she told him she was going to quit on November 5— the morning before she went to jail.

By the time Amanda got to Merlin, Meredith and her friends had already whirled on to the disco Domus, where they met up with some other British Erasmus students from the University of Manchester. There they stayed until just before five in the morning, when Amy Frost remembers that she, Robyn Butterworth, and Meredith walked home— leaving party animal Sophie behind to close the place down with Shaky.

"I remember that at five I was already in my bed," Amy told police later.

AFTER HE WAS ARRESTED, Rudy Guede told police his own Halloween-night story. According to him, that's when he made a vampire connection with Meredith. At the time, he was still pretending to be South African. "We saw each other that Halloween night in some kids' house. I didn't recognize Meredith because she was dressed up like a vampire. When I recognized her, I told her, 'Wanna suck up my blood because you lost the cup?' And she started laughing because just weeks before England had lost to South Africa in the rugby final, and that's the night we met, we hung out the entire night, and we made a lot of jokes together."

The British girls didn't remember Meredith meeting Rudy on Halloween night. Rudy's lawyers would insist that in the crowded, smoky student parties that night, with everyone in an alcohol haze, the fact that no one remembered this chance romantic encounter was hardly surprising.

There was a reason why the pretty vampire might have caught his eye again. Well before Halloween 2007, Rudy had already gone "vampire" himself. He'd made a video of himself, eyes rolled back, bared teeth, saying in English, "I'm Count Dracula. I'm going to suck your blood." His friends had posted it on YouTube, where it could still be found in 2011. He had also joked on his own Myspace page that he was a vampire and liked to drink blood.

Meredith's Halloween party picture, one of the last ever taken of her, in vampire costume with blood dripping down her chin, was beamed around the world in the first weeks after her death. That picture and the headlines gave the "murder game" story a lasting power that would burrow deep into the Italian psyche.

HALLOWTIDE ROLLS INTO PERUGIA on a cold fog, bringing early darkness to the winding, tilted lanes. Students leave town to visit their families and permanent residents retreat indoors, pulling up old memories behind shutters. There is no reason to be outside in the elements. By nightfall, the streets are nearly empty. The shopping is done, and umbrellas are stowed by the doors, dripping.

In 2007, November 1 fell on a Thursday. According to the *Corriere dell'Umbria,* Perugia temperatures that day would reach a high in the midforties, and skies were cloudy with moderate winds.

The astrological weather for Amanda Knox, a Cancer: "Erotic feelings grow. You receive a proposition from a person who never pressed before."

The astrological weather for Raffaele, an Aries, a bit more ominous: "A day of high tension with inflexible adversaries."

If the two lovers strolled past a newspaper kiosk that morning, they might have noticed bold-type headlines about five young anarchists arrested in nearby Spoleto exactly one week before in a major operation involving a hundred ski-masked carabinieri and, according to witnesses, four helicopters.

The news on November 1: a judge had ordered the so-called Spoleto Five to trial. Perugia Public Minister Manuela Comodi (soon to become famous in the Kercher murder trial) would prosecute the alleged ringleader, twenty-one-year-old Michele Fabiani, an anarchist from a well-known Umbrian leftist family. Like the rest of their countrymen, Italian Communists practice *nepotismo:* Fabiani's father was a well-known local Communist who for decades had been organizing labor across Umbria dressed in Che Guevara army fatigues and who, like Don Quixote, still battled capitalism daily in the Berlusconi era.

For months before his arrest, the red-diaper baby Michele Fabiani had been organizing protests against plans for an ugly high-rise building a wealthy Perugia family wanted to build on the outskirts of the nearby medieval town of Spoleto. He was having some success. Five hundred people had turned up at one protest. Then someone had sent a threatening letter with bullets in it to a magistrate from a building where Fabiani was known to work. Police descended, arrested Fabiani, and branded him an anarchoterrorist. (In a weird coincidence that conspiracy theorists seized upon, Fabiani and the Spoleto Five all had a connection to the lawyer Paolo Brocchi, whose laptop and phone Rudy Guede had turned up with in Milan. Brocchi represented one of the environmental organizations fighing Spoleto development, alongside Fabiani.)

After his arrest, authorities inexplicably placed him in solitary confinement for eighteen months. Fabiani denied involvement in the bullet mailing while continuing to write pamphlets about anarchy and revolt from his prison cell. Police never turned up any proof that the five young men had armed themselves, but Fabiani spent years under house arrest, awaiting trial.

Protests against the building ceased after the arrests, and the high-rise was erected at Spoleto without further incident.

AMANDA AND RAFFAELE, THE "two little lovebirds," as Sollecito's lawyer would eventually describe them, were oblivious to the doings of the local anarchoterrorists and couldn't have cared less about unimpeded construction in medieval towns or the weather. They were burrowing into a shared fantasy world, involving, Amanda would later write,

"Eskimo kisses" (rubbing their noses together), reading Harry Potter in German, smoking hash, wandering around the *centro,* learning new guitar music (Amanda), downloading cartoons (Raffaele), and occasionally taking breaks to eat, sleep, and have sex. Sollecito couldn't keep his hands off Amanda. The virginal doctor's son was living in a libidinous fog. Every new day was a sexual fantasy come to life.

AMANDA RECITED HER VERSION of Halloween and All Saints' Day repeatedly after the murder, in e-mails, in the questura, and to Mignini after she was arrested. And until the fateful night of November 5, her story was remarkably consistent, especially given that one of the first effects of cannabis is an alteration of the sense of time.

It went like this: She woke up at Raffaele's the morning after Halloween and made her way home, leaving him sleeping in his bed. She did some homework. Late in the morning, Meredith came into the kitchen with Halloween fake blood still on her chin. She and Amanda chatted. Raffaele came over and made pasta for lunch. Amanda played her guitar. Meredith took a shower, got dressed, and left.

Raffaele and Amanda stayed on alone at the Pergola house for the afternoon, while, "I played and sang," Amanda recalled, in an e-mail she wrote several days after the murder. Around five o'clock, Amanda said, the couple left to go to Raffaele's apartment, a five-minute amble up Corso Garibaldi. It was dusk and chilly. They downloaded and watched the French art house movie *Amélie,* about an eccentric young woman and the man who falls for her, because Raffaele said Amanda reminded him of the main character. A police analysis of the computer confirmed that Raffaele did indeed download the movie from an illegal sharing site called eMule. A witness confirmed that they had been in the apartment in the early evening: a woman had rung the doorbell and heard their voices on the intercom. That friend was a woman who cleaned his apartment twice a week. She clocked the two students at Raffaele's apartment at 5:45.

Patrick Lumumba sent Amanda a phone message, saying she didn't need to come to work. At 8:38 P.M., Amanda sent an SMS reply to him: "*Ci vediamo piu tardi, buona serata,*" the literal Italian translation of the slangy English parting salute "See you later, good night."

After that, both Amanda and Raffaele's phones stopped receiving signals and were presumably turned off around the same time. The defense tried to claim that the lack of signal was an anomaly due to the fact that they hadn't used the phones, not that they had turned them off.

At some point in the evening, Amanda said, her lover cooked a dinner of fish—a rarity in landlocked Perugia—and maybe even got some blood on his hand. "I remember it [the fish] was very good," Amanda recalled, but in interviews with police, she wavered on the time of the meal, putting it as early as 9 P.M. and eventually as late as 11 P.M. As Raffaele was washing dishes, a curious thing happened: the pipes under his sink burst, and water overflowed onto the kitchen floor. "The pipes detached, and Raffaele put them back together," Amanda recalled. "To get the water off the floor, we took some rags, but it was too much water. I went into the closet to see if there was a mop." There was not. "I said, 'Don't worry, I have a mop at our house and tomorrow morning we can pick it up and I can clean up.' After this, Raffaele was a bit pissed about the pipes, and he asked what I wanted to do. I lay on his bed, he prepared a joint on his bed. We chatted, smoked a joint, had sex, and I fell asleep in his arms."

At some point before that, they read Harry Potter in German, or tried to. The last human interaction with Sollecito's computer that night, according to Italian tech experts, was at 9:10 P.M., when *Amélie* ended. The next interaction was at 5:32 the next morning, when someone connected to the iTunes Store.

ON THE OTHER SIDE of the Perugia *centro,* at a student apartment on via Bontempi (in English, the Street of Good Weather), an elegant curving old walkway of wide, cascading steps, Meredith and the British girls were relaxing together at the apartment Amy Frost and Robyn Butterworth shared. Amy and Robyn had spent the day in their pajamas, sleeping off the Halloween revelry. Sophie wandered in at four, Meredith followed at four-thirty, and the girls settled in to watch a DVD of Nicholas Sparks's tearjerker *The Notebook*.

Amy popped a ham, eggplant, and cheese pizza into the oven, and while it was cooking, Meredith and Sophie took turns using Amy's computer to check in with their Facebook friends. The girls followed the pizza with an apple crumble one of them had prepared. They were together until sometime before nine o'clock, when Sophie and Meredith left together.

Meredith didn't mention anything about a date or a meeting. On the contrary, she seemed as hungover as the rest of the girls. "We were very tired," Amy recalled. "My impression was that we were all tired and that she had to go to bed, too." However, Meredith tucked a borrowed history book into her purse on her way out the door, and "I had a feeling she wanted to read it," Amy recalled.

Meredith confided in Amy that the boys downstairs had left town and that Giacomo had entrusted her with watering the cannabis plants, a duty she wasn't entirely comfortable with. She had the keys to their apartment in her purse.

"Meredith asked my advice, whether she should or not," Amy later told police. "The boys had asked her not to say anything about the plants. I think they told her not to say anything even to Amanda or the girls that lived in the house." Amy never explained what she had told Meredith to do about the watering or whether she planned to do it right away, that night, and the police didn't press her on the point.

Meredith and Sophie walked together down via Bontempi and via del Roscetti, passing the Brocchi law office. Neither girl could have known that one of the boys Meredith had seen at a downstairs party, Rudy Guede, had just a week before been caught with stolen goods from the same site.

Sophie saw her friend for the last time at that juncture, where the Street of Good Weather ended at the massive half-medieval, half-Etruscan city gate known as the Arco dei Gigli, which some believe is the Gate of the Sun referred to in Dante's *Divine Comedy*. There they waved good-bye, and Meredith walked off, her blue jeans and light blue sweatshirt with the glowing white Adidas logo fading into the gloom.

After Meredith left Sophie, she turned left on via Pinturicchio, a level, more trafficked street. The windows in the three-story stone buildings were shuttered to repel the damp cold, and the street would have been dark, except for a few streams of golden light escaping between the fastened slats over the windows. After about a quarter mile, she would have turned right down a set of stone stairs descending two flights, passing a lane called via Melo, lined with more shuttered three-story town houses. At the bottom of those stairs, she was facing her own house, 7 via della Pergola.

At 8:56 P.M., Meredith Kercher's cell phone called her mother's phone number in Coulsdon, Surrey. The call never made it through, and nobody knows whether Meredith was actually trying to call her mother or if the call was simply made by accident, speed dialed in her purse and then cut off during a struggle. At ten o'clock, Meredith's cell phone connected to the number of her bank in the United Kingdom and hung up. Thirteen minutes later, the phone established an Internet connection, apparently automatically, as it received an automated SMS from an advertiser.

Meredith Kercher returned home alone on that chilly, foggy night. British, far from her family, and not Catholic, she wasn't celebrating the Day of the Dead. Her house was dark, and her female and male Italian housemates were absent, marking the holiday with families and friends. Everyone had left town for the weekend but one: the only other non-Italian, the boisterous, eccentric, guitar-strumming American roommate named Amanda Knox.

Sometime in the nighttime hours linking All Saints' and All Souls' Days, in the middle of Hallowtide, Meredith Kercher was brutally murdered. Her killer left feces in the toilet and the imprint of a man's right shoe, an American brand, Nike, in ever-fainter spots of blood down the hall from the murder scene and out the door. In the bathroom, a single bare footprint in blood stained the fuzzy blue bath mat.

Meredith Kercher's murder is a private tragedy for her family and friends and a hideous act of violence against a young woman. It is also a Halloween story. Meredith was killed by a half-shod person or people on a Thursday night at Hallowtide who seemed to have entered through a high window without leaving a trace, who left feces in the toilet and the inexplicable blood of an animal—a black cat—smeared on a wall in the apartment below. All those signs taken together meant much to those who could read them.

CITY OF SPIRES

PART THREE

STVDIVM GENERALE

11
MIGNINI

They who dream by day are cognizant of many things which escape
those who dream only by night.

—*Edgar Allan Poe*

GIULIANO MIGNINI, PERUGIA'S *PUBBLICO MINISTERO,* one of Perugia's town
magistrates, whose job it is to investigate and prosecute crime, had just
finished eating the lunch his wife had made, and he was preparing to
take his half malamute, Argo, out for a post-*pranzo* constitutional walk
in the cold, prematurely dark afternoon when the phone rang with news
of a body found. Mignini had drawn holiday office coverage that weekend, so the call to duty was no surprise but certainly neither planned nor
welcome. He was clad in his customary clothes: soft suede shoes, rumpled linen jacket, rumpled ample pants. Compared with many Italian
men, whose fastidious attention to style borders on gayness or at least
dandyism, the Perugia magistrate was an unmade bed, albeit dignified.
He had already pulled on a scarf and his padded khaki-colored jacket to

fend off the cold humidity, but his bald pate with its fringe of curly gray hair was exposed to the raw air.

Mignini was a believer and a traditionalist, and the day before, All Souls' Day, he and his nonagenarian mother, his wife, and their three teenage daughters had gone together to lay flowers at the graves of previous generations of Migninis buried in the local cemetery. Beyond their own graves, Migninis have a unique connection to the Perugia cemetery. Giuliano broke the mold and chose a career in the law—most Mignini men before him were sculptors. The Perugia cemetery contains a great funerary pyramid designed by Romano Mignini, his great-grandfather, in the nineteenth century, back when Europeans were fascinated by Egyptian symbolism and filled their cemeteries with sphinxes, obelisks, and pyramids, at the same time as linguists were beginning to decipher the hieroglyphic script and revealing to modernity the ancient Book of the Dead.

The magistrate's own father had died in a car accident when Mignini was four, and he, too, was buried in the Perugia Cemetery. Mignini knew his father mainly by the stone slab marking his final resting place.

ON NOVEMBER 2, 2007, the magistrate was fifty-seven years old, and mortality was much on his mind after the All Saints' Day lunch: his own, his aged mother's, that of all the family members long departed—among them his grandfather on his mother's side, the man who had been like a father to him, the man with the German blood in his veins from whom the magistrate had inherited his own large blue eyes.

Also gone: his uncle on his mother's side, a Fascist with colorful and redemptive war stories he shared with the boy. He had served in the Italian army under Benito Mussolini and was such a committed Fascist that he had nearly frozen to death fighting Communists in Russia. "A very beautiful story," Mignini said, the one he remembers best: his uncle was with his fellow Fascist fighters, surrounded by partisans in the Ukraine, freezing cold, certain of death. They prayed for help from the local Madonna delle Grazie, the lady of favors—she of the light, strange, distracted eyes, crowned in her glass box inside the Perugia duomo. After praying to her, he found a way out, evaded the partisans, and managed to save his companions. A small miracle.

That uncle and many other important individuals from the magistrate's life had passed on, but much of the family remained, including his three teenage daughters. He sometimes sang in the choir of the duomo, and he felt at home in many of Perugia's churches—San Lorenzo, San Domenico, and San Pietro, his favorite, the dark, moody church of his wedding day, located in a monastery dating to the tenth century, with carvings by Raphael and a massive fresco by Antonio Vassilacchi, *The Triumph of the Benedictine Order.* The medieval gardens behind it are planted with alchemical herbs and a tree of the knowledge of life and death.

The magistrate's life was made up of many small miracles, and he was disposed by nature and education to put faith in such events. His mother had been widowed at age thirty and left with two small children. Giuliano could well have grown up poor or with a wicked stepfather. His mother had fielded proposals from many men, rejecting all suitors, and supported herself and her children with her own stenography school.

The Mignini Stenography School was in a three-story brick building that shared a back wall with a sixteenth-century massive stone dungeon known as Torcoletti Prison. Torcoletti had served the city as a jail for debtors, thieves, spies, heretics, and during the Fascist years left-leaning political prisoners. By the 1950s, it was a women's prison—the *carcere femminile*—and home of many Italian murderesses.

A woman named Caterina Fort was Torcoletti's celebrity inmate when Mignini was a boy. In the 1950s, she was the most notorious female killer in Italy. A jealous beauty, she had bashed her lover's wife to death in a Milan apartment with a tire iron, then taken out his three children, including an eight-month-old sitting in a high chair, in the same manner. Caterina, nicknamed the Beast of San Gregorio because the massacre occurred on Milan's Via San Gregorio, confessed to killing her rival, but even sodium pentothal never weakened the wall constructed in her mind to protect her from the memory of killing those children. Italian psychiatrists studied her for years and wrote textbooks devoted to her case. They wanted to understand how the human mind could so thoroughly erase guilt.

Mignini clearly remembers his mother pointing out Caterina Fort, the stunning, infamous murderer of children. For years, the boy had only to look out his window and see her and other incarcerated women exercising on the roof below. That he did with great curiosity until he grew old enough that his mother admonished him for it.

The prison for female criminals was out back. The headquarters of the carabinieri was across the street. Between them, the prison and military police provided the social and physical structure of Mignini's childhood world.

He was too young to understand his father's funeral. On that day, the carabinieri came from across the street, in their stiff blue-and-red uniforms, with their neat white gun holsters, and took the boy away from the scene of family grief, entertaining him with games until it was over. He never forgot their kindness. To this day, he prefers working with them to Perugia's nonmilitary police force, the *polizia*.

A policeman, not a carabiniere, called to tell him about the body on the afternoon of November 2. Marco Chiacchiera, the forty-one-year-old chief of Perugia's anti-Mafia and vice squad, said the body had been found inside a bedroom at the very edge of the Perugia *centro*. When it came to corpses, Mignini was more used to dealing with suicides, and not in the *centro*.

This was definitely not a suicide, Chiacchiera said, but a murder.

The policeman picked him up at around two in the afternoon; Mignini wouldn't see his dog or his home again until three the next morning. Chiacchiera steered the curves of the looping mountain road easily. As he drove, the policeman explained the situation: a dead female, presumed to be one of the female students living at the house, found in a bedroom, stripped from the waist down, a gash to the neck. Looked like a sex crime. The National Scientific Police were on their way up from Rome.

As the policeman spoke, the public minister looked out the window, taking in the wisps of mist threaded through the olive groves like wedding veils or shrouds.

Chiacchiera pulled up to the house. Police cars, an ambulance, and press were already on the scene, as well as a number of civilian cars, parked on the driveway and on the street, which had already been taped off as a crime scene. People huddled in grieving, shocked groups on the gravel outside. Somewhere among them Amanda Knox and her boyfriend, Raffaele Sollecito, hugged, kissed, and snuggled in full view of the telephoto lenses of the photographers and videographers from the local media.

Mignini doesn't remember seeing the pretty American who was destined to become his most famous defendant on that first afternoon. He first noticed a lawyer he knew standing by the door, comforting a distraught brunette. The girl was Italian, one of the roommates who lived in the house, and the lawyer was her legal representative. Filomena had lawyered up, in American parlance, in the first hour after the crime was discovered. "She appeared to be suffering for the dead," Mignini would later recall. "I put on paper shoes, because we were all very concerned about contamination, and I went inside."

The girl "suffering for the dead," Filomena, had rushed home from the Day of the Dead market on the flats below Perugia. The market is an annual event held by vendors in a vast asphalt parking lot near the Perugia basketball stadium where Rudy once played. Tables are piled with cheap clothes, kitchen gadgets, and regional food specialties. Before she'd had a chance to browse, Filomena's cell phone rang. It was Amanda calling to say that someone seemed to have been inside their house, there was blood in the bathroom, a burglary. Filomena had trouble understanding the American, but she comprehended enough to freak out and called her boyfriend, Marco Zaroli, who agreed to head over to the house with his friend Luca Altieri. Luca had the wheels.

Filomena was not happy that it was Amanda at home when things were going crazy; *mamma mia,* she thought, Amanda, the exuberant hippie, the *cretina.*

When Amanda had been in jail for a month, in early December, Filomena sat with Mignini and shared her memories of that afternoon. Around 12:20 P.M., as she walked into the Day of the Dead market, Amanda called, saying, in English, "There is something weird in the house. I went there, found the door open and blood in my bathroom. I took a shower, but now I am scared, what should I do?"

Filomena told the American to check the house, but at that point, communication between the Italian speaker and Amanda broke down. "I couldn't tell where she was," Filomena told Mignini. "I was taking for granted she was there [in the house], but she told me she had left. I couldn't understand. It was weird. Paola saw me go white and asked what happened, and I said, 'Amanda's at home, and she's the most stupid [*cretina*] one of all, and she went in the house and there's blood in the bathroom and the door is open and now she's worried.' And I was starting to worry, my friend tried to calm me. Paola even said maybe Meredith just cut herself and went to the bathroom. Maybe she ran out to the pharmacy and left the door open."

Filomena tried Meredith's two cell phones and received messages that they were off. Then she called back and told Amanda, in English, to check the house. "Amanda said she and Raffaele would go and do that."

At about 12:40, Filomena estimated, she tried Amanda and got no answer. Then she tried again, and Amanda answered and told her that she was inside the house, Filomena's window was broken, and it seemed that burglars had been in the house.

Only at that point, Filomena recalled, did she tell Amanda to call the police. Then, panicked, she and Paola scurried back to the parking lot.

Police, trying to create a tight timeline of events on the morning of November 2, pressed Filomena on her time of arrival at the house. She couldn't be specific. "It must have been one, or maybe before. It took me a while to get up there. I was panicking, and I couldn't find the car."

On the way to the car, she remembered, she called her boyfriend Marco. It is unclear from her statement whether Filomena told Amanda to call the police first or whether she called her boyfriend first and then told Amanda to call the police.

Italians have a natural resistance to dealing with the police. Filomena would not have been eager to advise her goofy American roommate to bring police into their house—a house where pot plants were known to be growing downstairs—if she could avoid it.

Filomena's friend Paola Grande remembered that when Amanda called about the break-in, Filomena wanted "immediately to call a lawyer." In fact, Filomena's lawyer was already on the murder scene when Magistrate Mignini showed up.

"I didn't trust Amanda as much, to say the truth," Filomena told Mignini after the arrest. "I called Marco, my boyfriend, and I said, 'Marco, *Madonna mia*, Laura is not there, we can't find Meredith, and Amanda is there and says there was a thief. Please, please go to Amanda to see what happened.' Marco told me he would go right away, and they arrived before me."

By the time police took control of the crime scene, Filomena had, by her own admission, already entered her room at least twice. First, before Meredith's body was found, she had scurried, in a panic, to assess the damage and look for anything missing. She sneaked back in later, with police on the scene, to retrieve her laptop, which she later testified had been destroyed by whoever rifled through her room.

Filomena's later testimony that there was "glass on top of my clothes" was the key pillar of the theory that the robbery had been "staged."

"We all thought it was staged," Mignini said time and again.

Police and prosecutor felt that no logical-minded thief would select such a high window that also faced the road. It was fifteen feet off the ground. But a lower window grate offered a convenient ladder for anyone with the climbing skills of a *ladro acrobata* or a trained athlete.

THE PUBLIC MINISTER WAS directed to the doorway of one of the small rooms. He was careful, he would always recall, not to step inside. The National Scientific Police in Rome—still on their way to the scene—had ordered that no one go into the room or touch the body, not even the local coroner, who had been allowed in only to establish rigor mortis and then been banished outside, waiting to start taking temperatures with which to establish time of death.

It was small enough, anyway, to not have to strain to see inside.

The killer had covered the body with a blanket, a sign, the prosecutor felt, of feminine *pietà*—sympathy. Later, Italian criminologists would bolster this notion and say publicly that killers who cover their victims with blankets are usually female. American criminologists say that gender has nothing to do with it, that any killer who is inexperienced and feels bad about what he or she did might cover the victim.

A member of the police lifted the blanket for the prosecutor.

He saw a pretty girl lying on her back, a gash to her neck, a puddle of blood by her head, blood splatters on the wardrobe, a bloody smeared handprint on the wall. Her head was turned to the side, eyes wide open. One hand, balled into a fist, covered with dried blood, rested near her shoulder. Her long brown hair, matted with dried blood, was stuck in strands to one side of her face, which was also smeared with blood. Her shirt was pulled up to her neck, revealing tiny, girlish breasts. Blood-soaked towels were crammed against and under her upper body, as though someone had tried to stanch the bleeding or clean it up.

One leg was straight, one leg bent at the knee and fallen open. A pillow was wedged beneath her lower back, so that her perfectly hairless private parts—waxed or shaved—were aimed upward and toward the door, a gaping dark slash of pornographic invitation that drew attention away from her face and everything else in the room. There was no turning away from that *solcatura del sesso*—the furrow of sex. It grabbed and held the eyes. There was something deliberate—staged—about that obscene display; the magistrate felt it, and so did anyone else who stood at the door.

It was difficult for the magistrate to look at the naked, lifeless girl and not think of his own three daughters, on the cusp of womanhood. He looked at the walls, at the array of taped-up photos of young people, laughing. An English-Italian minidictionary was near the woman's foot, speckled with blood. The girl was a student, no doubt, but beyond that he knew nothing. It was difficult for him also to know how many people had already been inside this room, inside the house, since the murder had happened.

"*Merda, merda,*" he kept muttering softly, *shit*.

FOR MIGNINI THE BATTLE of good versus evil—in the mind, in the body, in the books, and out in the streets—is omnipresent. One of his favorite novels is familiar to Anglophones as *The Lord of the Rings*.

Born in 1950, Mignini was a Cold War baby. The atomic age had just begun, and in poverty-stricken Italy cars were replacing donkeys as the chief means of transport. The Church's grip was as strong as ever, the defeated Fascists were in hiding, but they had clandestine supporters everywhere, still gripped by fierce hatred of the Left, and vice versa. Italians experienced the Cold War years in a much hotter way than did Americans. They call those years the *anni di piombo*, the years of lead, when a terrorist war was being waged between the country's Communists and Fascists. Mysterious groups exploded bombs in train stations and public squares, and other shadowy groups kidnapped or assassinated officials.

Official commissions as recently as 2003 attempted to determine culpability for those *stragi*—slaughters—but no official conclusions have been reached to explain the worst attacks. Some accused right-wing groups masquerading as leftists. Some blamed the CIA, which viewed Italy's Communist Party as a threat to European capitalism during the Cold War. Others blamed the terrorist Left. Reams of evidence have been produced to support each view.

The pitched political atmosphere in Italy during those years left no one unaligned, especially during the leftish mass rebellion of youth. Mignini himself was eighteen in 1968, a seminal year for protests across Europe.

Mignini insists that he did not participate on either side of the political fence, but he doesn't deny that his youthful inclinations leaned to the right. "I was in high school and pretty young, and I didn't have clear ideas. I wasn't politically active. I had my ideas, but they weren't relevant in my life. I was thinking of studying, I wasn't political." (Italians scoff at such evasions: local journalists are sure he was a teenage Fascist.)

Mignini earned his law degree from the University of Perugia when he was in his midtwenties, after a five-year course of study in undergraduate college. He practiced as a private lawyer for only a year before deciding to be a judge, a magistrate.

"A magistrate and a lawyer are two entirely different things. A lawyer takes care of the interests of his own clients, and I didn't like that fact. A prosecutor is someone who takes care of the interests of all Italians. What I need is the truth."

Mignini's job—any Italian magistrate's job—is to be both investigator and prosecutor. But neither he nor any other magistrate in Italy was trained in crime detection, only in law.

He passed the magistrate's test in summer of 1979 and took a *pretura* posting in Volterra, a town some hundred miles north of Perugia, near Pisa. Mignini liked the *pretura* position. It was a post with a long and august history dating back to ancient Rome, and he would have been happy to do it forever. The *pretore* served as both investigator and prosecutor in relatively minor cases. But the Italian judiciary abolished the position during a modernization effort in the 1980s. Mignini was sorry to see an ancient legal tradition go.

Mignini rarely traveled outside Italy, but on his few tourist excursions he always chose Germany, a country and language he preferred to all others. His year in Volterra was the first and only time in his life he lived outside Perugia. "I have a beautiful memory of Volterra. Etruscan city. *Bellissima.* I felt like I was in a different world."

Up in Volterra, he sowed some oats. Although he had left a girlfriend behind in Perugia, he found another *fidanzata* in Volterra. He eventually broke that heart, returned to Perugia, and married his first girlfriend, a pretty brunette. His wife is fifteen years younger than he. At the close of the Knox trial, at the end of 2009, Mrs. Mignini became pregnant for the fourth time at the age of forty-five, giving birth to a fourth daughter in summer 2010.

WHEN MIGNINI WAS GROWING up in Perugia in the 1950s and 1960s, the city was as it had been for centuries: a closed community with family names that dated back centuries. Residents had ancestors who had weathered the city's feudal history and harsh papal rule and had sided with either the Fascists or the partisans during World War II.

By 2007, all that had changed forever. Perugia was still a walled city, but the barbarians were within the gates. "There are a lot of drugs now," Mignini said, acknowledging that Perugia had become a staging city for cocaine headed to Rome, a crossroads for heroin coming up from Naples, and infested with low-level dealer gangs, many from North Africa. Besides the drugs and Mafia, Perugia had also served as a gathering point for Islamic and other terrorists. Their plots to blow up trains or poison water supplies were a periodic concern of Mignini as well. In 2007, Mignini was also part of an investigation on financing terrorism activities through drugs.

The work of handling these big problems plus hundreds of petty and not-so-petty drug and gang and domestic violence cases every year was overwhelming. Mignini said he personally oversaw more than a thousand cases a year, without interns or assistants, because of a shortage of young lawyers trained as magistrates in the region.

Mignini's legal colleagues in Perugia regarded him as a rigid moralizer, but he had a reputation for honesty. He was certainly not corrupted by the usual vices that afflict men in positions of power, such as avarice and lust. By the summer of 2009, though, some of his colleagues thought the shadow of triumphant evil represented by a dormant and possibly dead serial killer had distorted his judgment.

BEFORE MEREDITH KERCHER WAS murdered, Mignini's career had brought him into contact with depravity—drugs, terrorism, prostitution, organized crime. His greatest obsession, though, was a notorious unsolved crime in which a serial killer or group of killers terrorized the limpid Tuscan *campagna* around Florence in the 1980s, shooting young couples who were making out in cars and surgically removing the genitals of the female victims.

The so-called Monster of Florence shot and butchered sixteen people before the killings stopped in 1985. For the following two decades, countless investigators and journalists tried to solve the case; men were arrested, tried, acquitted, and convicted; and still the killer or killers were unknown. Speculations about motive included a wild array of theories: a Sardinian gang, a lone psychopath, an organized satanic cult that needed the body parts for their twisted rituals.

The Monster last killed a pair of French tourists having sex in the woods in 1985. In 2001, when Mignini got involved, the civilian police and the carabinieri who had been investigating it as part of a commission were split asunder. Around the same time, the latest chief inspector on the case, Michele Giuttari, was formulating an elaborate theory that a satanic sect with members among the highest levels of Florentine and possibly national power circles, was responsible for the Monster killings.

Besides actually investigating the case, Giuttari presented his sensational theory in a book that became a bestseller and launched him on a new path as a writer of crime novels. The Monster, he wrote, "struck his victims while they were making love. . . . In that precise moment [of orgasm], powerful energies are released, indispensable for the person acting out satanic rituals, which bring power to himself and to the ritual he is celebrating."

During his Monster investigation, Giuttari learned about the rites of the ancient Order of the Red Rose—a supposedly global esoteric society that conspiracy theorists believe controls levers of power and prominent individuals all over the world. Theorists think this powerful organization has existed for millennia, practicing black magic using symbols and bloody practices taken from pagan religions as far back as the ancient Egyptians.

To prove his theory, Giuttari disinterred a piece of evidence from the files of one of the Monster killings—a pyramid-shaped Tuscan doorstop deemed insignificant at the time—and claimed it was a key clue. Giuttari told *Corriere della Sera* that the object was "a truncated pyramid with an hexagonal base that served as a bridge between this world and Hell."

Mignini was a young lawyer and magistrate when the Monster killings started in the 1970s. He was aware of them, but they occurred just outside his jurisdiction. The murders were of enormous local interest. Perugians—like all other Italians—joined the speculation about the case.

In 1985—not long after the last Monster killing—a handsome, wealthy young local doctor named Francesco Narducci was fished out of Lake Trasimeno, which is in Mignini's jurisdiction. Police at the time believed that Narducci had fallen or jumped off his boat and drowned, either in a suicide or after ingesting drugs to which he was addicted.

He was a well-known member of the Umbrian upper crust. His wife was the daughter of Luisa Spagnoli, founder of one of Perugia's most famous local industries, the Luisa Spagnoli women's haberdashery, whose fine dresses and suits are sold throughout Italy. His father was a gynecologist.

The shallow, muddy waters of Lake Trasimeno are not good for swimming, but its placid shores and tranquillity make it an ideal picnicking site. Three islands in its center rise up like the smooth humpbacks of dark primordial beasts. Hannibal ambushed and massacred an ancient Roman army there.

According to local lore, certain cults practiced moonlit rituals on one of the islands. Such tales could have some real roots in pagan Umbria, but whatever the ancients did on the Trasimeno islands had long since faded from living memory on the day Narducci's body was fished out of the lake. The Monster never killed again, however, and local gossips began linking Narducci to the crimes.

Mignini would have occasion to remember that gossip when, more than fifteen years later, a local woman being extorted by some organized criminals reported that her tormenters had warned she might "end up like that doctor in the lake." On the basis of that threat, which suggested that the doctor's death had not been accidental (Mignini never explained why he believed small-time loan sharks would have inside knowledge of the Narducci case), Mignini joined Giuttari in an ambitious and highly controversial reopening of the Monster case. Operating out of a special suite in a Florence hotel, the men theorized that Francesco Narducci was the Monster and had been killed by fellow esoteric cult members who needed to shut him up before he cracked and revealed that he was the harvester of the orgasmic body parts they used in their demonic rites.

Mignini hypothesized that Narducci and his unnamed fellow cult members belonged to a deviant Masonic sect with local practitioners in the Umbrian and Tuscan regions, the same one that had long been rumored to practice ritual behavior on one of the mist-shrouded islands in Lake Trasimeno.

There are many rooms in the mansion of Mignini's rich cultural heritage, as there are in Italy's culture in general. Some of them, like the Uffizi Gallery, are open to tourists, some are to be found in books by Boccaccio or Petrarch, in the poetry of Dante. Others—Catholicism and the Vatican—can be glimpsed through stained glass but never fully seen. And then there are other rooms—darker, utterly closed and locked against the prying eyes of outsiders, rooms with keys that perhaps only native Italians hold.

In interviews, Mignini made no secret of his belief in the prevalence and possibility of conspiracy—both in the world at large and against him personally. He found the American tendency to ridicule or officially rule out conspiracy naive in the extreme.

"Why do they call it a conspiracy *theory*?" he asked. "What does 'conspiracy theory' mean? How can you call a conspiracy theory the fact that more than one person did a crime together? Why are they called conspiracy theories? Caesar was killed by twenty senators, is that a conspiracy theory? It's normal that people work together. I remember Ruby and Oswald together. Ruby killed Oswald to shut him up. I could see that on TV. Why did he kill him? He was afraid he was going to talk."

Mignini got encouragement and theoretical assistance in the esoteric aspects of the Monster conspiracy case from an unusual source: Gabriella Carlizzi, a wealthy Roman woman and courthouse gadfly whose day job consisted of running a Catholic charity that worked with prisoners. Carlizzi, who died of cancer in 2010, was, like Mignini, a serious, practicing Catholic herself who had dedicated her life to exposing and fighting satanic sects.

Before her death, Carlizzi operated out of a home office in a spacious apartment on one of the most ancient roads out of Rome, replete with white grand piano, bronze statuary, and fluffy lap dog. She made herself up in what Americans might recognize as high Staten Island style, with designer eyeglasses, lip liner, and ample tanned cleavage on display. Childhood polio had left her with a limp and a dedication to art, literature, and a form of Christian spirituality that recognizes agents of Satan in an astonishing array of modern-day organizations and societies.

In the 1900s, Carlizzi's family had poured its money into the projects of a mystic priest who performed exorcisms and worked with prisoners in Rome. After his death, Carlizzi took over the priest's work in the Roman jails. Italian magistrates and courts found her moderately useful as a person who could perhaps extract useful gossip and even confessions from incarcerated criminals.

Carlizzi claimed she had participated in numerous trials and aided police over the years. Her avocation, though, was not terrestrial crime fighting but the study of evil and the cults that perpetuate it through black magic. Over the years, she compiled and disseminated a list of dozens of organizations linked to the Order of the Red Rose, including Scientology, Hare Krishna, the Mormons, and dozens of lesser-known, obscure sects: the Arance ("the orange ones," somehow connected to a scandal involving arms deals and Lockheed), Le Nuove Amazzoni (who revere an alternative, female pope), the Ordo Templi Orientis (a group based in Bologna), the Nuova Acropoli (a group dedicated to the rebirth of the classical Greek religions), and the *roditori,* or rodents, who penetrate banks and institutions and "empty them from within."

Around the time Mignini heard about the vague threat about ending "up like that doctor in the lake," Carlizzi sent him a fax outlining her theory of the Monster case. Based on her own research into the esoteric sects, she said, she believed the Monster of Florence had been sent out to kill couples in the act of having sex.

When Mignini was working out his unorthodox theory of the Narducci case and the Monster of Florence, Carlizzi faxed him information about the practices of esoteric cults from her vast files. Mignini met with her at least once, but he says he did so only to see whether she had anything useful to share.

"It doesn't help to make those people angry," he said.

Carlizzi's files on the grisly rites of the secret societies certainly bolstered Mignini's theory that Narducci was a body snatcher for a deviant Masonic cult that needed parts for its midnight rites. But Mignini was embarrassed when an American writer, Douglas Preston, ridiculed his theory in a bestselling book in English. The prosecutor promptly had Carlizzi charged with defamation for bragging that she had advised him. He also grew increasingly sensitive to perceived criticism of his theories from Americans, and during the course of the Kercher murder trial he sued or threatened to sue a number of American journalists and writers across the Atlantic. In interviews with me, he often prefaced any conversation with long digressions about the motives of his critics in the United States.

Armed with his hypothesis, Mignini set to work looking into Narducci's death. He pulled out the old files and soon noticed a number of irregularities. The coroner had been kept away from the dock when Narducci's body was pulled out. A hearse taking the body into Perugia for examination was stopped by local police, who directed the driver to take the body to the wealthy doctor's family. The body was then buried in the family crypt, with no further examination. Pictures of the body on the dock seemed to show a man who was taller and fatter than Narducci. Police files were missing, normal procedures had not been followed. Mignini even found out that the wife of a now-dead judge had told friends and family that he had spoken of actually seeing female body parts in jars of formaldehyde at Narducci's villa.

Mignini postulated that the body pulled from the lake had *not* been Francesco Narducci's. He theorized that conspirators had killed Narducci to keep him from revealing his monsterly habits and the names of his accomplices and that another body—perhaps also murdered—had been thrown into the water to be found, then exchanged with Narducci's murdered body before the actual burial.

More than two decades after Narducci's death, Mignini decided on a sensational course of action: he asked the Narducci family to let him exhume the body and give it a belated autopsy. The family refused. "And this . . . made me more curious," he said. "Because it is very unusual that a family asks for investigations to stop as soon as they know there is an investigation on how their son died."

Using his authority as magistrate, Mignini got a judicial order to open the coffin against the Narducci family's wishes. At the scene, he might as well have been the good Dr. Seward in Bram Stoker's *Dracula*.

"We thought to find dust and bones because this is seventeen years after the death, and because in photos the body was ruined by the water so it had no hair, it was swollen. It was already decomposing. We opened the coffin. And he has blond hair. The pants were 48 when they photographed the body—when they found Narducci, they wrote that the pants size was 60. And inside the pants was a cloth wrapped around his stomach. According to an expert, it's a sign of punishment in Masonry. As if he were degraded, they had demoted him. He wasn't wearing any jewelry, any metal objects or goods."

Mignini ordered a new autopsy, which, he said, revealed something else that was very strange: "They found his brain completely well preserved."

By October 2007, the Monster of Florence case was Mignini's single greatest preoccupation, bordering on obsession. He had confronted stonewalling on all fronts. Such resistance only encouraged his conspiracy theory. His investigation had enraged the Narducci family and its allies. Judges in Florence were trying to stop him, and he thought he knew why.

They were Masons.

In America, the Freemasons are a curious organization of Main Street bourgeoisie with funny handshakes and hats who organize floats for town parades and collect money for kids with leukemia. In Europe, and especially Italy, they are taken much more seriously.

There are twenty-four Masonic lodges in Perugia, making it Italy's per capita center of Masonic activity. Perugians believe that members of those lodges secretly control most aspects of banking, business, and administration in their community—and that members get preference in promotions, loans, and jobs.

Mignini was not alone in his distrust of and suspicion about the Masons, although he took his suspicions to an obsessive level. Italians associate the Masons with both government conspiracy and occult ritual. Long reputed to have members in the highest levels of government and administration in Perugia, they have a secret handshake and a secret language. Italians share the nineteenth-century American conception of Masonry, when an entire political movement rose up to eradicate the society because it was assumed to hold too much power. Mussolini abolished Masonry in Italy in 1925, claiming it was a political organization. It has been allowed to return only in a supposedly neutered form.

In the 1980s, a large, occult Italian Masonic lodge known as P2, for Propaganda Due, pursued a quasi-Fascistic, surreptitious takeover of the Italian government, involving members in the highest levels of the military and government and money-laundering activities in which the CIA and the Vatican were implicated. Its members were also named in a nationwide bribery scandal called Tangentopoli, in a Vatican bank scandal involving the CIA, in the murders of a journalist and a banker. The full history of its activities is unknown and, like the CIA, rife with conspiracy theories. It was sometimes referred to as a state within a state. Silvio Berlusconi and three heads of Italian intelligence services were all members of the now-disbanded lodge. It also had members in various Latin American dictatorships and was implicated in Argentina's so-called Dirty War.

In Italy, the Masons thrive because of an Italian fact of life. Outside of family connections, or *nepotismo,* membership in small gangs and cliques is the key to success. The founder of the Italian Communist Party, Antonio Gramsci, wrote that Italians traditionally ignore the interests of the nation as a whole in favor of more intimate allegiances. "Italians prefer joining organizations of a different type, like cliques, gangs, *camorras, mafias,*" Gramsci wrote. These small groups are so powerful in Italy that "they know no other limit to their power than the power of rival groups. They play a free-for-all game practically without rules or referee."

Masons trace their society back to a medieval mystery sect called the Knights Templar, formed in the eleventh century as a fighting order to protect Christian pilgrims to Jerusalem. They captured and hoarded treasure from the Holy Land and became Europe's first bankers, eventually loaning the Church and various royal families large sums of money, until the Church charged that they practiced Satan worship, homosexuality, and deviant initiation rites, and burned its leaders at the stake in the 1500s.

Perugia is an important Masonic city because it was on the "Templar path" between southern France and Spain and the ports from which the Templars sailed to the Holy Land. The Templars of Perugia initiated one of Catholicism's more bizarre cults. In 1259, a year of black plague and starvation, Perugia Templars (who may have learned the practice among Shi'a Muslims in the Holy Land) led ten thousand people through the city streets, all whipping themselves bloody. The mania moved north and the flagellant movement spread throughout Europe, traveling alongside the Black Death for a hundred years before the Church banned it.

The Templars left their mark on Perugia with obscure symbolism such as the half-eagle, half-lion griffon, an ancient mythical creature with roots in the Orient, with a mysterious duality associated with both good and evil. The griffon still represents Perugia's pride and authority. A majestic statue of a griffon clutching a papal helmet in its claws in a park near the southernmost edge of the city commemorates the city's overthrow of papal control in the 1800s. Griffons decorate most public buildings. A local dairy factory is called "Grifo Latte," and a Perugia travel agency is called "Grifo Viaggi."

Besides the ubiquitous griffon, the Templars left other curious symbols in Perugia. Buildings along Corso Garibaldi, where Raffaele lived, are decorated with pentagrams and alchemical symbols, symbols that survive today in Masonic pins.

Mignini grew up around those signs and symbols, and because Church and Italian history fascinated him, he knew them better than most. His Monster of Florence theory involved a Masonic conspiracy going all the way up into the police and judiciary.

Within the Italian judiciary system, judges and magistrates such as Mignini are regulated by one another, by region. The judges and magistrates of the Florence area have the duty of regulating Umbria's Perugia-based system, Perugia oversees Rome, Genoa oversees Florence, and so on. The logic is that outsiders are better able to police local corruption.

In Florence's reluctance to reopen the Monster case and let him follow his instincts, Mignini detected further proof of a Masonic conspiracy. He joined forces with Giuttari, and together they authorized various wiretaps, including of journalists and fellow members of the judiciary.

The wiretaps—ubiquitous in Italian investigations because anti-Mafia laws have expanded such authority—proved to be Mignini's official undoing. In 2010, Mignini and Giuttari were convicted in Florence of abuse of office. Mignini was given a suspended jail sentence and was in danger of losing his magistrate position, pending appeal. A Perugia judge then tossed out the Narducci body-switching case, and that was the end, for the time being, of Mignini's Monster theory.

Before his conviction, the magistrate had begun to see the deviant cult's conspiracy in many nooks—maybe even as far away as Seattle, U.S.A. "What I am looking for now," he said in 2009 during the Knox trial, in one of many hours he spent explaining the complexities of the Narducci conspiracy to me, "are the people who know the answer about Narducci. And they might even be someone from the Friends of Amanda Knox [an organization set up in the United States to support Amanda and her family]. In both cases, there are desperate people, and I can see them doing stupid things."

AFTER VIEWING MEREDITH KERCHER'S body, Mignini was directed to another room off the long, narrow hallway, the one with the broken window he had noticed from outside. Like the first room, a woman lived in it. Clothes were flung on the floor and on the bed, shopping bags were overturned on the floor, a large rock was wedged under a table. A laptop computer lay on the floor amid shards of glass.

Here the magistrate encountered Monica Napoleoni, the chief of the Perugia police murder squad. Usually sharply dressed in skintight street clothes like a vice cop, deeply tanned year-round, and with jet black, shiny hair swinging in bangs above her brows and cascading down her back, the policewoman's style is part dominatrix, part Donatella Versace with a badge. Napoleoni doesn't look or dress her part, but there is no doubt about her fitness for the job. Policing is the family business. Her father had been a Perugia police officer for decades.

Napoleoni, clutching a little notebook in her hand and a large Vuitton tote on her shoulder, ceased her investigations long enough to fill in the magistrate on what she had gathered so far. In court testimony, she shared her first impressions of the crime—including the idea that she immediately perceived that the break-in had been "staged"—with the world.

"I arrived with a doctor and a nurse—a woman doctor and a male nurse. The postal police were already there, and they told me they had arrived and found Amanda Knox and Raffaele Sollecito outside the house, saying they were waiting for the carabinieri because there was something weird in the house.

"I entered the room immediately on the left, and I took one step inside and noticed right away that the breaking in couldn't have been made from the outside. Pieces of glass had fallen on stuff that was on the ground. It seemed to me they had broken it after they went through the room. There were even pieces of glass on top of the windowsill outside. There was this big rock, I saw it almost completely, inside this Sisley bag.

"I went toward [the murder scene], and I made one step inside the room while the emergency doctor pulled up the blanket, and I saw this girl on the ground with her face to her left, her eyes open. And she had this horrible wound, it was horrible to see. I tried to photograph with my eyes what I saw inside that room, to understand what had happened.

"The girl was half naked, her shirt pulled above her breasts and lots of blood. There were splashes of blood on her breasts as well. One of her legs was slightly open. Then I noticed the desk with Vaseline on it in a little pot, closed on top."

At the mention of Vaseline, the magistrate was confirmed in the instinct he had had about the body, displayed so obscenely to anyone at the door of the murder room. Italians use Vaseline for one thing only. And that thing—anal sex—is not normally discussed in polite mixed company.

"Then we saw pieces of toilet paper, cotton balls on the desk, under-wear of the girl, and a bra with obvious spots of blood at her feet," Napoeloni continued. "It was right away obvious they had taken it off after they killed her. The bed had almost nothing on it; there was a sheet, a bag, some books.

"I noticed Knox and Sollecito entering the house on the left, but they were separate from the others, kissing and cuddling. At one point Sollecito came to me and told me that his girlfriend had taken a shower in the bathroom that morning and had noticed feces in the bathroom and that when she came back she didn't see them anymore. I went back inside, and two or three minutes later the Scientific Police colleagues arrived."

When the Roman scientific police arrived at dusk, they took command of the crime scene. Napoleoni and other Perugia police officers retreated to the questura (their headquarters at the bottom of the hill) to begin interviewing the victim's friends—"people informed about the facts," in police parlance—to try to understand, first, who the poor girl had been.

12
QUESTURA

In my mind I saw Patrik [*sic*] in flashes of red images. I saw him
near the basketball court. I saw him at the front door. I saw myself
cowering in the kitchen with my hands over my ears because in my
head I could hear Meredith screaming. I've said this many times to
make myself clear: these things are unreal to me, like a dream and I
am [scratched-out line] not sure they are real things that happened or
are just dreams my mind has made to try to answer the questions in
my head and the questions I am being asked.

—*Amanda Knox*, from a handwritten four-page statement she called
"a gift" to the police after naming Patrick Lumumba as the killer

The essential American soul is hard, isolate, stoic and a killer.

—*D. H. Lawrence*

WITHIN HOURS OF THE BODY being found, journalists from three countries were on the scene. Television trucks lined up in the *centro*, disgorg-

ing correspondents with lights and microphones. From within the high
Etruscan walls, it felt as though the whole world was watching Perugia.

"*Sgozzata in Camera da Letto*"—"Slaughtered in Bedroom"—read
the headline in the local *Corriere dell'Umbria* on November 3, followed
by twelve pages of coverage. The dead girl, reporters revealed, was "a
brunette, sensitive and beautiful," who had donated to the orphans of
Darfur. Halloween-night pictures of kids in costumes illustrated stories
about the local English community's reaction—"Fear Among English,
Many Return Home," *Il Giornale dell'Umbria* reported—and the details
of Meredith's "last dinner before death."

Without a suspect, with a killer at large, the media focused on
dread and fear. "Eleven Years of Blood," read one local headline, listing
the town's murders over a decade. "The Home Is Especially Dangerous," read another headline, reeling off statistics about violence against
women. "Female Students Fleeing City," read yet another headine.

Already the first odor of xenophobia was in the air. One Perugia
paper rued the "transformation at the heart of old Perugia" wrought
by *stranieri*. Under the headline "The Neighborhood of the Horror,
from *Torta al Testo* to Kebab," a local reporter described the multicultural scene between the murder house and on up Corso Garibaldi, the
street passing where both Raffaele and Rudy lived. Traversing the old
Sant'Angelo neighborhood, renowned in earlier years as the quarter
inhabited by the most wicked, he wrote, "Many businesses testify to
the presence of immigrants: Internet points for telephones and Western
Union services."

The British press picked up on the nativist fears, too. *The Daily Mirror* ran a story blaming Perugia's violence on immigration. Erasmus
students in Perugia spoke to the newspapers of their newfound fear in
Perugia, a city, reporters wrote, of "light and darkness."

The president of the Regional Council of Umbria, Mauro Tippolotti,
decried the party scene and called Perugia an "Ibiza for university students," referring to the Dionysian island off the coast of Spain frequented
by Kate Moss, Mick Jagger, and other moneyed Euro-hipsters. "The

Slow Decadence of Perugia and the Silence of the Authorities," read a headline in *Il Giornale dell'Umbria,* identifying "the true problem in this case: drugs." While students were holding a candlelight memorial to Meredith Kercher in the town square, the bishop of Perugia, speaking at a separate service in memory of local Saint Ercolano, blamed "the culture of juvenile immorality" for the sensational crime.

Graphic designers made logos for the story—little boxes with the words "L'OMICIDIO DI PERUGIA" over a picture of Meredith grinning in her vampire costume—and they decorated each of the eight or ten pages newspapers were devoting to the crime each day.

A half-dozen British and a few American journalists in the Rome-based press corps were on the scene, followed by a dozen or more flown in from London. Italian reporters from Rome and Milan were in town, too, all making forays into the windy streets for quotes and visiting the prosecutor, who was trying to make sense of the senseless.

THE GULF BETWEEN GIULIANO Mignini, fifty-seven, conservative Catholic, and the digital-age party animals who trip through his hometown cannot be overstated. When Mignini looked at the American exchange student Amanda Knox, born in the 1980s in the American West, with her father issues and writerly fantasies and yogi agnosticism and blithe disregard for all he held dear, the chasm yawned even wider.

Getting in to see *il dottore* was serious business. His office is on the third floor of the Office of the Procura della Repubblica, a white stone Fascist-era building trimmed with gold eagles across the street from Perugia's main bus stop. The *procura* office was one escalator flight below the yellow brick building where he grew up, where his mother, in her nineties, still lived, and which still housed the Mignini Stenography School.

An exemplary Italian son, Mignini ate lunch with his mother at least once a week.

Anyone wishing to meet with the man first had to pass muster with a guard behind bulletproof glass on the first floor, a man with a huge gold chain and giant cross nestled in the black hairs of his very tanned chest. After offering bags and briefcases for inspection and stepping through a metal detector, visitors took an elevator directly to the third floor—bypassing the second floor, which was utterly off limits to the public, reserved for the regional office of the Anti-Mafia Commission, which has offices in procuras across Italy.

His desk was heaped with sheafs of files in disordered, willy-nilly piles. The windowsill was lined with sinus remedies, for he suffered greatly and could sometimes hardly speak two sentences without clearing his throat.

A framed copy of the duomo's Madonna delle Grazie hung on the wall behind his back, casting her strangely distracted, cultic, pale-eyed gaze upon whoever faced him. On the wall to his left, he'd hung a large framed color photograph of Giovanni Falcone and Paolo Borsalino, assassinated Sicilian prosecutors, in 1980s pastel polyester suits and droopy mustaches. These "superprosecutors," killed by the Mafia, are judiciary heroes whose deaths provoked sweeping changes in the Italian justice system, changes that, among other things, made it easier for men like Mignini to order wiretaps. Kitschy mementos of the carabinieri—little plastic helicopters, police cars, an old calendar with a Norman Rockwell-esque watercolor of two uniformed officers helping a pretty girl across a street—were scattered everywhere.

It fell to Mignini to try to figure out what had happened at 7 via della Pergola on that horrible night. And his chief witness, on the morning of November 2, was the strange, light-eyed girl who had been first on the scene. The girl bore an uncanny resemblance to the town Madonna delle Grazie on the wall behind him.

The story she was telling made no sense to him.

AT THE QUESTURA, PERUGIA police were in a frenzy. All hands were on deck. Three dozen of them would sign off on arrest papers in four days.

The investigators were a motley crew of Mafia experts and vice police, more accustomed to dealing with dead Albanians and drug smugglers than with an international cast of party-animal students.

Monica Napoleoni, the head of homicide for the flying squad, took control of the case. Her staff in the questura included the policewomen Rita Ficarra and Lorena Zugarini, a thick-bodied woman (later to become the subject of East German swimmer comparisons in the press corps) who was photographed kicking in the locked door of the downstairs apartment in the hours after Meredith's body was found.

The policewomen had seen an awful lot of violence against women in their work, but it was mainly domestic violence involving men and women who were partners. In January 2009, Napoleoni, speaking at a roundtable on the domestic violence crisis in Italy, stated that she had seen a lot of women violently attacked by men in her time. She observed that it was easier to save prostitutes than married women from cycles of violent attacks because police could arrest prostitutes before it was too late. In her experience, abused women came to the police to seek refuge rather than justice.

Like Mignini, the Perugia police were most accustomed to dealing with *stranieri* criminals—Albanian gangsters, low-level mafiosi, the occasional Moroccan street dealer.

At some point, members of the national police force also came to Perugia, including the chief of the Serious Crimes Unit in Rome, Eduardo Giobbi. Giobbi, the senior man on the case, was technically senior to Napoleoni. After years in the police business, he relied on demeanor to identify suspects. From behind one-way mirrored walls, he settled in to watch the interviews.

Police rounded up every person who lived at 7 via della Pergola and all of Meredith's friends. The Italians made sure to bring lawyers or family members with them. Amanda and the British girls did not.

The waiting room at the questura was bare except for a row of four plastic chairs bolted to the wall and, for some reason, a poster of Città di

Castello, a nearby town, maybe prettier than Perugia. There was almost nowhere to sit. The room was wired for surveillance.

They called Amanda first.

At 2:30 P.M., less than two hours after her roommate's body had been found, Amanda Knox sat down for the first time with the Perugia police. Her boyfriend, Raffaele, made his first statement in a separate room, time stamped at 3:45 P.M. They were still just "persons informed about the facts," not suspects, but police would begin wiretapping their phones from that day forward.

"This morning around ten or eleven, I went to my place to change and take a shower," Amanda said. "I noticed the door was completely open. . . . I thought this was weird because we all locked the door when we left. I started calling the girls, and nobody answered. I thought maybe one of the girls had left to throw trash or go to the boys downstairs, who have an apartment under ours and who we sometimes see.

"I closed the door and went to the bathroom next to my room. I noticed on the floor some drops of blood and a spot of blood a little bigger on the mat outside the shower and another spot as if somebody had wiped a hand on the sink. This seemed to me very weird, for the simple fact that all of us girls are very clean and neat and usually clean up after we use it. I had piercings done on my ears about a week ago, and I remember touching my ear right away to see if it was bleeding. I touched the blood on the sink, and it didn't come off. I thought it was the menstrual blood of some girl, and because I was grossed out by it, I didn't clean it.

"I went into the other bathroom to dry my hair, and I noticed there were feces in the toilet. I thought this was very weird. I did not flush it. Then I picked up the floor detergent that was in a little closet and I left the house to go to clean up my boyfriend's room because the night before we had dirtied it. When I left, it must have been around eleven thirty. I can't be precise, I wasn't looking at my watch.

"When I arrived at my boyfriend's place, we stayed there for about an hour, enough time to clean up the kitchen and have breakfast. After that we went back to my house. I would like to be precise, I told my boyfriend right away the weird things I saw in my house and he told me to call the girls. I called Filomena to see if she knew anything about the blood in the bathroom, and she said no, she had slept at her boyfriend's place.

"After that I called Meredith three times. I called her first on the English cell phone, the first number she gave me and one I memorized. And it rang and then stopped. I then tried her Italian number, and the phone rang but no answer. I tried a third time on the English number, and no answer.

"At that point I was worried for Meredith because she was the only one I didn't have news from. We went home, and we started opening the doors of the rooms. I opened Filomena's room, we saw the window was broken. There was broken glass everywhere, and I was scared. I thought maybe a burglar had come in."

Amanda said she looked around to see if anything was missing without actually going inside the room. She then knocked on Meredith's locked door, noting that "Meredith would close (or lock) her door only when she would come out of the shower and had to dress; in all the other circumstances, she would maybe leave the door closed but not locked."

When Meredith didn't answer, Amanda said she crawled out on the terrace of the bathroom, craning her neck toward Meredith's window, but couldn't see anything. She peered through the keyhole and saw "only the bag on her bed." The purse, it turned out, was inches away from a bloodstain on the white sheet.

Amanda then said she went downstairs to "see if Giacomo had news of Meredith, and he wasn't there." Then Raffaele tried to kick down Meredith's door. He failed. He called his sister, and she advised him to call the carabinieri, a recorded call logged in at 12:51. While they waited, the postal police arrived on the scene. (The police later estimated that they had arrived at 12:45 and moved that back to 12:35 after the students were arrested). At 12:48, Amanda made the first of five calls to her mother, waking her up at 3 A.M. Seattle time. Prosecutors later found it suspicious that Amanda made the first call to her mother before Raffaele called the police, before Marco kicked down the bedroom door.

ALL AFTERNOON AND INTO the night, shocked friends huddled together in the questura waiting area, waiting to be called in for questioning. The British friends were crying, as were the roommates Filomena and Laura, who had arrived with lawyers. Later, everyone agreed, only Amanda failed to behave like a grieving roommate. Quite the contrary: she sat on Raffaele's lap, rubbing noses, sticking out her tongue, giggling, nuzzling. She seemed to brag or boast about her role in discovering the murder when speaking in English in a way the British girls found offensive and, in retrospect, even chilling.

"I wanted to kick her," said Robyn Butterworth. "She seemed to be going insane."

Some of the girls had met Amanda before that night; others had only heard about her.

Natalie Hayworth, a British friend of Meredith, later told police she had been horrified when Amanda interjected herself into a teary discussion among the girls in which one of them had said she hoped Meredith's death was quick.

"What the fuck do you think?" Amanda burst out. "She had her throat cut."

The bravado cracked, but at suspicious moments. At 3 A.M., after she'd been there twelve hours, the police officer Fabio D'Astolto, who spoke pretty good English on account of having lived in Australia as a boy, led Amanda upstairs to be fingerprinted. Everyone who lived in the house was providing their prints for elimination purposes. Suddenly, the previously stoic American grew visibly agitated. Walking to the fingerprint room, away from her boyfriend and the grieving friends, she started smacking herself in the forehead over and over.

"What's wrong?" asked D'Astolto in English. "Do you need anything?"

"No, nothing."

Eventually, that small detail became significant. Mignini concluded that she had been hitting her head that night in a desperate bid to knock the memory of her role in the murder out of it.

At 5:30 A.M. on November 3, with dawn illuminating the cobbled streets, police sent Amanda and Raffaele home, fifteen hours after they'd first arrived at the questura. Deliverymen were stocking the green wooden newspaper kiosks around the city with stacks of newspapers bearing the lurid headline about the *studentessa* slaughtered like a farm animal. In London at around the same hour, the *Daily Telegraph* was hitting the streets, reporting the death of an English girl in Italy. The Perugia officer Marco Chiacchiera was quoted, promising "a manhunt" and sharing the first theory: "The most plausible hypothesis we have is that Meredith met someone at the Halloween party. She expressed a desire to meet him again."

In the first days, they were looking for a male killer. The police raced to understand who the victim might have attracted, which men she had spent time with, and which ones had just watched her from the smoky shadows and corners across the crowded bars.

The British girls gave up a harvest of Halloween photographs that only deepened the eeriness. Police pored over images of Meredith in her black cape, dripping fake blood, grouped with different young men and women. Who were all those leering young men, some masked, their arms draped over the shoulders of the pretty vampire?

Inside the questura, police made lists of men.

Amanda offered up one particularly shady character who fit the Perugia crime stereotype nicely. An insistent, dark foreigner. An Arab. "I met Hicham—we girls would call him Shaky, in mid-October. I recognized him yesterday in your office." She told police that Shaky had once offered her a ride home on his motorbike at 2:30 in the morning after her shift at Le Chic, but instead of taking her home, he had driven to his house and spent an hour trying to persuade her to have sex. She told police she'd had to argue with him to take her home.

"The other girls had met him more than me, and I do not know their level of friendship with him, but from what I know Meredith never had a problem with Shaky. She thought of him as a nice guy because on one occasion he drove Meredith and a friend home from a disco. She told me the same thing had happened to Sophie as to me."

Mignini asked Sophie to look at the Halloween-night pictures with him. Sophie had a hard time identifying the people in the pictures she had taken. As the *pubblico ministero* flipped through them, she tried.

"I can't remember. I can't remember. Some random guys at Merlin's. I can't remember."

Mignini asked about boyfriends.

"I am sure Meredith only had Giacomo, but I know Amanda's brought other men there," Sophie said. "Meredith would tell me about it."

After that statement, the prosecutor and the police grew a little more interested in the habits of the *ragazza americana* who had been first on the murder scene. Mignini was still aiming at his more familiar criminal quarry: foreigners, immigrants, the *stranieri* lowlifes he knew from experience with hundreds of cases to be associated with crime in Perugia. But now he understood that the light-eyed American might have associated with the swarthy set.

"Was Meredith annoyed with this? What would Meredith say about those boys?" Mignini asked Sophie.

"She would tell me one of the guys was a little bit weird."

"Who?"

"He worked in an Internet café."

"Was he Italian?"

"I think so, I'm not sure."

"Did she bring home foreigners, immigrants, for example?"

"I don't remember details."

"Did Meredith ever tell you about somebody being violent, weird, or insistent?"

"No, she never told me anything in particular, but there was Hicham, the Moroccan guy, and I didn't like him that much, and also Meredith, Robin, and Amy told me they didn't like him much. The girls told me to be careful of that guy."

Police had already hauled in Shaky at 2:30 A.M. the night after the body was found. The terrified little Moroccan had an airtight alibi: he'd been working at a pizzeria until midnight.

When police interviewed Shaky, they had him look through the Halloween-night pictures, too. He identified two of the men with arms around Meredith's shoulders, grinning. One was the brother of the owner of Pizzeria Da Gennaro on via Bartolo, near the Umbra Institute. The guy with him was his friend.

"I saw Gennaro's brother and Meredith together, often and alone," Shaky told police that night.

If the *polizia* followed up on Shaky's tip, there is no record of it in the case archive.

The Da Gennaro pizzeria owner and his brother were prominent relative newcomers to Perugia, successful local businessmen who had moved to Perugia from Calabria, the home ground of the notorious 'Ndrangheta mafia, a group with tentacles into legitimate businesses worldwide. A British journalist in Italy described the 'Ndrangheta as "bigger, more deep-rooted and more powerful than the Mafia." The owner of Da Gennaro also owned Merlin Pub.

Police quizzed the boys downstairs, each of whom showed up at the questura with family members or professors in tow. Police had found blood in one of the bedrooms downstairs. The boys all had weekend alibis with their families in Marche. But their lives and habits were clearly intertwined with those of the four girls upstairs.

Police grilled Stefano Bonassi and Meredith's boyfriend, Giacomo Silenzi, at least twice in the days after the murder. On November 3,

Stefano admitted that he smoked joints but denied using harder drugs. They quizzed him about the blood on his bed and bedroom wall. "I do not know what to say about the blue pillowcase stained with blood because I left it clean and hanging in my room," he said. "We have two cats. One is more savage and stays outside. The black one stays inside. The black one had hurt himself on Friday, October 26, and had a wound behind his right ear. He lost a lot of blood while he was eating and shaking his head."

Forensics would confirm that the blood—bewilderingly copious amounts halfway up the wall—was feline.

Giacomo Silenzi was next, and he didn't live up to his surname. He was pretty open about the drug use. He told police, "Me and my friends use hashish. Meredith used hashish too." He said that he and the other men usually procured the drug on the duomo steps, as the girls were in no condition for commerce. "The women would often come home drunk," he said.

Giacomo inadvertently also gave police a key lead that probably got them thinking about kinky sex early on. In the first days, the Vaseline by the body, coupled with the condition of the body, suggested anal rape. Giacomo had boasted to his roommate Marco Marzan that he'd tried anal sex with her. Marco had dutifully shared that with the police, and the police then quizzed everyone about the pot of Vaseline and Meredith's potential for kinky sex. Eventually, the police asked Amanda a question about Meredith and anal sex, to which she responded, in an e-mail home describing the questioning, "wtf?"

Stefano was the first to mention the "South African" who went by the name of Body Roga or the Baron. The police took note, but they didn't know the man's real name until much later.

AT 11 A.M. SATURDAY, the day after the murder was discovered, Rudy was traveling north by train to Milan, and Amanda and Raffaele were at the questura again. Police drove Amanda back up the swerving road to via della Pergola. They asked her to put on paper shoes before entering the crime scene. She slipped them over her shoes and did a giggly, swively move, even uttering an "oopla," police thought. The flirty display shocked the police. She didn't look as happy in long-lens press photographs taken that same afternoon, though. Photographers captured her standing outside the crime scene, talking to Mignini, biting her nails, pressing her hands together, wearing the same clothes as the day before.

That afternoon, back at the police station, Amanda was becoming a person of interest, and she didn't even know it. She talked to the police again starting at 2:45 P.M., and besides her usual questioner, Rita Ficarra, important police were at the table: homicide chief Napoleoni, vice officer Chiacchiera, and detective Giobbi from Rome.

In this interview, Amanda inexplicably lied about Giacomo's relationship with Meredith. "None of the boys has shown an interest in us girls, only Marco sometimes, to joke around and flirt."

She also lied about smoking pot. "I do not know if Meredith smoked joints, but I never saw her smoke. She said she quit because it was unhealthy. I personally don't smoke cigarettes or joints. I saw that the boys in the house downstairs would roll cigarettes, but I assumed it was tobacco."

Amanda wasn't the only student to get cagey about the topic of illegal drug use. Police don't usually arrest users in Perugia, focusing instead on sellers, but it was not so easy to tell the police about hash use. Amanda reasonably would have feared admitting breaking Italian laws, and also could have gotten the boys downstairs and her roommate Laura into trouble by telling police that they provided her hash.

At the trial, Filomena genuflected with spiritual remorse over her occasional puff in an exchange with Raffaele's lawyer Luca Maori.

MAORI: Did the boys downstairs use hash?
FILOMENA: Yes.
MAORI: Did you use it?
FILOMENA: I have to say the truth: I sinned once. I sinned.

MAORI: We are all sinners.

FILOMENA: I sinned.

JUDGE: Continue, lawyer.

Eventually the police persuaded Sophie, Meredith's party buddy from Leeds, to talk about the sin.

"The only thing Meredith was scared of was drugs," Sophie began, talking to police. "When we arrived in Perugia, we were all a bit scared. Meredith had seen needles in the garden next to her house, and we saw a person shooting up heroin right next to my house. But we never had any problem with anything else."

"Did she use drugs?" Mignini asked.

"She smoked cannabis."

"Where did she get it?"

"I think from the boys downstairs. She would smoke once in a while, maybe, with the boys."

WHEN THE POLICE SENT them home early Saturday evening, Amanda and Raffaele went shopping. Amanda needed some clean underwear. She had her period and was still wearing the clothes she'd put on the morning before Meredith's body was found. She and Raffaele went to Bubbles, one of the cheaper of the overpriced clothing shops in the Perugia *centro,* a pink-walled emporium of Chinese-made teen fashion for teen girls who want to be *à la mode* without spending Versace cash. The underwear, lots of thongs, was laid out on a table. The loss-prevention camera captured Amanda and Raffaele together at that table at 7 P.M., picking through the lingerie, stopping to hug and kiss.

After they were arrested, that video was valuable and the owner sold it and his own narration, including his memory of Raffaele saying "Now we'll go home and have wild sex," to the Italian television networks, which looped it alongside the tape of the couple hugging outside the murder house. Raffaele's father sued Bubbles for releasing it.

With her new underwear, Amanda and Raffaele went out for pizza and then drove to an apartment where Amanda's roommate Laura Mezzetti had been staying. Everyone who had been on the scene—Filomena, Paola, and Luca—gathered there to debrief and mourn. Amanda talked in English for about twenty minutes, the Italians remembered later. But Raffaele's translation of whatever she was saying lasted only about four minutes.

The Italian girls were "confused" by Amanda at that point. Laura would later testify that even she, who had always taken Amanda's side before, found the young American "annoyed and annoying" at this gathering. The Italian girls lost patience with their odd little roommate, who didn't seem to have a grasp on the basics of proper grieving behavior in Italy or conduct while dealing with the police. If they tried to guide her on either subject, neither of them has ever admitted it.

When Laura later recalled this gathering for Mignini, she said Amanda had complained that the police were "being pushy and telling her that she lied." Right then, Laura began to understand that the police suspected Amanda. And, she thought, maybe she ought to think twice about the American herself.

"The questionings are different from person to person," she told Mignini after Amanda was arrested. "I was surprised that she knew details like, I don't know, the police asked if Meredith had anal sex. And I thought this very strange of the police to ask her. They asked me some things as well, but because I was in Viterbo [when it happened] I understand why the questions to me were different. We did think it was not normal that a girl would come home and find the door open and find blood in the kitchen [sic] and bathroom and take a shower and . . . go back to Raffaele's house. We said, 'You take a shower? You see this mess, and you just go back to Raffaele's house?' We thought her story was a bit confusing."

That was the last time the two Italians would see their American roommate for almost two years, until the day they each testified for the prosecution in court and faced her as a defendant charged with murder. After her conviction, Amanda wrote a letter to me, professing shock that her Italian roommates didn't like her.

I have only to say about Laura and Filomena that I'm surprized [sic] by how they reacted and how quickly they turned their backs on me. I'm also surprized by how much they censured their habits to protect themselves. I mean our house was certainly not a slutty druggy house. . . . At the same time, it's also absurd and unfair of them to claim that they had smoked 'one or two' joints and that I was the only one to bring friends over to hang out. Laura had guy friends come over, and no one had ever told me that my friends, of which there were 4 in total, one of which was a girl . . . were cause of alarm. . . . I don't understand their behavior if not to forget about and distance themselves from a really traumatic, tragic event that has caused scandal. In the end, I understand and don't hold anything against them. They are just trying to rebuild their lives. . . . I had felt they were big sisters to me—always affectionate, helpful and generous. Then nothing.

That same night, at 3:45 A.M., with two days of freedom left, Amanda fired off a long e-mail to twenty-five friends, laying out her version of the events of the murder night and after. By then she had been spending five to twelve hours at a time in the police station and fielding increasingly worried cell phone calls from her relatives. She gave no hint that she sensed that she was a suspect or that she was aware that her access to e-mail was about to be extinguished, along with her physical freedom.

"This is an email for everyone, because I'd like to get it all out and not have to repeat myself a hundred times like ive [sic] been having to do at the police station." She "required" them not to share what she was going to tell them with journalists.

"I have to get this off my chest because its pressing down on me and it helps to know that someone besides me knows something, and that im not the one who knows the most out of everyone." The reunion of the three roommates was "a hurricane of emotions and stress." In a separate e-mail she confessed to a friend, "I'm falling apart."

She devoted exactly one sentence to what she had done on the night of November 1. After describing seeing Meredith alive for the last time in their house, she wrote, "after a little while of playing guitar me and raffael went to his house to watch movies and after to eat dinner and generally spend the evening and night indoors. We didn't go out."

Generally spent the evening indoors, the *colpevolisti,* those who believed Amanda guilty, would always note.

ON THE CHILLY SUNDAY morning of November 4, church bells chimed from steeples and towers across Perugia, calling parishioners to Mass and reminding nonbelievers of the advancing hour. At the kiosks, newspaper headlines were still fixated on the murder of the English student. News trucks were parked all over the *centro.* Salacious secrets from the "house of horrors" were being revealed. The *Corriere della Sera* had an interview with Stefano Bonassi, in which he told about the *ragazza americana* Amanda Knox having sex with his cousin from Rome. *La Repubblica* reported that police now thought the killer was in fact "two men."

The police were still making suspicious-man lists. At 2:45 P.M., Amanda signed a statement naming the men she had brought into the house. She named five men: Juve; Spyros; Daniele; Pasquale Alessi or Pisco, the owner of Merlin; and a friend of the boys downstairs named Giorgio.

The translator Aida Colantone later testified that she had encountered Amanda in the questura hallway before this episode, sitting in a chair and looking alarmingly pale. The young American told her she had her period.

At four that afternoon, Napoleoni told Amanda that she, Laura, and Filomena had to return to the house. Mignini was present. Again they gave Amanda the CSI paper booties to put on. She did not repeat the giggly swivel. Inside, the police wanted to show Amanda the household knives. Were any missing? They went into the kitchen and opened the knife drawer. In the face of all that sharp shiny steel, the "ta-da" girl suddenly fell apart, shaking and sobbing. The scientific police worried that they might have to perform an EMT maneuver of some kind, get out the glucose drip. They laid her on the couch. She recovered without medical assistance.

Back at the questura early Sunday, Raffaele was waiting for Amanda. The normally shy Italian boy was belligerently demanding that he be allowed to get his shaken girlfriend some pizza. The police showed them into a bugged room and listened in, again coming up empty-handed. If they were guilty, the two students never let slip a clue, even in apparently unguarded moments.

In future reports of the conversation, reporters cherry-picked the first paragraph and published it alone, ending the dialogue before it became clear that Amanda was talking about Juve, the Arab guy who'd gotten her the job at Le Chic, and not some unnamed malevolent "he."

RS: What are you thinking?

AK: That I don't want to be here. I want everything to be over because I want to know who his friends are, he doesn't have many friends. Now it's like this, and it's interesting. He doesn't have any friends now, he didn't go out, he didn't talk to many people, all he could think about was his girlfriend. That's what he told me.

RS: I could take good care of you. I have a lot of friends. If I tell them to take care of you . . . That's the difference. . . . I have good friends, not his friends.

AK: I know, but he gets crazy when . . . when he thinks about breaking up with a woman . . . strange to me. He says he trusts his girlfriend but he doesn't like it when he sees her talking to a guy he doesn't know. Even when they've just broken up with each other . . . [incomprehensible part]. He

looks at her and gets crazy. He forced? [translator not sure
about this] me all the time. He's terrifying. He says that he
doesn't mind seeing his girlfriend talking to another man
that he doesn't know, but then he gets arrogant with me.

RS: That's ridiculous.

AK: Frankly, I don't like him anymore. I mean, it was nice of
him to get me a job, and it was nice of him to play the
guitar with . . . when I went home . . . [incomprehensible]

RS: Oh wait, are we talking . . . are we talking about your
friend from Le Chic or—

AK: Friend from Le Chic?

RS: No, I'm talking about that guy who—

AK: Who?

RS: I'm talking about that guy—

AK: Spyros?

RS: No, Shaky, Shaky, eh, eh. (Giggles.)

AK: Oh!

AK: I don't like him. He's not . . . I hate that guy. (Giggles.) He
tried to have me.

RS: I thought you were talking about Shaky.

AK: Shaky, Shaky.

　　(. . .)

RS: Yeah, uhm. (Giggles.)

Amanda left to go to the bathroom. When she returned, her cousin
from Germany called. Raffaele spoke with her on the bugged phone, in
the bugged room. The cousin asked him to take care of Amanda. "I can
do nothing when we are at the questura," the Italian student said. "They
are squeezing my brain, literally kicking me in the head."

THAT SAME AFTERNOON WAS the last time Brett Lither talked to her friend
before she was arrested. Amanda was on a cell phone in the questura. "I

just remember her being really freaked out, because she had been in the house. The police basically told her that the murderer could have been in the house when she was there or something like that. She was scared. When I say she was freaking out, I mean she was in shock. Like a bomb went off next to her, that was the bomb of her life. That was the closest she'd come to total complete craziness. Ever. I don't really know what else to say about that, except that she was in shock. She was scared. She was really scared. Her voice wasn't normal. She hadn't eaten. She hadn't slept. It was pretty clear that she was ragged by what was going on."

THAT EVENING, A LOCAL coroner named Luca Lalli was finishing up a seven-hour autopsy. The doctor had been kept away from the body for the first twelve hours after it was discovered so the Rome-based CSI team could do its work. Because the body had been cooling for hours, Lalli was never able to pinpoint a time of death. He did determine that Meredith had died of asphyxiation, choked to death on the blood leaking into her lungs from the deeper of the two knife wounds. He found signs suggesting recent sexual activity, but there was no sperm and he couldn't determine whether the sex had been forcible or not.

MONDAY MORNING, NOVEMBER 5, Meredith had been dead for three days, and the three surviving roommates tried to return to business as usual. Laura and Filomena went to work at their law office. Amanda showed up for her nine A.M. Italian class at the University for Foreigners. She was now remaining in Perugia against family advice, and, unlike her two roommates, she hadn't contacted a lawyer nor, apparently, consulted with anyone in Italy who might have suggested she get one. Her phone was tapped, and the police knew her aunt had urged her to go to the U.S. Embassy. They also knew that her mother was en route to Italy.

She arrived at class on time wearing Raffaele's track suit, and looked troubled, resting her head on her desk. Her teacher, Antonella Negri, gave the students a typical intermediate Italian language class assignment to write a "casual or formal letter." Amanda scribbled a letter to Edda Mellas, who was due to arrive in Perugia the next day, starting with "Ciao Mamma." Negri later turned the assignment over to the police, who gave it to reporters, who interpreted it as further evidence of Amanda's cold-bloodedness because she wrote only of herself and of needing to shop for clothes and of being "confused." Like everything Amanda wrote before and after the crime, her written words were ambiguous, revealing what the reader chose for them to imply.

"I need to reconstruct my life, but I feel like I've forgotten how I lived before," she wrote in the class exercise letter. "I hope you will be able to help me. Maybe we can go shopping for some new clothes and you can meet my roommates. . . . Despite my situation, I would like to remain in Perugia. I know that you want me to come back to the United States, but I am not finished here, I am not afraid of Italy. I am not afraid of anything in particular. I am afraid because I am confused. What happened is a mystery to me."

Police had instructed her not to discuss details of the case, and perhaps that's why she didn't say more about Meredith's death in the assignment. Or perhaps her intermediate Italian vocabulary allowed her only to write about shopping and not murder. In any case, the teacher and classmates were shocked to realize that a member of their own class had had any involvement at all in the notorious murder. Antonella Negri would tell police that Amanda stayed behind after class to talk to her about it. Out on the street, Amanda ran into Patrick Lumumba, who was handing out flyers—not to his bar but to a candlelight memorial for Meredith planned for the duomo steps that night. Patrick asked Amanda if she would be willing to talk to some of the reporters who had been hounding him about the case. Amanda declined and kissed him goodbye on the cheek. Lumumba's lawyer later compared this moment to "the kiss of Judas."

At two in the afternoon, Raffaele's maid saw Amanda and Raffaele at his apartment.

At 8 P.M., a hundred mourners gathered on Corso Vannucci and walked to the duomo steps, where a giant photograph of Meredith was laid out, surrounded by candles. Amanda and Raffaele were not among them.

At 10 P.M., the police called Raffaele's cell phone and found him at a restaurant, eating pizza with Amanda. They asked him to come back to the questura for another round of questions. He asked if he could finish eating, and they said yes.

The very last time Filomena talked with Amanda was by phone later that evening. The American called her from the questura at 10:39 P.M., and Filomena answered, calling her *"Bella, bella."* The defense played the surveillance tape of that call in the closing hours of the trial. Amanda lapsed into English at every three or four words, incapable of completing even a single sentence in Italian. *"Io ricevuto un . . .* aah, ahh, call," she started. Filomena responded in Italian only.

"She told me her mother was coming, and then she asked if we could still live together," Filomena later recalled. "I think she said she had been in the questura and that Raffaele was in, and I was surprised by that. I said, 'Why are you still there?' I said, 'You must have patience and simply explain how things happened when you came in. They are only trying to do their job.' I said, 'Explain this well.' And I told her it wasn't clear to me either. I am sorry, you hear a person say the door is open, she goes into the house and there is blood. I take a shower and go out? I don't know about you, but I don't think this is very normal at all. Why do you go in and take a shower if the door is open?"

The police were thinking the same thing.

ON THE NIGHT OF November 5, their last night of freedom, given Raffaele's daily habit, the students had likely smoked up for relaxation. It had been a pretty stressful week, by anyone's measure. They finished their pizza, and Amanda willingly went to the station with Raffaele.

The defense has since claimed that Mignini himself was present at the police station from shortly after ten that night. But he has always insisted that he was home in bed when the two students were invited into the questura for their last round of questioning.

The police had been listening in on their conversations on phones and at the bugged rooms at the questura, but in four days, they hadn't said anything incriminating to each other. From phone surveillance, police knew that Amanda's mother, Edda Mellas, was making her way toward Perugia, due to arrive by train the night of November 6. Thus, November 5 might be the last night the strange, pale-eyed girl who'd given Inspector Giobbi from Rome such a bad feeling would show up at the questura without a parent or a lawyer; or, worse, she might retreat to the refuge of the U.S. Embassy.

The police and Mignini always maintained that the questioning on the night of November 5 didn't require either videotaping or the presence of lawyers because the students were still only "persons informed about the facts," not suspects. But the police and their contacts knew better. Erika Pontini, who covered the case in Perugia for *La Nazione* of Florence and who was close to Officer Napoleoni, recalled, "On the night of the fifth, we knew, journalists knew, something was going to happen. They thought Sollecito was the fragile link in the chain."

MOST OF THE NAMES on the doorbells in the gated seashore apartment complex where Dott. Francesco Sollecito lived begin with the four letters "Dott." Travelers to Italy needing medical attention should not assume that this honorific refers to a medical degree, though, because on the Appennine peninsula, students earn the right to the *dottore* if they graduate from the equivalent of an American four-year college in any subject. Dott. Sollecito, however, was in fact a medical doctor, residing in upper-middle-class comfort in a spacious, ultramodern apartment decorated in shades of blue with his buxom blond second wife, Mara. Theirs was not a sumptuous apartment by Roman standards, but in poverty-ridden Puglia, everything about the doctor said money.

He wore a delicate bracelet of a gold watch, chewed on a Cuban cigar, and kept his jaw clenched. A pale-eyed, pale-skinned man living in sunny, dark-skinned Puglia, one of the poorest regions of Italy, Dott. Sollecito was married to a member of one of the richest families in the region, and both his children had inherited their father's fine features, high cheekbones, and small nose.

Nothing in his upbringing, personality, or athletic experience had prepared the doctor's son for a November night at the Perugia questura. Police put the stoned young man into a room by himself, took his Nike Outbreaks off, and told him his shoes matched the bloody crime-scene footprints. They sent his little knife out for analysis, too. His father had warned him by phone several days before not to take his knife into the police station, but Raffaele had replied that the police were "too stupid" to notice it. The police had heard every word of that the conversation on wiretap.

Now they had him where they wanted him. The room was cold, he was barefoot, and he was freaking out. It didn't take long to break him down.

Giacinto Profazio—a burly cop soon to make the Rome papers for extracting a false rape confession out of a pair of Romanians who spoke no Italian—was one of his interrogators. At around 10:30 that night, before the effects of the predinner *spinello* had waned, the fine-boned rich boy from Bari gave the police what they wanted: he couldn't really be sure Amanda had been with him throughout the evening on the night of the murder.

"Everything I told you before is a sack of shit"—*un sacco de cazzate*—the police wrote. Raffaele signed his name under those words sometime after 10:30 P.M. The exact time is not on the statement.

Raffaele's only other prior statement to the police was the one he made on November 2, the afternoon of the discovery of the body, when he told police he and Amanda had spent the night of November 1 at home. In a letter to his dad written from jail in the early days after his arrest, Sollecito would write that "Amanda told me to say she went to work," but it's unclear when he ever said that she went to work, since no other statement to police is in the record. His November 6 recounting of the night of the murder almost exactly matches his description of his and Amanda's doings on Halloween night, when he did in fact separate from Amanda around 9 P.M. while she went off alone, reconnecting with him at around 1 A.M., and he would later say that he'd confused the two nights under police pressure.

Besides the two conflicting police statements, he also told one published lie about what he'd been up to the night of the murder. A British reporter for the *Sunday Mirror,* Kate Mansey, found him in a bar near Piazza Grimani a day before his arrest, and she reported that he said he and Amanda had been "at a party with a friend" on the night of the murder. He never told that story to police, though, and he later denied it in letters to me.

The police were so suspicious of Raffaele, and so sure that he'd be spending the night of November 5–6 at the questura, that some of them were already inside his third-floor Corso Garibaldi apartment before midnight on November 5. Computer forensics analysis showed that whoever had been inside his apartment—police, apparently—turned on his computer while he was still handing over his shoes and knife and destroying Amanda's alibi—and his own as well—at the questura.

In the early-morning hours of November 6, someone on his computer googled ANSA, the Italian news agency, apparently checking to see whether the arrests had been announced.

By the time he was arrested, Raffaele was such a veteran hash smoker that he'd grown pretty immune to its more debilitating effects. In a letter to me, he scoffed at the notion that the hash he and Amanda had smoked during the day and evening on November 1 could have provoked memory loss and a psychotic act. "I wasn't 'High' that night because I only smoked one or two joints during the day and I was relaxed and calm. In the joint/joints there were less than 1 gram of hashish in total and in my opinion it's ridiculous to be 'high' this way."

Raffaele attributed the differences between his first statement

(Amanda was with me all night) and his second statement (she was out between nine and one) to police bullying, which prompted him to become confused and to recite to them the chronology of Halloween night, the night before the murder, when Amanda had in fact been gone between nine and one. "During the second and last time in the police station they asked me the same questions as the first time. It made me surprised and caused me confusion to which day we were talking about and my movements. They said awful things about Amanda and that they had hard suspects [sic] on her, thus in their opinion, I was covering her. In this way, after many hours of questioning me, I said that maybe Amanda was at work, because she was there every Tuesday and Thursday, but I also said I was not sure on it. . . . In the end me, Amanda, and later Patrick, were in the police station alone for about 20 hours without sleep and we cannot talk with family or lawyers or anyone. It's difficult to explain and there's a lot to say about 5th November 2007."

WHILE HER BOYFRIEND WAS destroying her alibi, Amanda was outside the interrogation rooms, doing yoga stretches in the hallway. An interested male cop watching her asked if she could do a cartwheel, too. Amanda obliged him. A number of female police, including Ficarra and Napoleoni, later said they had witnessed this gymnastics display and that they had been horrified. They had already developed a distrust of the loud American with the cool arrogance, the sudden tears, and the flirtatiousness with men. Now she was doing what looked to them like *velina* moves, right in the hall of the questura, practically dancing on the corpse of her friend.

Rita Ficarra approached and asked Amanda if she would open her cell phone and go through the names again. Amanda did. Then Ficarra asked if she would like to come into one of the interrogation rooms and talk.

Amanda went willingly.

She sat down in a small room with the middle-aged, almost motherly Rita Ficarra, the door-busting Germanic blonde Lorena Zugarini, and a low-ranking cop named Ivano Raffo of the Serious Crimes Unit of Rome, a sexy Johnny Depp look-alike whom cynics think the policewomen brought into the room to lure the man-focused Amanda into a confession.

They started looking at the phone, clicking through old outgoing texts (Amanda told them she had habitually erased incoming messages). They focused on a message Amanda had sent at 8:38 P.M.: *"Ci vediamo piu tardi, buona serata."* See you later, good night. She'd sent it to Patrick Lumumba after he had texted her to say business was slow and not to come in to work. Unfortunately for Amanda, Italians don't use that phrase unless they really mean to see each other later. The all-purpose farewell salute "See ya later" in American idiom doesn't translate literally into Italian. The police thought the message meant that Amanda had an actual appointment with a murderer.

Amanda tried explaining that she had sent the message to Lumumba and why. But now the police had almost exactly what they'd been looking for from the first afternoon they'd found the body: a brown-skinned *straniero* male, possibly linked to the scene at the very hour of the murder. They had promised the press a manhunt. They were not going to let the opportunity pass.

Then they dropped the bombshell: they told her that Raffaele was now saying she had left his apartment between 9 P.M. and 1 A.M. on the night of the murder. At that point, without an alibi, she probably needed a lawyer. Much later, she would say she did ask about the possibility, but that the police had told her that having a lawyer "would only make things worse for you."

Now the interrogation began in earnest, and the two versions of the night—Amanda's and that of the police—diverge. Eventually a dozen police were in the room at different points during the last all-night questioning episode. They moved in and out, crowding in, insisting, and shouting. An American former FBI agent, Steve Moore, an outspoken defendant of the students' innocence, has said the Italians were engaging in an interrogation practice known in the policing business as "leapfrogging," wherein pairs of fresh officers are sent in every twenty minutes or so to keep the pressure on consistent high as the interrogee slowly wilts without water, coffee, sleep, or bathroom breaks. "Frankly, I'm surprised she lasted as long as she did," he said.

Amanda claimed—for the first time to her parents when they first visited her in prison on November 10—that one of the policewomen had slapped her in the back of the head twice. She was never able to identify who had done the hitting. The police denied it. For stating that claim in public on the witness stand, police slapped her with slander charges. They also made the same case against Curt Knox and Edda Mellas for talking about the hitting to a British newspaper before the trial.

The police and Amanda agree that they waved the phone in front of her face, insisting that *"Ci vediamo piu tardi"* meant she had made an appointment to meet someone just before her roommate was murdered. A part-time English interpreter, Anna Donnino, a local housewife, a soothing civilian presence, held Amanda's hand, whispering in English that it was normal to forget the details of a trauma and translating the Italian questions that were coming fast and furious. Donnino whispered, "Amanda, let me tell you about a trauma I had. I broke my leg a few years ago in an accident. And I forgot how it happened. And I had to try to remember it. Maybe this is what's happening to you. Try to remember, because this was a trauma."

The soothing tone was misleading. The interpreters didn't like the girl at all. She gave them a bad vibe. One interpreter later told me, "Knox is a liar. She told so many lies she doesn't know what's true anymore." That interpreter knew about the lies because Amanda had lied about smoking dope during the session in which the interpreter had worked. The interpreter knew about other lies from reading about them in the newspapers later.

Her first interpreter, Fabio D'Astolto, described his first impressions in a deposition six weeks after Amanda was arrested: "I just remember that the girl seemed insincere and strangely cold after this tragedy that had hit a friend of hers with whom she shared a house."

In the end, the interpreters performed a crucial role in the case: they were a subjective sieve through which every one of Amanda's utterances in English had to pass before reaching the police and Mignini. And they were inclined—at least after the arrest—to put a certain spin on her voluminous writings in English, fully translating anything that burnished the "Foxy Knoxy" (they translated that nickname as *Volpe Cattiva*, literally, "wicked fox") image and merely summarizing the frequent innocuous passages, giving an overall sense that everything the girl wrote was strange.

AROUND MIDNIGHT, EVERYONE IN the questura could hear screams echoing in the fourth floor. "He's bad, he's bad! " Amanda suddenly wailed in English. And then she gave police a scenario, saying she had left Raffaele's apartment to meet Patrick at the basketball court at 8:30 P.M.

At 1:45 A.M., Amanda signed the following statement, written by the police in Italian:

> To integrate what I have already said . . . I would like to specify that I know other people whom I see and who have frequented my home. I will give their cell phone numbers. One of them is Patrick, a black man about 170 cm tall with little braids, owner of the pub Le Chic . . . the pub I work in Monday and Thursday from 10 to 2. On Thursday, November 1, the day I usually work, while I was at my boyfriend's home I received a message on my phone from Patrick, who told me the pub was closed. I answered the message that I would see him right away. So I told my boyfriend I had to go to work. In the afternoon, I had smoked a joint with Rafaelle. I was confused because I don't frequently use drugs or stronger drugs. I met Patrick right after in the basketball court of Piazza Grimana. I don't remember if Meredith was there or if she arrived after. But Patrick had sex with Meredith, he had a thing about her. I don't remember if Meredith was threatened before. I remember confusedly that he killed her.

The official version from the police is that at that point they called Mignini, who got out of bed, threw down some coffee, and rushed out into the night. The defense uncovered a document indicating that Mignini was with the police before midnight. In any case, at the questura, under the bright fluorescents, Mignini confronted the American girl, who was awash in tears, repeatedly hitting herself in the head. According to the *pubblico ministero,* everyone was treating the girl like a wounded baby bird. The sexy young Roman cop Ivano Raffo was even holding her hands.

"A very fatherly figure," Mignini said of Raffo. "He was calming her, petting her hands, she was crying. I had the impression she was terrorized by Lumumba. Then there was Mrs. Donnino, also very sweet, and there was a policewoman."

The minute Amanda named Patrick Lumumba, officers were dispatched to round up the "Congolese," as the newspapers consistently referred to him. Lumumba's arrest shocked the town almost as much as the murder itself. He was practically white Perugia's African mascot, had just started his own bar, and had a wife and baby at home. "He is an example of good integration, we might say," said Stefania Giannini, the silver-haired, supremely elegant president of the Università per Stranieri.

The police knocked on Lumumba's door at three in the morning on November 6 and dragged him off to the police station in his pajamas in front of his crying toddler and horrified spouse. He had no idea what was up. He figured it had something to do with Meredith Kercher, but he thought maybe the police were just rounding up all the local bar owners for questioning. Only when he got to the questura did he slowly come to understand that Amanda—his smiling, flirtatious American waitress—had fingered him as Meredith's killer.

AT 5:45 A.M., AFTER Amanda signed a second statement, she apparently stopped crying and hitting herself in the head. The head hitting would always obsess Mignini. Hitting oneself lightly in the forehead is a part of the Masonic initiation rite. Throughout the investigation, gathering evidence for his case, he often asked police to describe how Amanda had been hitting herself in the head.

Ficarra took Amanda to the police canteen for espresso and sweet brioche, the customary Italian breakfast. When they came back upstairs, the police placed Amanda under arrest. The entire *squadra mobile*, thirty-six members of the Perugia police force, showed up and signed the arrest document. It had been an exceedingly tense and tough four days. Everyone needed to be acknowledged.

The police continued to investigate the case for another year, as the law allows them to do, but the entire case developed out of what had been said in the questura during the night of November 5–6, when Amanda and Raffaele went from being interviewees "informed about the facts" to interrogees, suspects.

In a letter to me from prison almost three years afterward, Amanda said that trying to write about the events of November 5–6 was still traumatic. "I had to stop because I felt like I was suffocating. The whole rest of the night, I just laid in bed and stared at the wall, trying to calm down. The terror of the experience . . . lingers, and is expanding by the anger at realizing, over time, how much I was being manipulated and used without realizing it. I absolutely did not waltz into the police station spouting accusations while the police served me tea and crumpets." She wrote that at the time, she "didn't understand what was going on, why they were calling me a liar, why they were insisting that I had met someone, why they were insisting that I was traumatized and had amnesia. . . . They spoke to me as if I were another victim, the key witness, not as if I were a murderer. In fact, I didn't know I was accused of murder until I was in front of the judge for the first time, after three days of complete isolation. I was told that I wouldn't be let go, that I had to remember, that I had to tell them who I met that night (referring to the message on my cell phone)."

Eventually, whenever the Italian press reported on Amanda describing police abuse, they reminded readers or viewers that the Americans were waterboarding prisoners in Guantánamo.

AMANDA THE ASPIRING WRITER had finally produced some writing that really mattered, not only in her private literary fantasy, not only on her website, but out in the real world, where an audience of millions would take her words seriously. She couldn't stop herself. Even as the police were writing up her arrest papers, she needed to keep writing. She asked for pen and paper and told Ficarra she wanted to give her a *regalo*—a gift. She proceeded to write three more pages, reiterating what she was now calling her "vision" of meeting Patrick, being in the murder house, hearing the screams.

By the time she finished, she had signed two statements for the police and handed over a third rambling statement in her own handwriting, all before dawn on November 6, 2007, all putting herself on the scene of a bloody murder in what she called "a vision."

LATER THAT DAY, MIGNINI confronted a more somber duty. The British consulate from Florence brought Meredith's mother, Arline, and sister, Stephanie, to meet him at the morgue. He ushered Arline into the cold room, where she formally identified the body.

"She asked *me* if she could kiss her," he recalled, wiping away a tear. "Can you imagine, she felt like she had to ask me if she could kiss her poor daughter?"

ON TUESDAY MORNING, DOZENS of television network crews, photographers, and reporters, exhaling fumes of the espresso and cigarettes that had fueled them through the morning's fast-breaking news, crammed into a questura conference room where more than thirty police were assembled behind Napoleoni and Giobbi.

Perugia's police chief at the time was a stout Fred Flintstone look-alike named Arturo De Felice (soon to be transferred south to Catanzaro, his birthplace, in Calabria, the poorest region of Italy). Before the Kercher murder, the chief's duties consisted mainly of organizing large events such as regional soccer cups. De Felice hadn't cut a stellar path in Perugia. The local journalists and police who would discuss him uniformly described him as "stupid."

Caso chiuso, said De Felice, stepping forward with a Cheshire-cat grin, giving the reporters the names of Amanda Knox, Raffaele Sollecito, and Diya "Patrick" Lumumba, a rudimentary outline of the group sex and violence theory, and no motive. "The motive is sexual, very much so," he told the assembly, clarifying that Meredith was "morally innocent."

Reporters shouted questions, but they would get nothing more out of the police—officially, anyway.

Except for the photographers: at one point, Officers Zugarini and Ficarra, holding Amanda with a sock cap pulled over her eyes and wearing Raffaele's Chicago White Sox sweatpants, paused in the doorway of the press conference room long enough for photographers to catch a snap. The sexy cop Ivano Raffo was standing behind her, an unlit cigarette in his lips. The photographers had another chance for the perfect shot outside as each of the alleged perps was walked out of the questura and into a separate car for the ride farther down the mountain and out onto the fruited Umbrian plains fifteen minutes away, where three isolation cells were being prepared in Capanne Prison.

"It was like opening the kennel doors for a bunch of hunting dogs," said Vanna Ugolini, the crime reporter for the daily *Il Messaggero* in Perugia, among the journalists that morning. "They just went off."

Now even the journalists without plane tickets to Italy were busy, because the perps had—thankfully—posted personal pages on the social networks, available from any corner of the globe. In November 2007, this case was a lot more interesting than the unrest in Pakistan following the disputable reelection of Pervez Musharraf or the news that President Bush wanted to increase the number of troops in Iraq. A drugged-up, pretty American girl orchestrating the sexual assault of her pretty English roommate in a fantastic medieval town trumped the War on Terror.

Amanda and Raffaele hadn't been in Perugia's isolation cells for twenty-four hours before reporters found a photo Amanda had posted of herself in a yellow halter dress, wielding a World War II machine gun at a Nazi history museum in Germany and grinning maniacally, and another image from Raffaele's blog, the young man posing as a mad doctor swaddled in white sheets, brandishing a meat cleaver. The photos went up alongside those of the victim in her vampire costume.

The words on Amanda's self-titled "Foxy Knoxy" Myspace blog provided almost too much grist for the mill. Anglophone reporters didn't have enough column inches for it. She wrote that her mother was her hero and that she loved good wine, making coffee, doing yoga on a rainy day, soccer, and Harry Potter. She also wrote about smoking dope and having sex with an Italian stranger on a train. She had posted two creative writing exercises, a pair of dark, strange short stories dealing with rape and stalking.

To counter this avalanche of self-created innuendo, Amanda's family took down the website and her supporters began creating an Amanda Knox who might have been a Mormon, sexless, drugless, drinkless, studious. "She's a health-conscious vegan on the Dean's list!" one of her supporters wrote. "She would never smoke pot."

Raffaele's blog was also a rich source of imagery and information. Out came the meat-cleaver-wielding surgeon snapshot and the blog mentioning seeking "stronger emotions that surprise you again"—words that would be interpreted as the musings of a man capable of murder.

WHILE REPORTERS WENT HUNTING on the Internet, the police were collecting more evidence. One of the officers inside Raffaele's apartment on the morning of November 6 was Perugia Assistant Police Officer Armando

Finzi. Finzi later testified that the apartment had reeked of bleach when he entered it. He opened a kitchen drawer and pulled out a large knife, selecting it from all the rest of the cutlery in the drawer based on his understanding that the cut in Kercher's neck was very large. Looking at the kitchen drawer, he experienced what he later called an "investigator's instinct" about that particular knife. He handed it off to a more senior officer, Stefano Gubbiotti, who had spent the earlier part of the day at the murder house. No forensics expert, Gubbiotti first stored the knife in a calendar box, then repacked it and stuck it in a closet, and finally sent it to the crime lab in Rome. In a week, the scientists said the knife had Amanda's DNA on the handle and traces of Meredith's DNA on the blade. Besides that knife and Raffaele's penknife, no other knives were tested, or, if they were, the police never put the results into the record.

AMERICAN SUPPORTERS OF AMANDA Knox expended a lot of energy and television time attacking the Italian judicial system, a PR tactic that appalled Italians and backfired badly. The truth is that Italian justice is theoretically at least as fair and as filled with checks and balances as the American system, and certainly more lenient to some criminals. Rehabilitation, not punishment, is the goal, in keeping with the national instinct toward compassion. Murderers can be back on the street in less than ten years. And, as the Italians are quick to point out, they don't have the barbaric death penalty. In criminal cases, there are many stopgaps along the way.

One difference: Italy allows preventive detention. Suspects can be jailed for up to a year without charge while investigations are ongoing. Authorities may throw them into isolation cells and deny them lawyers until arraignment—tactics created to combat Mafia collusion that Mignini applied to Lumumba and the students. But prosecutors must periodically report to judges on their investigative progress. Eighteen judges eventually ruled on the investigation, allowing it to go forward each time defense lawyers challenged the investigation.

To detain the students, Mignini had to produce reasons within hours of the arrest. A judge then reviewed his evidence and decided whether the arrests were valid. Amanda's statements in the questura sent her to jail and kept her there.

While Amanda was trying to explain her "vision" to the police and herself—thrashing deeper and deeper into the briar patch by scribbling down more thoughts—Mignini crafted, and at 8:40 A.M. time stamped, a theory of the murder, placing Amanda at the center of it.

Amanda Knox, he wrote, had been a full participant in sexual violence and murder. "The sexual relations between Meredith and Patrick must be considered violent in nature," he wrote. "And Knox must be considered a contributor to Patrick in the infliction." He recommended detention for all. Patrick and Amanda, as foreigners, were flight risks. Raffaele had to stay in custody because he'd lost his alibi in two ways: via Amanda and by claiming to have received a call from his dad at 11:30 on the murder night that he'd actually received on Halloween night, and not least because the little knife in his pocket might be compatible with the wound to the victim's neck.

Mignini saved his most thoughtful and complex reasoning for "Knox," who, he wrote, had to be detained not because she was a foreigner but because she had demonstrated *spregiudicatezza*—in English, roughly behavior that combines heedlessness or absence of thought for consequences and lying. She was also culpable, he wrote, for corrupting her Italian boyfriend: "for involving in such a serious episode *il giovane* [young] Sollecito."

That report landed on the desk of a tense, soignée brunette in her forties, Judge Claudia Matteini. After policewomen Napoleoni, Ficarra, and Zugarini, Matteini was the next—but not the last—Italian female to hold the fate of the young American in her hands. Like all the women before her, Matteini seemed to instinctively distrust the peculiar roommate. Amanda, Matteini wrote, had an "attitude the consequence of a mixture of shrewdness and naiveté."

On November 8, Amanda, Raffaele, and Patrick briefly left their cells and appeared before her. They also met their lawyers for the first time. The next day, Matteini formally affirmed the arrests, opening with a paean to Perugia's freedom and vitality that seemed like a press release for the international journalists.

"Perugia is a city that is proud of its long and consolidated cultural tradition, civilization, and hospitality," she wrote. "Its streets, squares, and bars are full of the echoes of free, multiracial, and happy voices of a multitude of students of all ages and origins who attend its two famous universities. But liberty presupposes responsibility and responsibility in its turn a mature awareness. If both are not present, risky situations can occur, especially when these impulses are not assisted by some form of ideality. The case we are examining here reflects one of those risks which unfortunately ended up in tragedy."

IN AFFIRMING DETENTION, MATTEINI relied on much evidence that would be proven inaccurate or meaningless later. She noted that Raffaele's penknife was the murder weapon and that the shoe prints in the murder room were "almost certainly" Raffaele's. They were not. She believed that Raffaele had written a blog about needing "new sensations" a month before the murder, not a year before. If she had seen the entire piece of writing, she did not consider his repeated references to studying, to taking care of his grandmother, to cleaning his apartment, and other indications of good citizenship and psychological normalcy. She believed that Amanda had had an appointment with Patrick, which she had not. She believed that a parking lot video camera showed Amanda walking toward the house at around the hour of the murder. It did not.

She had, though, Amanda's statement placing herself inside the house, hearing the screams, and she had the prosecutor's references to her strange behavior, so at odds with that of a normal grieving Italian girl. In ruling that there was sufficient evidence to detain the suspects while authorities conducted a thorough investigation, she presented the sex-game narrative that took hold worldwide and that would—except for the replacement of one suspect with another a few weeks later— survive a nine-month trial.

She contrasted a sketch of Meredith's personality—serious, studious, a model of sexual fidelity—with Amanda's frivolous, promiscuous character. "Amanda Knox, the other roommate at via della Pergola, is much more of a restless person: she didn't have problems with multiple and occasional relationships; it happened for example . . . with a friend of the four Italian boys: he spent the night in Amanda's room."

With that example of a "restless" one-night stand as a springboard, Matteini laid out the crime theory: "It is possible to reconstruct what happened on the evening of November 1. Sollecito, Raffaele, and Knox, Amanda, spent the entire afternoon smoking hashish. In the evening, around 8.30 P.M., while Knox found herself at the house of Sollecito, she received a message from Diya Lumumba, who . . . confirmed the appointment that evening, having obviously agreed beforehand that the girl would provide him with help in having an encounter with her friend Meredith."

THE PERUGIA AUTHORITIES HAD no problem detaining Amanda for a year based on her "vision" about being inside the house. Raffaele was a different story. Originally, Raffaele was detained on the basis of his penknife, which turned out not to match the wound or the bloody bedsheet print. He was then held in jail because of the presumed match between his Nikes and the bloody shoeprints. When the Sollecito family hired an expert who explained, on national TV, that the actual shoe print almost certainly belonged to a half-size-larger Nike, the authorities in Perugia held a press conference within days to announce the finding of a new piece of damning evidence on which to hold Raffaele. Six weeks after the first CSI team had scoured the murder room, scientific police went back in and recovered Meredith's severed bra clasp, which they had noticed in their first sweep but mysteriously left behind on the floor. When they went back for it, in the supposedly secured crime scene, the clasp wasn't even in the same spot as it had been in when the first CSI team had videotaped it. An unknown number of investigators had been into and out of the house and room since then. The crime lab in Rome tested it and found a trace of Raffaele's DNA on one of the metal hooks. And as soon as the shoe prints were out as evidence against Raffaele, police announced the DNA on the bra clasp.

WITH AMANDA'S *MEMORIALE* OF the murder night in hand and Raffaele's DNA on the bra clasp, some of the police considered their job done. Within months, Serious Crimes Unit chief Eduardo Giobbi hung Amanda's framed portrait in the hallway in the Rome offices of the national police among those of some of the nation's most vicious mafiosi.

FIVE DAYS AFTER THE arrests, Perugia newspapers began reporting what police had known within the first week after the arrests—that none of the fingerprints or DNA they had picked up in the murder room belonged to any of the three people they had in jail. On the contrary, the prints belonged to a Perugia man whose fingerprints were on file but who was currently nowhere to be found.

By November 11, police revealed to selected reporters that there was "a fourth man" involved. According to the London *Telegraph,* he was "a North African musician" who could be seen in parking garage video footage heading toward the murder house just before nine at night.

The man was not Moroccan, he was not a musician, and he would be identified not by the faulty video cameras of the parking lot but by his own fingerprints. As soon as the National Scientific Police had the prints, the Perugia police had his name. It didn't take long to find him.

RUDY HERMANN GUEDE, TWENTY-SEVEN, the son of an Ivory Coast immigrant bricklayer, the onetime adopted son of the richest citizen of Perugia, was feeling homesick. On November 4, he had taken a train out of Perugia, and by November 10, he was freezing in Germany, sleeping on barges or bunking in refugee flophouses. Later he would say he saw bloodred every night when he closed his eyes.

He nearly saved himself by burrowing anonymously into Europe's undocumented immigrant underworld. In Germany, he was well on his way to gaining a new identity, according to a story his lawyer sold to a British writer. But he saw himself on international TV, portrayed as a killer on the lam, and he couldn't resist Skyping for three hours with his childhood friend Giacomo Benedetti back in Ponte San Giovanni on the bottom of the hill below Perugia. Unbeknown to him, Giacomo was Skyping him from a Perugia police station. During that call, he still felt the need to protect his reputation, a reputation belonging to a person— Rudy Guede—he was in process of erasing.

On November 11, 2007, with police monitoring it, Rudy and Giacomo had a Skype chat. Giacomo had been instructed to get Rudy's location and arrange a meeting, preferably in Italy, where police could nab him.

GIACOMO: Hey, Rudy.

G: Where are you?

G: Do you feel like talking?

R: I don't have any money, but as soon as I can I'll call you.

R: I have nothing to do with this story.

R: But I'm scared.

G: You need to stay calm.

R: I was there when it happened.

R: I have nothing to do with it.

G: Where did you end up going now?

R: I tried to help her, but then I escaped.

G: If you try to explain better, I can help you.

G: But you need to stay calm.

R: Listen, whatever they are saying in the newspapers is bullshit.

R: Right now I'm not in Italy.

G: Right.

G: And where are you?

R: Not that I don't trust you, but right now I can't tell you.

R: I'm sorry, but I'm scared.

G: Of what?

G: You have nothing to do with it.

G: If you try and trust me, you'll get out of this.

G: But you have to help me.

R: The weird thing is that I tried to help her, it happened when I was in the bathroom taking a shit.

R: I tried to stop it from happening.

R: But then he ran off.

G: He? Who?

R: Then I tried to help her.

G: Who ran off?

R: Giacomo, I'm at an Internet point, I don't have much money, as soon as I can I will call you, I promise.

G: Wait.

G: Don't be stupid.

G: You are going to make things worse.

G: Trust me.

G: Everyone here is convinced you didn't do it.

R: Listen, I'm not in Italy but beyond Austria.

R: What's—

R: Please don't betray me.

G: I would never do it.

R: I have nothing to do with this, I will tell you everything later.

R: I was in the bathroom when everything happened, I tried to do something, but I wasn't able to, Amanda has nothing to do with it.

G: But you need to tell me who was there.

R: Because I fought with a guy.

R: And she wasn't there.

G: And who was there?

R: I don't know, I didn't see him in his face.

G: Italian?

G: Patrick or Raffaele?

R: I think so.

R: I don't have much money.

R: Patrick no.

G: Raffaele?

G: I can send you the money.

R: The guy was Italian because we insulted each other.

R: And he didn't have a foreign accent.

R: And as—

G: So was it Raffaele, the one in TV?

R: I think so.

R: But I'm not sure.

R: And another thing, I didn't rape her.

R: We wanted it.

R: Both.

G: I believe you.

G: I know you well, I know you have nothing to do with it.

G: You need to understand that I can help you.

G: If you don't tell me where you are, you are going to make things worse.

G: I can send you some euros through the mail.

R: If I'm here it's because I'm scared, I don't want to go to jail, they wrote that I'm obsessed with American and British girls, so not true!

G: I know.

R: I'm in Germany.

G: It's all bullshit.

At that point, Rudy asked for money, and they discussed how to get a hundred euros to him in Düsseldorf. Giacomo asked why he had disappeared, and Rudy replied, "I was scared because I knew I was going to be accused of something I didn't do." Then they said good-bye.

In that, Rudy's only known prearrest statement on the subject, he stated that "Amanda had nothing to do with it," although he left the possibility open that he had seen Raffaele in the house.

On November 19, the *Corriere dell'Umbria* reported that the police had apprehended Rudy Guede in Mainz, Germany, where he had boarded a train without a ticket. By November 21, he was telling a new version of the events of November 1 to the Germans. It was a most interesting tale indeed.

Back in Perugia, police searched his house and turned up an empty Nike box from shoes almost identical to and a half size larger than Raffaele's. They never found the actual shoes. It now seemed that the first and ugliest instincts of the magistrate and the police—that the killer of Meredith Kercher had been an *extracommunitario*, a dark, non-Italian male—had been proven right. Italy's nativisits were vindicated. The Umbrian branch of an extreme right-wing party, Alleanza Nazionale, immediately plastered the alley walls of Perugia with large posters of an old police shot of Rudy Guede, sporting some rapper bling, over a caption that read: CONTRO OGNI DROGA—against every drug. And beneath that, the party slogan, a Fascist slogan used by Mussolini: DIO PATRIA FAMIGLIA—God Homeland Family. Rudy Guede now made the perfect bogeyman, the foreign monster that many Perugians, and certainly many Italians also, secretly fear and, equally, don't want to believe threatens their part of town.

Police released Lumumba, who had an airtight alibi, a Swiss professor who had been sitting at the bar with him during the murder hours. "The Congolese" soon announced that he'd file a slander charge against Amanda Knox. He closed his pub.

With Rudy in and Patrick out, the Perugia police and Magistrate Mignini had a choice: to step back, admit error, and revise their theory or add the new man to their existing theory and forge ahead. They chose the latter path. The rest is tabloid and Italian legal history, or, as one of the Italian papers put it, black man out, black man in. The two white students stayed in the case, too. And in jail.

13

LA SIGNORA DEL GIOCO

It's a complex fate, being an American, and one of the responsibilities
it entails is fighting against a superstitious valuation of Europe.

—*Henry James*

Brutal murderer or just too sexy for the cops? Is the suspect in an
Italian murder case innocent or a narcissistic sociopath?

—*MSNBC headline*

WITHIN HOURS OF HER ARREST, Amanda Knox's face was flashed around
the world. It was a perfect, heart-shaped face but with a mysterious expression, one that viewers could only subjectively read. One American
who went on to start a website devoted to Amanda Knox's guilt said she
took one look at it and thought, "That girl's a killer."

The American writer and Italophile Mary McCarthy, in her 1950s
paean to Florentine art, *The Stones of Florence,* wrote about the other
famous female face out of Italy. McCarthy (coincidentally also a Seattle

native) connected the mystery of the Mona Lisa smile to alchemy and medieval sorcery. Of Leonardo da Vinci's painting, she wrote, "Everything is in a state of slow metamorphosis or creeping transformation, and the subject of his most celebrated painting, the *Mona Lisa*, smiling her enigmatic smile, is certainly a witch. That is why people are tempted to slash her, to draw moustaches on her, to steal her; she is the most famous painting in the world, because all the deceptions and mystifications of painting are summed up in her, to produce a kind of fear."

Mignini always included witch fear in his murder theory, and only reluctantly relinquished it. As late as October 2008, a year after the murder, he told a court that the murder "was premeditated and was in addition a 'rite' celebrated on the occasion of the night of Halloween. A sexual and sacrificial rite [that] in the intention of the organizers . . . should have occurred 24 hours earlier"—on Halloween itself—"but on account of a dinner at the house of horrors, organized by Meredith and Amanda's Italian flatmates, it was postponed for one day. The presumed assassins contented themselves with the evening of 1 November to perform their do-it-yourself rite, when for some hours it would again be the night of All Saints."

Eventually, Mignini's number two, the chain-smoking, no-nonsense Manuela Comodi, persuaded him to drop the references to Satanism. But no one forgot about it, not the jury, not the judge, not the press, not the Perugians, not the court spectators, who could never look at Amanda and Raffaele without wondering whether a whiff of sulfur surrounded them.

UN FESTINO DI GIOCHI *proibiti*—literally, "a party of forbidden games." The phrase first appeared in the *Giornale dell'Umbria* the day after the arrests, November 7, 2007, and was quickly picked up worldwide. Amanda Knox, Raffaele Sollecito, and Diya "Patrick" Lumumba had killed Meredith Kercher after, police said, playing a forbidden game. Later that cumbersome phrase—*un festino di giochi proibiti*—was simplified to *gioco erotico*—"erotic game."

The first story to refer to the sex game ran next to the famous picture of Amanda Knox peering at the camera with Raffaele in profile to the camera, his hand on her arm, petting her. There are trees behind her, and she looks pretty and elfin, like a wood sprite or a pretty goblin. Her lips are fuller than in other pictures, as if maybe she's just been kissed, and her expression is sad or accusatory or shocked, impossible to define precisely, inscrutably unhappy. The headline read, in Italian, "They Are Three Kids from Good Families."

THE POLICE AND PROSECUTOR would have to wait weeks for the DNA evidence. While they waited, they had much circumstantial evidence— the shifting stories, the fact that the two students had turned off their phones at the same time on the murder night, their strange delay in calling the police on the morning of November 2 after Amanda saw blood and they found the broken window.

They also had what they could see with their naked eyes and measure with rudimentary science. What they saw was a dead girl inside a bloody room inside a house that had been unlocked and seemed to have been wiped clean. There didn't seem to have been a fight anywhere but in the murder room. A large bottle of water stood open on the kitchen table, a few cigarettes were in ashtrays, a chair was knocked over in the dining area, but otherwise the place was spic and span. Two of the four bedrooms were completely intact.

The Perugia police didn't have the CSI expertise to deal with what was clearly going to be a high-profile case. The National Scientific Police in Rome took over, headed by a raven-haired young forensic scientist named Patrizia Stefanoni. She and her team collected evidence on the day the murder was discovered, and Stefanoni's lab—an unaccredited lab, the defense would eventually point out—eventually reported back.

While they were waiting for the scientific analyses, this is what the public minister and his investigators had from inside the house:

Meredith Kercher was killed by a cut to the neck on a Thursday night, in her own bedroom.

There were five left Nike shoe prints in blood on the pillowcase that had been shoved under Meredith Kercher's hips.

There were three more bloody left shoe prints on the tile floor around the body, matching those on the pillowcase.

The shoe prints looked very much alike.

There was one bloody bare right footprint on the fuzzy blue bathmat in the smaller bathroom. It was from a large foot and therefore also presumably male.

There was a small but visible dried smear of blood on the bathroom faucet.

There were unflushed feces in the toilet in the larger bathroom.

There was blood on a wall in the downstairs apartment, soon determined to be that of a black cat.

The police dusted the house for fingerprints. Dozens of prints turned up, too many to categorize. Police paid attention only to the ones for which they had matches—the girls in the house, the boys downstairs. The only identifiable prints in Meredith's room were Rudy's, although fourteen prints were unmatchable. Investigators tried to match the prints only to the known visitors or inhabitants. As Prosecutor Comodi put it later in her trademark frisky way of talking, when asked how wide a net investigators had cast in testing fingerprints in the cottage, "We didn't compare them with Obama's fingerprints, why would we?"

Police found Amanda Knox's prints in one place only, on a water glass in the kitchen.

There was no visible blood or strands of hair or threads of torn cloth on the broken glass bits still in Filomena's windowsill and no fingerprints on Meredith's locked doorknob, although there was a smear of her blood on the latch.

To the superstitious-minded, it might seem that whoever had come in through that window—if anyone had—possessed superhuman powers of levitation and an uncanny lightness of touch that had left not a single organic or inorganic trace on the narrow, jagged entrance.

TO UNDERSTAND MIGNINI'S WORLDVIEW, to get what he saw when he looked at the crime scene with its bloody prints from a single shoe, a mysteriously broken window without human traces on it at Hallowtide, on a Thursday night, with cat's blood downstairs, and to see what led him to think of a woman leading a sex game, we must dig far back into the history of the long battle of Catholicism versus alternative spirituality in Italy and know its signs and symbols as well as he does.

The conflict between paganism and Catholicism persists in the minds of true believers like Mignini, and, judging from past prosecutions involving Satanism in Italy, there may well be modern-day people there who still revere and even practice deviant aspects of the "natural" religions that predate Christianity. Some of the more benign practitioners may be found among the secret societies, including the Masons, whose initiation rites supposedly draw from pre-Hebraic religions as well as Christianity.

From his research into the Narducci case, Mignini knew more about the Masons than most. Masonic initiation rites are rooted in a hodgepodge of alchemy and ancient religious practices and texts, from the Mithraic mysteries to the Egyptian Book of the Dead and the Bible itself. Members can attain several "degrees," and at each degree a separate initiation rite takes place. Initiates are blindfolded and asked to leave their worldly belongings at the door. They either untie their shoes (being "slipshod" is part of the rite) or actually remove one shoe. At certain rites, they either strike themselves in the forehead or are hit in the forehead, apparently to commemorate a blow to the head suffered by the original builder of Solomon's Temple. They also wear aprons, another throwback to the initiation rites of various pagan cults.

The removal of one shoe during Masonic initiation is a piece of pagan symbolism so ancient that historians don't even understand its significance. After studying numerous statues with one sandal and myths such as Cinderella, involving lost shoes, or the laming or hobbling of one foot, as in Achilles' heel, the Italian cultural anthropologist Carlo Ginzburg theorized that the ritual laming of a foot or the removal of one shoe was a symbol of stepping into and out of the underworld. In certain rituals, taking off a shoe offered "more immediate contact with the ground, to achieve a relationship with the subterranean powers." Symbolic visits to the world of the dead were part of many initiation rites, such as the Dionysian and Eleusinian mysteries. So-called mono-sandalism abounds in ancient imagery and old stories, but its original ritual or spiritual meaning has been lost. In the *Aeneid,* Dido removes a sandal before killing herself after Aeneas leaves her. The Etruscan god of the underworld, Hades, leads a cohort of soldiers with one bare left foot. Jason the Argonaut appears before his usurping uncle Pelias wearing one sandal after an oracle had warned Pelias to "beware a man wearing one sandal." Medea removes a shoe when summoning Hecate, an underworld deity. The Greek historian Thucydides mentioned the practice, but even he wasn't clear on what it meant because the symbolism was already so ancient.

Mignini, of course, was very familiar with Masonic ritual. At 7 via della Pergola, the track of single bloody shoe prints leading out the door was the first, most visible clue.

Mignini was also comfortable with the notion that his Catholic Church still battles the forces of paganism, and chief among the Church's traditional pagan foes was an old cult in Italy that revered the fertility goddess Diana, which was a primary target of the Inquisition. Ginzburg, after poring over thousands of pages of records from the Catholic Inquisition, in which accused witches described elaborate rituals involving magic and the resurrection of slaughtered animals, decided that

these witches probably belonged to a pre-Christian Diana cult rever-
ing a forest deity practitioners referred to as La Signora del Gioco, the
Lady of the Game. He found evidence that nominal witches—at least
in the early years of the Inquisition—were still practicing old rituals intended to ensure abundant crops. Italian women executed as witches in
the 1300s referred to their leader as the Madonna dell'Oriente (a term
that comes from the Latin *Domina Oriens,* for the moon goddess) or La
Signora del Gioco. In their confessions about these gatherings, both
men and women said they followed a "white goddess" or a "lady of the
game" into the forest at night, where they practiced animal transformation, becoming beasts that could fly, and traveled long distances, entering houses through windows and walls, drinking wine, leaving behind
feces, and waking up in their own beds the next morning unsure of how
they'd gotten home.

The practitioners called those gatherings "games."

For some unclear reason, the game nights traditionally fell on
Thursdays.

During the coming months, while the young people were in jail,
Mignini hoped at least one of them would break. He thought Amanda's
"vision" of being in the house during the attack was flawed as a confession but was a key element of the truth of the actual event. The fact
that the two students recanted their November 5–6 statements within
days of being jailed was a problem, not insurmountable since he had
their statements, but he hoped they would eventually confess. That they
never did so baffled him even as the trial began. *"Sono perplesso,"* he said
in interviews. "I'm perplexed." It made no sense to him that at least one
of them wouldn't break for leniency.

He concluded that perhaps they feared something worse than the
wheels of human justice. In interviews he sometimes proposed that a
fourth person, a sort of master of horror ceremonies, never apprehended,
had been on the scene and that the defendants were too terrified of this
sinister mastermind to dare mention him or her.

American supporters of Amanda Knox have always claimed that the sex-game theory came from Mignini, their bête noire. But the first hints of it probably came from the police and, even more specifically, from the minds, the instincts of the female police officers.

Luciano Ghirga, the garrulous, gap-toothed Daniel Webster of Perugia and Amanda's first Perugia lawyer, thought the policewomen themselves had come up with the sex-game theory. "Mignini probably went with what the police were already thinking. He was there, listening. All the witnesses were asked sexual things, mostly, and it was coming from the policewomen. I can see them thinking, look at this little bitch, she thinks she can fool us. She had unconventional behavior."

Mignini also eventually said the sex-game theory came first from the police: "From the beginning when they saw the body, what they found on the crime scene, no bra, the shirt pulled up, it was clear there was a sexual imprint on it. The bra straps that were cut. And they thought it was one or more people. Then there's a Vaseline jar on the desk. Open."

The sex-game theory depended upon Amanda's propensity for sadosexual behavior. In investigative interviews he conducted with Meredith's friends, Mignini homed in on Amanda's hypersexuality and Meredith's response to it. He worked carefully to distinguish between Meredith's sex life and Amanda's, as in the exchange with Filomena below.

"She brought this guy Juve, who worked at the pub Le Chic," Filomena said in response to questions in December 2007, after Amanda had been in jail for six weeks. "At lunchtime she would come in and eat a sandwich and change and they would go out, it happened, like, twice. And then Laura told me, on a weekend when I wasn't there, she brought a guy named Daniele, a friend of the boys downstairs, where Meredith's boyfriend—"

Mignini interrupted: "The *fidanzato*."

Filomena hesitated.

"They hadn't known each other very long, that's a big word—"

"Yes, it's an important word," Mignini replied.

"Everybody liked Meredith. She might not have been this great beauty, she was nice to be with. Amanda, on the other hand, was a bit insistent, nice, but after, a bit . . . a bit—"

A carabiniere named Danilo Paciotti, one of Mignini's most trusted attachés, also at the table, interrupted, "Heavy."

"Yes, a bit heavy," Filomena agreed.

THANKS TO A DIRTY trick Italian authorities played on her during her first month in jail, intended to uncover any sexual relationship she might have had with Rudy Guede, we know exactly how many men Amanda had had sex with in her life and their first names. In November 2007, an apparently fake prison doctor told her she had tested her blood and told her she had HIV. Terrified that she was dying, she listed the names of all her sex partners and tried to remember whether or not they had used condoms. She named seven men. The list was promptly leaked to the press, and some British newspapers printed that Amanda reported having had sex with seven men in her four weeks in Italy. The list of seven men was a lifetime count, meaning that after Kyle, she'd had sex with six more men over a period of two years in Washington and in Italy. She was no virgin, but her record was certainly within the norm on college campuses in the United States, where, in 2010, a Duke University senior gained infamy and a book deal for very publicly rating more than a dozen athletes she'd bedded during her four years of higher education.

After Kyle, Amanda joined a rock-climbing group and befriended a tall, muscled, but insecure young man named David "DJ" Johnsrud. They were friends for several months before he worked up the courage to stammer out how he really felt about her. Soon they were taking camping trips into the Cascades and developed what passes on modern American campuses for a committed relationship.

DJ left for China at the same time Amanda left for Italy. Before they parted ways, they agreed that they would set each other free while they lived abroad. They still hooked up regularly by Skype (the British girls would later say that Meredith was horrified by the fact that Amanda

Skyped DJ naked). Still, the long-distance relationship didn't restrain her from cutting what authorities considered a pretty scandalous sexual swath in Perugia.

In four weeks in Italy, she had bedded not only Raffaele but Daniele, the boy from Rome, and a man named Elis, an Albanian she had met in a bar (Elis would go on to sell his story to the British tabloids, describing a one-night "sexual marathon" with oral sex and multiple orgasms). Still, DJ remained her "boyfriend," which meant, she confided in Lumumba and Meredith, that she felt guilty for her headlong romance with Raffaele, if not the one-night stands.

The day before Meredith Kercher was murdered, Halloween 2007, local women organized a rally in Perugia *centro* in honor of the millions of women executed as witches by the Inquisition. Dubbed "Never Forget the Female Holocaust," the event was meant to commemorate nine million women—according to the organizers—who were burned alive during the Inquisition simply because they possessed a female power "closely connected with the natural world" and lived as healers, midwives, and herb gatherers and "officiated at fertility rites."

Umbria's Councillor for Equality was behind the rally, and its leader was a gynecologist and staunch Italian feminist, Marina Toschi. Toschi, a vigorous fiftysomething redhead, took credit for forcing the Perugia public health service to provide free female condoms to local prostitutes. It took her a decade, but she finally succeeded. She blamed the southern Italian Mafia bosses and their protectors within the local government for keeping the flesh trade alive in the Umbrian region. "We are now a colony of Calabria. All the public health chiefs here are Calabrian," she said. "They don't kill you, they just make your life impossible."

Toschi was a strong advocate of female sexuality and empowerment. One might think that Amanda Knox—vilified for, among other things, having seven sex partners over two years—would have found a natural champion in her. The equality councillor was indeed outraged by the coverage of the case, but not for the way the American murderess's sex life was brought forth as evidence against her. She was appalled that Meredith, the victim, was portrayed in the press as a sexually active young woman, as if that had had something to do with her death. But after the Perugia court convicted Amanda in December 2009, and as the Americans were crying foul, Toschi went around Perugia with a petition, urging people to sign it in support of the fundamental fairness of Italy's justice system.

Like everyone else in Perugia, Toschi had been reading about Amanda Knox in the newspapers since November 7, 2007, and she was convinced that the young woman was a sick product of America's excessive morality, a repressed girl who had gone murderously wild as soon as she landed on the more liberated European shores. "Americans think the Bible, the truth, God is with them," she said. "The pictures of Amanda Knox on Myspace, holding the machine gun in Germany, they reminded me of Abu Ghraib. That was really disturbing to me."

THE ANCIENT WALL

PART FOUR

11

THE DREAM TEAMS

She seemed to believe that truth would prevail, so why waste
time spinning a lot of fancy theories? Whereas Zen knew that
truth prevailed, if at all, only after so much time had passed that it
had become meaningless, like a senile prisoner who can safely be
released, his significance forgotten, his friends dead, a babbling idiot.

—*Michael Dibdin*, in *Ratking*

IN EARLY NOVEMBER 2007, THE U.S. and British embassies dispatched representatives on opposite missions. The British consul arrived on November 2, as soon as the embassy received word of a dead British citizen. Before the end of the week, the British authorities had removed the British girls from Perugia. The diplomats also steered the Kercher family through the sad trauma of police, prosecutor, and morgue. Meredith's father, John, refused to view the body, so Meredith's mother and sister identified her. None of Meredith's family spoke a word of Italian; an embassy representative had to be present constantly.

The British Embassy gave the Kerchers a list of lawyers who had worked with British citizens before. One of them was Francesco Maresca, a short, stylish Florentine who raced motocross on weekends and, with dimples and copious dark blond locks, looked as if he'd stepped out of a 1970s Bain de Soleil tanning oil ad. He spoke no English, but he had represented the British "soccer hooligans" who'd disrupted a World Cup match in Italy some years back. When the Kerchers reached out to him, he was doing a lot of medical malpractice defense, but, like any Italian defense lawyer worth his fee, he'd also represented mafiosi. He might even have been a little more familiar with the ways of *omertà* and the criminal clans than other northern Italian defense attorneys, since he hailed from Naples, where his father had been a police officer. The fact that he shared a surname with a notorious female Camorrista, Assunta "Pupetta" Maresca, who had earned her leadership status by shooting a man in broad daylight when she was six months pregnant, probably didn't hurt his defense business, either.

The Kerchers picked Maresca to lead them through their Italian nightmare.

The U.S. Embassy had a similar list of lawyers, which it e-mailed to Chris Mellas in Seattle. Mellas started at the top, calling them one by one, selecting the first lawyer with an office manager who spoke English. The office belonged to Carlo Dalla Vedova of Rome, who turned out to be a very un-Italian Italian—cosmopolitan, suave, prematurely gray, low-key, and undramatic. He spoke perfect English, thanks to his Irish mother, and had spent a semester at Harvard. His father was a dean of Italian jurisprudence. He'd thrived in post–Berlin Wall, corporate, Eurodollar Europe, spending several years in Bulgaria creating the legal framework for that counry's nascent market economy, becoming fluent in Bulgarian.

The U.S. Embassy also sent an attaché to interview Amanda in jail and ascertain that she was not being abused, but that was all the aid it could offer. Every year about three thousand American exchange students are arrested abroad, and the State Department rarely rushes in. American supporters of Amanda have asked why the U.S. Embassy didn't get more involved in her case. After all, the girl was alleging police brutality in the first days after her arrest. Edda recalled that the American officials discussed the possibility of filing a complaint about the police brutality charge, but Italian defense lawyers overruled that. "She'll be out of jail in a few weeks, why piss off the police?" was the logic.

To be sure, there were bigger and better reasons for the United States to stay out of that particular briar patch. The diplomatic relationship between the United States and Italy in 2007, especially the personal understanding between George W. Bush and Silvio Berlusconi, didn't allow for an open difference of opinion regarding the arrest of a young American who had at the very least been using illegal drugs. Berlusconi was an important European partner who had committed troops to the "Coalition of the Willing" in Iraq. The Knox family had neither the connections nor the stature to initiate the slightest ripple in the diplomatic relationship between the nations.

The third defendant in the case also had a little help from the diplomatic world. A Perugia lawyer, Dottor Valter Biscotti, happened to be in Abidjan on business when Rudy Guede was arrested in Germany on November 19, 2007. He got word of the arrest during a chance meeting with Ivorian diplomats, who he said connected him with Roger Guede back in Perugia. He took the case gratis, since the young man and his family had no money. He would, he knew, be rewarded in the nonfungible but more glamorous and valuable currency of fame.

Like any good defense lawyer anywhere, Biscotti has a few acquaintances on the local police force. The Perugia police might even be a little more predisposed toward him than other defense lawyers, because he once won a large settlement for a member of their own club—one of the last undercover agents murdered by a Red Brigades terrorist on a train between Rome and Florence in 2003. He knows how to work them, too. He has claimed to know, through his police sources, who really killed the Italian political leader Aldo Moro in a brazen terrorist kidnapping in the 1980s, still unsolved. Biscotti has warned that the Red Brigades might rise again, information he also credits to his police contacts.

Biscotti is tiny and tense, radiating the unease of a man who has come a long way in life and finds his perch precarious. His parents hailed from the impoverished South of Italy but moved north to start a restaurant in Turin in the 1960s. He served pizzas before he went to college. In 2009, he was a veteran middle-priced Perugia lawyer operating out of a fantastically frescoed, authentically aged eighteenth-century office with a wrought-iron balcony above Corso Vannucci. His cases had ranged from high-profile *cronache nere* to bread-and-butter Albanian mafia drug and fraud cases.

Biscotti's physical and temperamental opposite, a roly-poly bear of a man with a four o'clock shadow, Nicodemo Gentile, was already on the case up in Perugia when Biscotti returned from Africa. Gentile, who hailed from the land of the 'Ndrangheta in Calabria, was a cousin of the owner of Pizzeria Da Gennaro and Merlin Pub and of one of the young men pictured with his arm around Meredith Kercher on Halloween night. Gentile also had a history as an advocate for the small Ivorian community in Perugia. Before Rudy was arrested in Germany on November 19, when he was still just a fugitive, Ivorian community leaders had called on Gentile first.

Together, Biscotti and Gentile took Rudy's case. Anglophone reporters took to referring to them by the English translations of their names, Cookie and Nice. At first glance, they looked like a bumbling Mutt-and-Jeff team. Without their work, though, the case against Amanda Knox and Raffaele Sollecito might not have been viable.

By the time Rudy was arrested, the centrality of the pretty girl was obvious to anyone following the case. Claudia Matteini had confirmed Mignini's sense that Amanda was the ringleader who had led the sexually besotted *giovane Sollecito* into murder. Amanda's sexual history, her Foxy Knoxy page, Meredith's alleged dislike of her—all the memes were being broadcast. Rudy, attentive to television coverage of the Perugia murder he was monitoring from immigrant hostels and flophouses in Germany, was keenly aware of what police thought about the crime.

As soon as he had his Perugia lawyers, he started to put the *cronaca nera* female star around the house or even inside it during the murder, depending on when he was talking. Contrary to what he'd told Giacomo on Skype before he was arrested—"Amanda has nothing to do with it. . . . She wasn't there"—Rudy began what would be a two-year-long evolutionary process of putting Amanda Knox into the murder picture, at first tenuously (in one statement, he thought he heard her outside), then with more eyewitness details, putting her inside and arguing with Meredith. Writing in the German jail, he admitted having been in the house at the hour of the murder but claimed he had been there at Meredith's invitation. When he arrived, he now wrote, Meredith was complaining that Amanda had been stealing her money. He calmed her down, he says, with some consensual heavy petting. Stopping short of actually ejaculating inside her, he had retreated to the bathroom with a sudden cramp. After popping on his iPod (he helpfully explained that whereas some people read newspapers, he listens to music on the toilet) and listening to three tracks, the sound of screaming interrupted his business. He came out with his pants still undone to find an Italian white man running past him, crying out, "Black man found, black man convicted!" Rudy tried to stop him, but the man slashed at his hand with a knife—hence the tiny scars still on the fingers of his right hand (which defense forensic experts would attribute to his hand slipping from the handle to the blade of the murder knife as it got slippery with blood). He grabbed a chair to defend himself—much as Christian Tramontano said he had done when he found Rudy in his house after dark—and the man ran off.

Rudy wrote that he then ran into Meredith's bedroom to find her bleeding on the floor, tried to stop the bleeding with some towels. "Her neck looked like a river of blood," he wrote. He admitted he washed his hands (putting himself in the bloody bathroom) before he left.

He lamented his departure but insisted on his innocence. "This story added to my childhood and adolescence is an explosive mix for me, I cannot sleep any longer, I cannot close my eyes because I see all red, I never saw so much blood, like a river. . . . Only once before it has happened that I've seen so much blood in my life, when I was a child in Torgiano [a town near Ponte San Giovanne] because I was living in that area. My 'father' smashed a stick over my head. There was so much blood coming from my head and pouring down on the ground that I looked like a fountain. But that has nothing to do with that evening and is nothing on comparison."

He added: "I didn't rape her because I really respect women as I never had a mother, but had many female figures who acted as my sweet, loving mother. I went there just to talk to her. I won't deny that I liked her."

In May 2008, with Biscotti and Gentile at his side during a meeting with Mignini and Comodi, Rudy recalled new details. This time he put Amanda inside the murder house. He said that while he was in the bathroom, the door opened and he heard Meredith saying "We have to talk" and Amanda replying "What's the matter?" He then heard their argument escalate through the music coming from his iPod, until the final bloodcurdling scream.

Biscotti and Gentile had to let their client put himself on the scene. His handprints were on the wall in blood. His DNA was on Meredith's torn-off bra, inside her purse, and on her sweater, as well as in her body, and on the toilet paper in the unflushed toilet. His left Nike shoe print in blood led out the front door.

The lawyers could have advised him to say he was too high to remember what had happened and to throw himself on the mercy of the court, a tactic that, given Italian leniency toward drug abusers, could have got him a sentence of less than ten years. Instead, they opted for a higher-stakes game, with Rudy pleading innocent, but also implicating Amanda in "a fast-track trial," a legal maneuver similar to an American bench trial. Rudy would repeat the story that he had indeed been in the house during the killing, and had been in the bathroom when he heard

Meredith screaming. When he came out, he claimed, the white male ran past him. In this version, he thought he had heard Amanda, possibly outside the house. He added that he had tried to help Meredith by stanching the blood with towels. Mignini didn't cut Rudy any slack on the first round, but asked for and got the maximum fast-track sentence, thirty years. Had Rudy gone to trial, Mignini could have asked for life. The judge that convicted Rudy also agreed with the prosecution that there was enough evidence to try Amanda and Raffaele in a separate trial.

MIGNINI WOULD EVENTUALLY CALL Rudy to testify against the students, but when he went to court he refused to speak. But on December 22, 2009, with Amanda and Raffaele convicted and sentenced, Biscotti predicted that Rudy would finally reveal the whole truth—a truth that just happened to coincide perfectly with what Mignini had been saying for two years. "She orchestrated it all," Biscotti said, referring to Amanda. She had done it for "sex," using "promises and enticements. Raffaele is weak." Rudy, he said, would continue to maintain that he was in the bathroom when the killers stabbed Meredith.

Rudy did speak at his own appeal, at length. He still pled innocence, but now he said he had seen Amanda at the crime scene and knew her to be the instigator of the murder. He repeated that he could never get the "red" from all that blood out of his mind and that he had tried to sop up the blood with towels (that detail was true to the crime scene). He apologized to the Kercher family for not calling for help but explained he had been too frightened for himself.

Later that day, the Perugia appeals judge knocked Rudy's sentence back to sixteen years.

When CBS requested an interview and tried to sweeten its request by asking Biscotti whether his client might need anything in jail, Rudy asked for a basketball signed by his American basketball hero, Byron Scott.

Biscotti proved himself both crafty about the potential inherent in his otherwise indigent client and exceedingly capable on the PR front. Talking to me, he first announced that he had his own three-hundred-page diary on the case to sell to the highest bidder. He then put a high price tag on any Rudy interview—300,000 euros—which no one met. NBCUniversal paid his way to New York to appear in an interview—and Gentile occasionally asked me to arrange for trips to New York. With no one offering to meet his price for an interview with Rudy, Biscotti struck out at the Americans—and the Sollecito defense team—who insisted that the most logical explanation for the crime was that Rudy had acted alone. He often threatened to sue anyone who tried to paint Rudy as the lone killer. Biscotti played the race card every chance he could, portraying his client as a victim of arrogant American power, much like the Italian nation as a whole ever since World War II. "The Americans are raising millions for Amanda Knox's defense and putting pressure on Italy's judges and police," he said in an interview in his office during the summer of 2009. "There is pressure from every angle. Rudy is just lucky he found two lawyers who care for him. We feel we are his big brothers now."

RAFFAEL'S FATHER HIRED A lawyer in Perugia named Luca Maori and eventually the doctor shelled out yet more money to hire one of the most high-profile lawyers in Italy, Giulia Bongiorno. The lawyers' first decision was whether to try to separate Raffaele's case from Amanda's. Because the two students were each other's only alibi, they decided to stick together.

The students' lawyers confronted a crime narrative of such *cronaca nera* perfection that nobody—not reporters, not the public—had the inclination or interest to dismantle it. Their biggest problem was the famous female defendant's own words—accusing an innocent man and putting herself in the house.

Confessions, according to criminologists, change every aspect of the investigations that follow, from police tactics to witnesses' memories to scientific analysis. Confessions can prompt witnesses to alter their memories completely. In one recent U.S. study, psychologists asked participants to witness a fake crime, a thief taking a computer from a room. They were then asked to pick the guilty person out of a lineup, although the actual guilty person was not in the lineup. Two days later they were called in and told that one in the lineup had confessed. Sixty percent of the individuals who had correctly stated that the culprit was not in the lineup changed their opinions after the confession.

Based on records of the Kercher murder investigation, from police-witness conversations that took place in the questura, and later, after Amanda's statement and arrest, the same phenomenon occurred. Amanda's chief accusers—the British girls—shared different memories before and after the arrest. In their first conversations at the questura, none told police that Meredith disliked Amanda. Only on a second or third round with the police did Sophie Purton—under pressure to give the police lists of men who might have encountered Meredith—even pass on the fact that she'd heard that Amanda had brought unknown men into the house.

Six weeks later, interviewed in Bergamo in northern Italy, with Amanda's confession widely disseminated, the British girls first began recalling Meredith's unease about Amanda's bathroom habits and her weird boyfriends. They also talked about their own impressions of Amanda in the questura, hours after poor Meredith was found, about watching her making out with Raffaele at the questura, her curious callousness.

BESIDES THE BEHAVIOR, THE case would be built upon forensics. No traces of the students were found in the murder room. But police had the knife, with its damning combination of Amanda on the handle and Meredith on the blade, and they had Meredith's bra clasp, a tiny piece of metal the Rome lab said contained traces of Raffaele's DNA.

Supporters of and lawyers for Amanda and Raffaele brought forth many experts from Italy, the FBI, and elsewhere, who repeatedly criticized the science behind the findings on both those objects. The defense teams also called expert witnesses who testified that the five cells on the knife blade were too small an amount to allow for an objective determination about who or what the material had come from. They dispensed with the bra clasp by arguing that after lying on the floor for six weeks, it had been contaminated, or that contamination had occurred at the lab. Some partisans accused the Italian lab of actually tampering with the evidence. The prosecution released documents from the lab late in the trial revealing that Stefanoni had actually tested both the knife and the small luminol-revealed footprints for blood—and found none.

Forensic scientists are as susceptible to being influenced by confessions as laypeople are. In 1988, a Pennsylvania defendant named Barry Laughman confessed to a rape and murder and spent sixteen years in prison before DNA evidence confirmed that he was innocent. Scientists found a blood type on the scene that was not his. Rather than contradict the confession, lab scientists went into contortions to make their evidence work. "The state forensic chemist went on to concoct four 'theories,' none grounded in science, to explain away the mismatch," wrote the American criminologist Saul Kassin. After sixteen years in prison, DNA evidence finally proved Laughman innocent, and he was set free.

A British researcher found the same phenomenon with fingerprint experts. In a study, the researcher re-presented fingerprint experts with pairs of prints from a prior case. Instructed that the suspect had since confessed (which suggested a match) or was in custody when the crime was committed (which suggested an exclusion), the experts changed 17 percent of their previously correct decisions.

"Confessions corrupt evidence," said Kassin. He pointed out that studies have shown that in all cases with confessions, 40 percent contained errors, and in false confession cases, 80 percent of the cases contained errors in forensic work, by informants or by witnesses. "Eye-witnesses change their memories to identify the confessor."

IN THE UNITED STATES, an organization called the Innocence Project has been taking the cases of convicted rapists and murderers and applying new DNA technology to old evidence. Their efforts have overturned rape and murder convictions in thousands of cases across the country. In 25 percent of these DNA exonerations, the falsely convicted convict had actually confessed. Furthermore, many of the false confessions contained publicly unknown facts about the crime scene, suggesting that police often feed details to suspects who later admit guilt.

Amanda could never prove that someone had cuffed her on the back of the head during the interrogation, and her defense lawyers did not try to prove that it had happened. Even so, one of them—Ghirga—was sued for defaming the police for repeating the assertion.

Leaving aside the issue of whether they hit her or not, the sequence of events she—and the police—consistently described as happening on the night of November 5–6 indicates that Perugia police were deploying an interrogation technique straight out of a handbook written for American police in the 1940s that is still used today.

The so-called Reid Technique is a three-step method that gets results through psychological pressure, with or without physical intimidation.

Step one: Police get a suspect to feel vulnerable to manipulation, provoking stress through isolation and lack of sleep or food. In Amanda's case, the fact that she had already been questioned for days, was in a foreign country and had nowhere to live, and couldn't understand Italian well would have been sufficient to create the requisite level of vulnerability.

Step two: Police present the suspect with false evidence. After Raffaele cracked in the next room and their mutual alibi crumbled, police told Amanda they had proof she'd been in the house during the murder—proof they did not have. According to Raffaele, the police were already telling him they had proof that Amanda was involved early in the night, even before they got him to say she might not have been in his house through the entire night of November 1 and 2.

Step three: Police introduce a discussion about psychology and memory, persuading an interrogee to question his or her own actual memory—or lies. The translator Anna Donnino provided the psychology element by describing her own traumatic memory loss and suggesting that Amanda was experiencing the same psychological phenomenon.

In a letter to me recounting the events of the night of November 5–6, Amanda said she felt that the police "spoke to me as if I were another victim, the key witness" and that she didn't know she was accused of murder until three days later, when guards led her out of isolation and before Judge Matteini. During the interrogation, she recalled, "I didn't understand why . . . they were insisting that I was traumatized and had amnesia."

The Reid Technique is quite effective, which is one reason it's been taught to police for more than sixty years in the United States. But in recent years, most police and forensic psychiatrists, including the American Psychiatric Association, agree that unless such interrogations are taped, it is impossible to tell how much of what the suspect said was spontaneous and true and what was actually introduced by police or even induced by the memory-loss suggestion tactic itself.

At the trial, translator Donnino stated that the young American had abruptly and inexplicably cracked, without any police abuse. She said that Amanda had gone from calm to screaming, from sitting up talking to lying in a fetal position screaming, right after police asked her about the "See ya later" cell phone text message to Lumumba. Donnino testified that she had not noticed the police abusing Amanda Knox in any way before she broke down.

Donnino went on to translate, by her own admission, at least six hundred of Amanda's letters from jail. At the trial, she described polite police officers who had never threatened Amanda with jail, never

deprived her of a lawyer, never lied to the girl. Under defense questioning, she replied that, "it doesn't seem to me" that she ever told Amanda
that the police had proof she had been in the house or could send her to
prison for thirty years. But she did remember—under questioning by
Amanda's lawyers—that she initiated a conversation about trauma and
memory loss with Amanda as a gesture of "solidarity."

> LAWYER: You were a victim of an accident where you
> broke your leg, do you remember telling Knox? Do you
> remember telling Knox you lived through a trauma and
> couldn't remember what happened?
> DONNINO: Yes, it's true I told her that. The first thing I take
> care of when I am translating is to make sure I have a
> relationship with the person. As a mother of two girls her
> age, I understood that she needed help.
> LAWYER: You told her that in a moment of trauma your
> memory leaves.
> DONNINO: I didn't say it to her that way. My principle is to assist
> people in these situations. I use my personal situations to
> help create this. I told her I had been thrown out of my
> bed to come to the questura. We even exchanged a couple
> words in German because she said she had been in Berlin. I
> understood she was in a difficult situation that needed a bit
> of solidarity.

Modern-day interrogation techniques have many psychological
aspects in common with those of the Inquisition. There's no rack and
thumbscrews, no eyeball plucking, but the psychological means of
extracting information from innocent or guilty human beings remains
as constant as human nature. The behavior of innocent people put to the
psychological rack is the same across ages and cultures. Like harmless
pagans confessing to black magic, innocent people do confess to crimes
in contradiction to evidence.

Criminologists who study the behavior of innocent people under questioning have noted that innocence seems more suspicious to interrogators than guilt because of the way innocent people believe in the power of justice to detect their innocence and in the power of their innocence to persuade. In studies of false confessions, the American criminologist Kassin found that the innocent were substantially more likely to sign a waiver of their Miranda rights (among others, the right to have a lawyer present) than those who were guilty—by a margin of 81 to 36 percent.

"It appears," Kassin said, "that people have a naive faith in the power of their own innocence to set them free." The innocent feel protected by what Kassin called an "illusion of transparency," a tendency to overestimate the extent to which their true thoughts, emotions, and other inner states can be seen by others.

> *This mental state leads those who stand falsely accused to believe that truth and justice will prevail. As a result, they cooperate with police, often not realizing that they are suspects, not witnesses; they waive their rights to silence, counsel, and a lineup; they agree to take lie-detector tests; they vehemently protest their innocence, unwittingly triggering aggressive interrogation behavior; and they succumb to pressures to confess when isolated, trapped by false evidence, and offered hope via minimization and the leniency it implies.*

It is not unusual for experienced police officers anywhere in the world to believe they have heightened powers of lie-detecting perception, although studies do not bear out their infallability. In Italy, according to culture chronicler Luigi Barzini, reading facial expressions is "an important art, to be learned in childhood," among everyone. "Italians are often disconcerted . . . in the north of Europe, and seldom know what is going on, surrounded as they are by blank faces on which little can be read," Barzini wrote. Eduardo Giobbi testified that he looked at Amanda Knox's face and, relying on his years of studying the subtle cues that guilty people exhibit, decided that she was in fact, a murder suspect. Giobbi, an Italian investigator who might convincingly claim to read the subtle verbal and physical cues exhibited by an Italian, never conceded that he could have mistranslated the nonverbal cues of a young woman who hailed from the other side of the planet and who didn't speak his language.

Giobbi's sixth sense turned Amanda from witness to suspect, and her questioners into interrogators, overnight. The interrogation produced an unforgettable result—Amanda's *memoriale* putting herself inside the house listening to Meredith's screams—that shaped the entire investigation thereafter.

15
TRIBUNALE

This is the simplest and fairest criminal trial one could possibly think
of in terms of evidence.

—*Stefano Maffei*, a lecturer in criminal procedure at the University of
Parma, to the *Seattle Post-Intelligencer*

A railroad job from hell.

—*Paul Ciolino*, an American investigator for CBS's *48 Hours*

In Italy, everything is theoretical.

—*A Perugia defense lawyer*, who asked to remain anonymous,
commenting on the rights of defendants

THE NARRATIVE WAS SUCH A perfect *cronaca nera*, it seemed a shame to
disturb it. So no one did.

Italy is a sunny place, but free speech is rather chilled. The nation was ranked seventy-ninth in press freedom in 2009. For years, major journalists who criticized Silvio Berlusconi were routinely fired. Prosecutors had the right to throw journalists in jail on fairly flimsy grounds, and most Italian journalists assumed that their phones were tapped. Couraegous, smart Italian journalists could be found on the front lines of stories about war and social issues, but those who did investigative work generally didn't take on the government. Judges—not journalists—were tasked with rooting out corruption.

Perhaps the greatest single systemic inhibition on the Italian press— and on any journalist operating in Italy—was the pervasiveness of the Mafia in economic and political life. Any journalist working in Italy was aware of the fate of an intrepid young writer named Roberto Saviano, who wrote a scathing and revealing memoir of life among the Camorra clans in Naples. The gangsters issued a Mafia version of a fatwa on Saviano. In 2009, he was hiding out in safe houses under constant police guard, in fear for his life. His girlfriend had dumped him, and he couldn't practice his craft, let alone go out dancing in Rome or eat at a restaurant. Though he was only in his early thirties, his existence as a free young man was effectively over.

Foreign journalists posted to Rome had even less incentive to get too nosy. The Roman beat is posh, luxurious, and amusing—too much fun to risk by violating the national journalistic norm. The basis of the beat is wine, travel, the occasional papal succession story, and endless sex scandals and Mafia stories taken from the Italian press. Smart Roman correspondents wanting to remain in Italy poke around at the peril of their lifestyles.

When Meredith Kercher was murdered, there was little incentive for middle-class, middle-aged professional journalists enjoying Italy's many lifestyle charms to shine too much light into the dark corners. Those who might have knew they could find themselves like Saviano, hiding behind armed men, exiled back to their cold countries of origin, or getting plastic surgery and new names. Thus, investigative journalism as practiced in countries like the United Kingdom and the United

States simply does not exist in Italy. That function is left to the judiciary, which is better able—after decades of assassinations, failed trials, and slow alterations in the Constitution that ironically make the judiciary less, not more, transparent—to securely investigate Mafia infiltration of government and businesses.

In the Kercher case, a powerful deterrent example was already in place. Mignini had recently plucked Mario Spezi, a Florentine newspaper crime reporter, out of his house and thrown him into solitary confinement for weeks after Spezi's investigation into the Monster of Florence case seemed to be deviating from the prosecutorial line. Mignini had also threatened an American novelist, Douglas Preston, in the same case, causing him to flee Italy, never to return. In the months after Meredith Kercher's murder, Perugia police hauled in a local reporter, *Il Giornale dell'Umbria*'s Francesca Bene, after she found witnesses with stories that cast doubt on the official theory in the Kercher case. Mignini also ordered a house search on a female Rome-based reporter for Mediaset, who had raised questions about the Kercher case early on. She never covered the case again.

In the Kercher case, the judiciary—lawyers and magistrates—leaked to favored journalists. Everything from audiotapes of surveilled conversations to videotapes of forensic workers at the crime scene, including garish close-ups of CSI workers swabbing orifices, was public before the trial even began. Crucial, potentially exculpatory other information—audio or video of interrogations, for example—never emerged. Added to the selective information download, many journalists approached the case with a casual attitude toward facts. If a lawyer said something, it was broadcast or printed, subject to debate but rarely if ever official correction. Nonexistent "evidence"—such as the girls' "mixed blood" DNA in the bathroom they shared, Raffaele's googling of bleach and blood in the hours after Meredith's murder, or a parking lot video of Amanda Knox arriving at the house around the murder hour—remained on the public record forever.

After the conviction, Amanda's stepfather, Chris Mellas, discussed this phenomenon in an interview with me. "I feel that there are a number of things the media didn't report appropriately. It feels like they didn't because perhaps it would have been akin to pointing out errors in the prosecution against Jeffrey Dahmer or Manson. They [the media] largely viewed us as supporting a murderer. There weren't too many in the media, at that point, who would believe us over the police or prosecution, which is not an uncommon position for the accused. What really hurt us in the media was the fact that not too many [journalists] would sit in court and report on that, but they would gather outside when court was over, and ask the prosecution and civil parties how it went. These people would flat-out lie to the press, get some good sound bytes out, and those were the big stories that made it to press."

In 2007, only two American correspondents were in Italy to regularly report the case. The Rome-based Barbie Nadeau, a longtime *Newsweek* contributor, got an additional contract from Tina Brown's website The Daily Beast to cover the case on an almost weekly basis, and the Bologna-based freelancer Andrea Vogt covered the case for the *Seattle Post-Intelligencer,* which had its own financial troubles and shrank from a daily newspaper to a Web-only journal during the trial. Both Americans hailed originally, like Amanda, from the American West, but both had lived in Italy long enough to be fluent in Italian and to have become more European than American in both style and craft. Nadeau, married to a UN official in Rome, had replaced all traces of her rural South Dakota accent with a cosmopolitan speech affect. Vogt, a statuesque redhead who could have played Brenda Starr, was married to an Italian professor in Bologna. They tried not to miss a single appearance by the girl or her family in Italy. They were appalled, if not embarrassed, at the way Amanda and the Knox family flouted Italian mores in speech, behavior, and dress. Both decided early on that Amanda seemed a crafty actress; "Watch her closely," one of them advised early on, "her every expression is calculated for effect." Eventually both would be in the *col-pevolista* camp, and one would write a book with the subtitle *The True Story of Student Killer Amanda Knox.*

The American reporters in Italy felt frozen out when Curt Knox hired a Seattle PR executive who limited access to the family to the American television networks in exchange—the Italian-based reporters believed—for favorable coverage of Amanda. Stonewalled by the Knox family, with editors demanding more and more access, the frustrated Americans perpetuated the notion that the Knox family had an expensive "PR machine" rather than the bungling, provincial effort it actually was by international crisis management standards.

Complicating matters, the story was monetized from the first weeks, and, for witnesses and journalists alike, its dollar value only increased as public obsession grew, inspiring yet more titillating comments, which provoked more headlines and attention. One Italian journalist called it "the supermarket of horrors." U.K. newspapers have far more correspondents based in Rome than do the Americans, and the British tabloid reporters were among the first on the scene in Perugia. Scores more reporters were dispatched from London to Perugia and Seattle within days of the murder and arrests. The British led the coverage for months, with headlines detailing Edda Mellas's supposedly scandalous marriage to a younger man, the Seattle police visit to Amanda's rowdy college house party, and other actually innocuous tidbits of personal information, all served up with unbridled tabloid innuendo. One of the most notorious articles insinuated that Amanda had competed with her mother for the affections of men.

American and British journalists theoretically operate in similar fashion; freedom of the press is, after all, an Anglo-Saxon invention. But a chief difference between the two styles of journalism is that British reporters pay for interviews, while in the United States paying for interviews is considered journalistic malpractice. Since the Kercher murder was so sensational and the stakes for newspaper sales were in the millions, huge sums were available for interviews. Reporters didn't even broker the biggest deals themselves; high-powered London agents did it for them.

Their biggest "get" was Patrick Lumumba, who, when he was released from jail, took a high-five-figure sum from a London tabloid to talk about Amanda. In that interview, key elements of which were picked up elsewhere and became part of the narrative of the case, he described Amanda as jealous of Meredith, said his own wife had decided that Amanda was untrustworthy based on one interaction with her, described Amanda flirting with customers, and suggested that he might have been ready to fire Amanda and put Meredith in her job.

American television producers also paid sources, not with suitcases of cold cash but with soft payoffs of meals, airplane tickets, hotel rooms, and luxurious trips to New York City for televised face time with anchors. CBS and NBC crafted hourlong "magazine" program investigations into the Kercher murder. NBC's entertainment division, which runs *Dateline NBC,* relied heavily on the English-speaking correspondents already in Italy, who were operating under local journalistic mores. In the first year, CBS produced an investigative piece casting grave doubts on the case against Amanda, using an American private eye who neither spoke Italian nor had any sources within the Italian justice system.

Even with money to spend, the American networks were as hampered as anyone else by the wall of innuendo passing as fact, the labyrinthine judicial bureaucracy lacking any official public face or any rules of transparency, the reams of legal documents in which were buried the useful factoids. And the language barrier made on-camera interviews nearly impossible.

Rather than invest money and manpower into unraveling the tangled case, the American networks channeled their assets into satisfying the short-term television need for video face time by shamelessly courting the chief "gets": Knox family members. Before the trial even began, Edda, Curt, and Deanna Knox and Chris Mellas had developed intense friendships with the three network producers assigned to the story.

By 2009, the family that had initially cowered away from the TV trucks outside their West Seattle homes when Amanda was first arrested now had network producers on speed dial. Each parent grew adept as the paid on-air talent at microphone checks and speaking in sound bites.

During breaks in the trial, when the morning shows were demanding live shots, it was not uncommon to see Edda Mellas exiting the court with a producer from two of the three networks literally holding on to each of her hands while a third tagged sullenly along behind, odd man out for the moment. After the conviction, the entire family appeared on *The Oprah Winfrey Show*. Later, Curt's wife, Cassandra, placed a framed photograph of the once-warring tribe—Chris, Curt, Edda, Cassandra, and Deanna and the girls, all together onstage in Chicago with the Queen of Media herself—on the family fireplace mantel.

Across the English Channel, the Kercher family grieved beyond the reach of the media. John Kercher, a tabloid reporter who had covered Madonna and Wham!, knew exactly how the hack pack would play it, and, besides testifying in court, he and his family rarely spoke publicly to the press in Italy or the United States. Kercher eventually wrote a short article for one of the British papers about the wrenching day when he learned his youngest daughter was dead. A year later, during the appeal, he published a furious essay in the U.K. criticizing what he felt was the celebrity accorded Amanda—who he made clear he believed had killed his daughter—at the expense of and in comparison to the fading public memory of Meredith. Like the Knoxes, none of the Kerchers (Meredith had three surviving adult siblings as well as her parents) attempted to learn Italian. The Kercher family relied on their Florentine lawyer to explain evidence and process. During and after the trial, which they attended only once to testify and again for the midnight reading of the verdict, their lawyer often praised them for maintaining what he called "the elegance of silence," in contrast to "the Knox clan," who, after an initial several months of silence—during which their daughter's fate was sealed in terms of negative public relations—almost never said no to a television appearance.

WITH AMANDA SEALED UP like Sleeping Beauty or Rapunzel while the perfect media storm raged outside prison walls, the star of the story was invisible to the press. Authorities confiscated and released her thirty-day "prison diary"; then she went silent. Almost a year passed without any sight of the pretty face. The Italian television networks endlessly looped the video of the couple kissing outside the house. Italian criminologists stepped into the void to share such notions as that only a female killer would pull a blanket over a corpse, in a sign of feminine *pietà*. The British press continued printing Myspace pictures of Foxy Knoxy at play with a machine gun in a Nazi German museum and a snapshot of her in a fluffy white prom dress doing a gangster hand symbol, surrounded by a pack of half-smashed boys sloshing red plastic cups. The American networks put up anything their producers could coax out of the Knoxes and friends in the way of old photos.

On September 19, 2008, the investigation reached a point at which the young people had to leave their cells and appear in public. On that late-summer morning, a scrum of hundreds of photographers and television sound- and cameramen scratched and elbowed one another for the optimal viewing point at the first pretrial hearing. No one knew if Amanda might have chopped off her hair in prison, contracted a skin disease, grown fat and saggy. Then the door opened to reveal the face, perfectly photogenic without makeup, clean, straight hair pulled softly back, small body encased in a virginal white peasant blouse. She was held at the elbows by two female guards whose light blue uniforms complemented her eyes and whose middle-aged frown lines only augmented her youth and apparent purity. Excited whispers of *"Bella! Bella!"* rose up simultaneously with the clicking of the cameras and flashing of bulbs.

The fact that the girl was now even prettier than she'd been when arrested gave the *cronaca nera* new energy. Soon afterward, an Italian magazine ran a national poll, asking its readers to vote for Woman of the Year. They selected Amanda Knox.

THREE MONTHS LATER, IN January 2009, Amanda Knox, thespian and self-described hippie, began her months of celebrity and reckoning in

Perugia's Tribunale, a medieval building hacked into the Assisi-facing side of Perugia's mountain. About eight hundred years prior, Saint Francis—the Western world's original hippie, a man who eschewed worldly riches and communed with animals—had been held prisoner on the very spot before founding his new order.

In the Tribunale, Giuliano Mignini, his disheveled bulk concealed under a knee-length black robe with gold tassels and epaulets, a ruffled lace collar tied around his neck with a string, finally faced his most famous defendant in public. He would have to persuade the two Perugian judges and six citizens facing him wearing red, green, and white sashes that Amanda Knox had led her boyfriend, "the young Sollecito," sometime after watching *Amélie*, around nine on the night of November 1, 2007, to break away from normal human behavior and stab Meredith Kercher to death; then, within a matter of minutes or hours, she had regained her senses enough to orchestrate the scrubbing away of almost every microscopic speck of her presence at the crime scene, leaving only Rudy Guede's bloody shoeprints, DNA, and fingerprints intact. He also had to convince them that the young students had then engineered a plot twist worthy of noir fiction, a sham crime scene, by throwing a rock through Filomena's window from the inside and trashing her clothes, to lead investigators away from them and toward a fictional burglar. And he had to do this while occasionally mentioning that a known burglar had already been convicted of the murder.

He was not alone with this complicated duty. To his left, in a black robe with silver tassels indicating her junior status, was Manuela Comodi, a short, curvaceous, chain-smoking, divorced mother who wore a massive diamond engagement ring that cast sparks around the room in time with her hand gestures. At a table directly behind them and close enough that Mignini could lean back for frequent whispered advice, was the Kercher family lawyer, Francesco Maresca. Maresca was almost more effective than Mignini and Comodi in laying out the prosecution theory of the crime, to which he added his own criminal psychology flourish. The defendants, he would say, in interviews at his baroque office in Florence with its twenty-foot ceilings, had come together as normal young people but had entered a netherworld of depravity that he called "nobodyland" once they got Meredith alone with their knives.

Also behind Mignini, but farther away, were tables for the two other civil party claimants: Patrick Lumumba and his lawyer, and the lawyer representing the owner of the via della Pergola house, the widow Tattanelli, who had lost considerable rent money since the day her property had become a murder scene on November 2, 2007.

The defendants sat at two tables to Mignini's right: Raffaele and his lawyers, Perugia's Luca Maori, and parliamentarian and superlawyer Giulia Bongiorno from Rome. On the other side of her, Amanda sat flanked by her lawyers, Luciano Ghirga and Carlo Dalla Vedova. Raffaele looked paler and more delicate than in his arrest photo, in which, after seventy-two hours of being worked over by Perugia police, he had resembled a werewolf with bulging bloodshot eyes and unshaven cheeks. He was visibly anxious throughout the trial, incessantly gnawing on his fingernails while occasionally glancing over at his former lover. Reporters took to remarking on his resemblance to Harry Potter because of his rimless glasses and boyish demeanor.

The chief judge on the case was Giancarlo Massei, the Woody Allen look-alike, whose small-town Catholic conservatism (his daughter Fiametta had what Italians consider a Fascist name, meaning "little flame") placed him as far from the Woodman as Perugia is from Manhattan. Massei and his number two, a stern female magistrate with cropped black hair and a reputation as a hanging judge, would eventually write a four-hundred-plus–page conviction memo.

Amanda—*I'm in love with smiles*—didn't alter her breezy style for the Italian courtroom. No one advised her to dress conservatively and look appropriately grave. Ghirga would later say that the trial wasn't about "appearances." She habitually showed up in jeans, sneakers, and T-shirts, hair hanging down her back, and flashed smiles at the photographers, the judge, the jurors. She wasn't one to wallow in anger or despair. She was confident she'd be set free in the end. That's what her lawyers and parents told her every day.

The courtroom was always open to the public, space allowing, except on days when autopsy photos were on display. The judge limited cameras to the first five minutes of each day. It rarely took photographers and television crews a whole five minutes to catch an Amanda smile on camera. When Amanda walked into the room, held by the elbows by two prison guards in pastel blue uniforms with white gun holsters, she made eye contact with whichever family members or friends were in the room and beamed.

On the first trial morning, besides her parents, hundreds of spectators and press tried to cram into the small room. Overflow reporters seated themselves in a cage usually reserved for mafiosi and other vicious types.

Mignini and his team had the floor for the first half of the year, from January to June 2009, with court meeting intermittently, usually once or twice a week. He started with the police, who recounted what they had found and seen and thought about it. Most of the police melted back into the scenery and didn't return to court after giving testimony, except for Napoleoni, who attended almost every court hearing in her designer plainclothes with a burly, balding bodyguard stuck to her side. Toward the end of the trial, she would sit behind the prosecutor and shoot glaring looks at the Knox family. Something about Amanda Knox had clearly gotten under her skin.

Three of the five main Perugia police on the case would leave the city before the verdict. The chubby Giacinto Profazio, the man who had "broken" Raffaele, had been the head of the flying squad, although he had arrived in Perugia only in 2007 and, after a stint in Sardinia, had moved on to a position in Rome. He testified about the shabby crime scene handling by the scientific police but came under attack himself for his heavy-handed interrogation style with Raffaele. The Sollecito family would publicly describe him as "a pig and an asshole," earning themselves the permanent enmity of the police.

The police tapped the Sollecito family's cell phones for months after Raffaele's arrest. They eventually went to all-out war against the family after garnering enough tapes of Sollecito family members cursing and venting rage at the police—"hang them by their feet in the public square" was one of the printable quotes—to enable the prosecutor to charge them with trying to influence the case using friendly politicians. That case remained open in 2011.

In May 2009, Profazio, in Rome, made the news again as one of two detectives who elicited false confessions about a rape from some Romanian immigrants who couldn't speak Italian.

TO PRESENT HIS CASE, Mignini called twenty witnesses whose memories created a picture of the night of November 1 and morning of November 2, 2007. Chief among them were an elderly woman who had heard a scream come from the direction of the house and people running from it; a homeless drug user who had slept on a bench at Piazza Grimana and who remembered seeing Raffaele and Amanda hovering in his vicinity sometime between nine and midnight on the murder night; a grocery store owner who recalled a year after the murder that a girl looking like Amanda had entered his store early on the morning of November 2 and headed for the cleaning products section; a tow truck driver who recalled seeing a car in the driveway of the murder house; and a young couple who recalled being bumped into by a black man running up the steps away from the house around 10:30 on the murder night.

At an undetermined hour late on November 1 on the third floor of one of the old brick town houses on via Melo, just above the via della Pergola house, an ailing widow heard a haunting scream. Nara Capezzali, sixty-seven at the time, was never able to be precise about the time, but she was sure of what she heard: "I woke up to go to the bathroom, and on the way I heard a scream, not a normal scream but a prolonged scream, it made my skin crawl. It left me disturbed. It was a woman's scream. Then I heard running." Two years later, she testified at the trial that she was quite certain she had heard the running feet of two people, one headed up the metal stairs beside her building and one running on the gravel walkway.

Capezzali was taking a diuretic medication that made her wake up and go to the bathroom two hours after she took it. Based on her estimate that she had gone to bed around nine, prosecutors in closing arguments estimated that she had probably heard the scream at around 11:00 P.M.

Capezzali had waited twenty days after the murder was reported in the newspapers to tell the police about the scream. After the conviction, she was revealed to be hard of hearing and suffering from a mental illness serious enough for her to be hospitalized in a psychiatric ward.

At around 10:30 P.M., a woman named Alessandra Formica and her boyfriend walked down the unlit stone stairs that led past the Piazza Grimana basketball court when they were nearly knocked over by a black man running up the stairs, in a big hurry.

Also around 10:30, Giampaolo Lambrotti, a tow truck driver, received a call to move a disabled car in the parking lot across from 7 via della Pergola. It took him fifteen to twenty minutes to arrive at the location, and when he arrived, he noticed a small car parked in front of the driveway gate at 7 via della Pergola. The gate was slightly open. He could not identify the type or color of car for sure, only that it was there and it was a dark color.

Antonio Curatolo regularly slept on a bench next to the basketball court at Piazza Grimana, which overlooks via della Pergola. Curatolo was an anarchist who in the 1970s had left the grid of Italian society to live on the streets. The gritty Piazza Grimana was his outdoor home. On the evening of November 1, 2007, he was perched on his habitual bench, notable for his long gray beard and long hair, squinting at a leftist news magazine by the light of a streetlamp, smoking cigarettes to pass the time. He did not wear a watch. All those years outdoors, without medical care or a roof over his head, had left him with a bad leg. He could barely walk. But he could see.

The piazza on that night was busy with young people, Curatolo recalled, but he had noticed one couple talking animatedly. They kept scurrying from one end of the basketball court to the other, peering over the side. He couldn't tell if they were arguing, but they seemed agitated. When he saw the pictures of Amanda and Raffaele in the newspaper, he thought he recognized them. But as an anarchist, he felt no compulsion to report it to the police.

Eventually a local newspaper reporter, Francesca Bene, thought to ask him what he remembered of that night. Fra Bene, as she's nicknamed in Perugia, is utterly disarming, the best weapon a reporter can possess. A wispy, chain-smoking, somewhat sickly woman, she's covered the mean streets of Perugia for years. She gave Mignini his first real eyewitness, six weeks after the murder.

Curatolo was pretty sure that Amanda and Raffaele had been in the square from about 9:30 P.M., but he wavered on how long they had been there. He himself was there until maybe 11:30, sitting outside. But he never heard the bloodcurdling scream that woke Mrs. Capezalli, who was indoors with closed windows in an apartment almost the same distance from the murder house. He also remembered that a bus was parked by the piazza, waiting to take partying students down to the discos. One problem with his memory: the party bus was there on Halloween night, not the relatively quieter night of November 1.

Perugia's intrepid local reporters served up another star prosecution witness in the form of a grocery store owner, Marco Quintavalle. Police had questioned Quintavalle, who owned a tiny Conad market on Corso Garibaldi, about halfway between Raffaele's apartment and the murder house, four times in the month after the murder. The police also brought photographs of Raffaelle and Amanda.

Quintavalle recognized the two but initially told police he had seen nothing out of the ordinary on the morning of the murder. He said that

Raffaele was a regular customer, and he even remembered seeing him with his new girlfriend. He remembered the girl, he said, because he thought it was nice that his regular customer, a sad-looking loner, finally had a girlfriend.

One year and three days after the murder, Quintavalle told a reporter for *Corriere dell'Umbria* that as he had raised the metal shutters on his store at 7:45 A.M. November 2, 2007, he had seen a very pale—*bianchissima*—girl with, he said, striking blue eyes, waiting outside. By the time he told this story, Amanda's face was not just locally but internationally famous. Quintavalle didn't remember what the girl bought, but, when pressed, he said he thought she had headed straight for the back aisle, where he stocked the cleaning products. Reporters persuaded him to tell that to the police, and he went down to the questura and made a statement. He then testified for the prosecution that the girl who had been in his shop that morning was the defendant, Amanda Knox—the same Amanda Knox who was claiming she had been sleeping in her boyfriend's bed on that morning at that hour.

Quintavalle hid from the press after his testimony, until finally a British reporter cornered him. Quintavalle then explained his tardy identification of the *bianchissima* girl he had seen at his shop on the morning after the murder: police hadn't shown him a picture of Amanda as she had been dressed that morning, wearing a blue cap. The pictures of Amanda wearing the blue cap had been in the local papers for months, but Quintavalle insisted he never looked at the local newspapers.

Perugia authorities eventually threatened Fra Bene with arrest for digging up other possible witnesses for the Kercher case, witnesses who didn't support the official theory. The police called her to the questura, harangued her for hours, then let her go, after she found and reported on witnesses who had seen a bloody man wandering around the *centro* the morning after the murder—a bloody man who was neither Rudy nor Raffaele but a local drug addict who'd been, police would later say, in a fight with his own girlfriend. Fra Bene was a bit shaken up but shrugged off the harassment as part of her job. Two years later, she was deep into studying the tarot, in addition to reporting on the Kercher murder trial.

Antonio Curatolo testified in court in spring 2009, swaddled in a hat, scarf, and coat, which he never removed even though the room was well heated. He was wheeled to the witness stand on a rolling office chair. He put the students on the piazza above the house from nine to almost midnight, effectively giving them an alibi, and said he clearly remembered there being a bus nearby waiting to take students down to the discos. The trouble was that on November 1, there were no buses and the discos were shuttered. Mignini later moved the time of death back to after eleven to better fit with Curatolo's memory.

After his testimony, the aging anarchist evaporated like smoke into the state hospital system. He was not seen in the piazza again, nor did he speak to the press. Even Francesca "Fra" Bene lost track of him. In their report explaining the conviction, the judge and jury made a point of noting that Curatolo's unconventional "way of living" in no way interfered with his ability to perceive reality.

A year after Amanda Knox was convicted, Curatolo reappeared in the Italian news when police arrested him and sent him to jail for selling heroin. It was then revealed that he had been under investigation for drug dealing since 2004. Reporters began describing him as a "serial witness" in not just the Kercher murder case but in at least two prior Peruguia murder cases, between 2004 and 2007. In one, the murder of a Perugia woman and landlord, Curatolo was called to testify he had bought the victim's jewelry from the accused. In another, he came forward to testify he had seen the victim—a Moroccan woman—and the accused together the night before she was murdered.

Besides the widow Capezzali, the grocery store owner, and Curatolo, Mignini brought in Hekuran Kokomani, an Albanian immigrant and convicted coke dealer who testified that Amanda, with Raffaele and Rudy, had jumped out at him from inside a trash bag on the road beside her house on Halloween—the night before the murder—and that

she had been wielding a knife. He said he had fended her off by fling-
ing handfuls of the olives he had been picking. Kokomani's testimony
went over like a Comedy Channel sketch, with reporters snickering for
days afterward. He had come forward as a witness just months before
the trial began, after a relative, Dishrim Kokomani, was charged, along
with some Italian bureaucrats, in an immigration fraud scheme. In a
small-town symbiosis, Rudy's lawyer Biscotti was also Dishrim Kokomani's lawyer.

The "British girls" arrived at the Tribunale together on February
13, 2009, tweedy, peaches-and-cream–complected sylphs who moved
as a pack. Their testimony was so similar that observers thought they
seemed robotic or coached. They repeated exactly what they had shared
with police in Bergamo back in 2008, when they'd described Meredith's
annoyance with Amanda's strange male visitors, guitar playing, and hygiene, and Amanda's callous behavior at the police station.

After the British girls testified at the murder trial, the day before
Valentine's Day 2009, Amanda Knox reportedly turned to her lawyers
and said, "Wow, it didn't take long for them to hate me."

She then rose and made her first spontaneous statement to the court,
as defendants in Italian courts are allowed to do. She didn't get up and
proclaim her innocence, though. She announced to the judge and jurors
and to the world press gathered behind her that the bunny vibrator had
just been a joke gift from a friend and nothing she ever really used.

The next day she showed up in court wearing a sleep T-shirt that her
stepmother, Cassandra, had sent her from Seattle, printed in red with
the Beatles title "All You Need Is Love." It was, after all, Valentine's Day.
The photographers went wild.

The day before, she had posted a letter to Raffaele, which the jailers
shared with the British Daily Mail. It indicated that the ex-lovers were
still trying to communicate across the chasm of the defense tables and
their guards. "It was good to see you again today," Amanda wrote. "We
got to exchange a few more glances than usual, though I have to admit,
I'm not good at reading the subtle messages that one passes through the

features of the face, nor can I read lips. I know what kind of girl am I?!? Those things are supposed to be my <u>first</u> language." According to the *Mail,* she added, "So, long story short, I must admit that I didn't pick up exactly word for word what you may have wanted to transmit my way." In another letter jailers shared with the *Daily Mail,* she closed by writing, "You know what would be wonderful? Do you think they would let us hug each other when the judge absolves us? I'm tired of not being allowed to look at you."

AFTER THE BRITISH GIRLS, it was Giacomo Silenzi's turn to be quizzed about his love affair with Meredith. Having been hounded by the press and terrified by the police over the previous year, the rocker–country boy had shaved off his long hair and shut down his Facebook page.

Speaking of sex and drugs to a roomful of adults, the boy was rendered nearly mute. The bejeweled, fortysomething assistant prosecutor Manuela Comodi, a mother of teenage daughters, knowing full well that police had already extracted every intimate detail of his "sentimental relationship" with Meredith Kercher, stepped with euphemistic caution into this minefield, walking Giacomo through the two weeks with his *fidanzata.*

"You had only just started this relationship when the murder occurred?"

"Yes, a few weeks before, two or three weeks before."

"Did you go out together with the girls?"

"Yes, we did have an evening together with the four girls from upstairs, together. And there were evenings when I was alone with Amanda and Meredith. Sometimes we would invite everyone for dinner. . . . We also did a few dinners to try and get to know each other better. . . ."

"Between Meredith and Amanda, how did they behave?"

"Well. Normal. I heard certainly there were complaints on the part of Laura and Filomena about Amanda. About how she behaved herself, about the cleaning of the house, those things."

"But Meredith Kercher and Amanda Knox?"

"Normal, normal friendship ties. I remember them going out to-gether to their classes. They did have dinners together before."

"When did you get closer to Meredith Kercher?"

"It was mid-October, in a discotheque outside Perugia called Red-Zone. Marco, Stefano, and Amanda with her friends."

"And that night at RedZone . . . did you exchange a kiss [in Italian dialect a euphemism for sex, *hai scambiato un bacio*]? I don't want to go into the details . . ."

"Yes, *abbiamo scambiato un bacio.*"

"You sealed the beginning of your story together with a kiss."

"Yes, with a kiss."

"After that?"

"I saw her upstairs, or she came downstairs. We talked of little things, how her exams and classes were, we didn't get to know each other that well."

"Where did you entertain each other?"

"In either the living room or bedroom."

IT FELL TO COMODI to present the scientific evidence, which came down, first, to the large knife from Raffaele's kitchen drawer.

There were two problems with the knife.

First, it didn't match the outline of a knife, in blood, on the sheet in Meredith's bedroom. That knife was smaller. Police dispensed with that problem by theorizing that there must have been two knives involved, a small one that had made a smaller nick on one side of Meredith's neck and the large one that had delivered the death cut.

Second, the amount of biological material on the knife was so tiny that even the supersensitive computer-generated tests were not deter-minative. Only after defense lawyers demanded to see raw data did the scientific police concede that the traces of DNA material they had identified as belonging to Meredith were what's known as "low copy number," meaning that the sample was actually too small to be objectively determinative of anything. Forensic scientists who deal with such samples must work in off-site or remote labs, fitted with positive air pressure and specialized lighting, to minimize the possibility of DNA contamination, according to the Forensic Science Service in the U.K. Stefanoni conducted the tests in her usual lab, which was not specially outfitted for such testing, with machines that had been testing dozens of other samples of Meredith's blood. The amount of material she eventually admitted she was dealing with on the knife was so tiny that one scientist who has written about the case, Mark Waterbury, estimated it was equivalent to $1/10,000$ of the weight of a grain of sand, whereas the amount of DNA in a conventional profiling test is about $1/350$ of a small grain of sand. In addition to the Italian lab not being equipped to guarantee a contamination-free test, all scientists working with LCN DNA must make subjective judgments about which genetic indicators are significant and which are not. Courts in the United Kingdom and the United States do not allow low-copy-number DNA as evidence.

Comodi called the crime lab chief to the stand to explain the DNA evidence. Patrizia Stefanoni was young and serious and had a nervous tic of coiling her fingers through the ends of her abundant long black hair. She described how she had tested for and found specks of DNA on the blade and handle of Raffaele's large kitchen knife, which she had determined to be Meredith's and Amanda's. She did not mention that she'd deemed the sample "low copy number" until defense lawyers forced her to six months later.

She also testified that her crime lab had identified a piece of Raffaele's DNA on Meredith's bra clasp. She was unable to explain why she and her fellow CSI investigators had left the bra clasp on the floor of the murder room for six weeks after the initial sweep for evidence. Besides the knife and bra clasp, the material evidence against the students amounted to two small bare footprints police believed to be Amanda's in the hallway revealed by luminol, which reacts to blood but also to bleach, a common denominator in all Italian bathroom cleaning products. Stefanoni did not initially testify that she also tested the bare footprints with a substance—tetramethylbenzidine (TMB)—that definitively identifies the presence of blood, and that these tests came up negative. The fact of that test was only revealed much later, in September 2009, defense expert witness testimony that no reporter or defense lawyer bothered to highlight until long after the conviction, in 2011.

Tests also revealed five spots of Meredith's blood in the bathroom—on the sink, the bidet, a Q-tips box, and a drain—that prosecutors contended were mixed with not just Amanda's DNA, to be expected in the bathroom they shared, but also with Amanda's blood. One of the most hotly debated "facts" in the case came to be over whether these so-called mixed blood spots were really mixed blood or Meredith's blood and Amanda's biological material, the latter innocently present because she lived there and used the bathroom. Various American forensic experts spoke out to say that there was no known scientific method by which the Italian lab could say the spots contained Amanda's blood, not just her DNA. The Perugia judge and jury, when convicting her, ignored the issue.

The police also sprayed the entire bathroom with another substance, phenolphthalein, which turns pink within a minute if it detects blood. If it does not turn pink within a minute, it is not detecting blood, and at 7 via della Pergola, it did not react all over the bathroom. But phenolphthalein eventually turns pink over time whether there is blood present or not. The police left the phenolphthalein on the bathroom walls for six weeks, until every inch of walls and sink had turned (innocuously) red, then released photographs of what appeared to be a blood-smeared bathroom to the media without explanation, giving the impression that Amanda Knox had blithely, if not psychotically, told police she had showered in a bloody room on the morning of November 2. One of the British tabloids published it anyway, without explanation.

.   .   .

TO ESTABLISH THE TIMING of the murder and the cover-up, prosecutors presented phone and computer records that contradicted Amanda's sequence of the morning-after events, in which she claimed she had slept in Raffaele's arms through the night, until 10:00 A.M. Both students had turned off their phones at around the same time, between 8:30 and 9:00 P.M. on November 1, and both phones began receiving signals again at 6:30 the next morning. Raffaele's computer indicated a final human interaction when the movie *Amélie* ended at 9:10, and then turned on again at 5:35 A.M.

But even this evidence was plagued by poor police work. In the days after the murder and arrests, police collected four laptops—Sollecito's two and one each belonging to Amanda Knox and Meredith Kercher. The postal police went to work on them. They pulled out the hard drives and hooked them up to a device that makes copies of hard drives. Incredibly, they accidentally hooked up the hard drives to the wrong side of the device, the side that delivers electrical voltage, rather than the side designed to record data. Smoke may or may not have erupted, but in short order, three hard drives were fried before the police realized what they had done.

That left only one working laptop: Raffaele's. It showed that the young couple had indeed illegally downloaded *Amélie* on the night of the murder between 6 and 8 P.M. But after 9:10 P.M., there didn't seem to be any definite activity on the computer. The defense expert tried to contend that Sollecito had downloaded one of his favorite animation flicks around midnight. The prosecution denied that. Everyone did agree that there was computer activity the next morning, iTunes Store access at 5:35 A.M. At dawn on the morning after the murder, someone in Raffaele's apartment had downloaded music. It was later rumored to be Seattle's own Nirvana.

Police also claimed that Raffaele had called the carabinieri only after the postal police seeking the owner of the phones had surprised the students in the act of trying to figure out what to do about the corpse.

They based this allegation on a digital clock in the parking garage video across the street that showed the time of the Postal Police car pulling up minutes before Raffaele's call was logged with the carabinieri. The defense later contended—and the prosecution did not deny—that the parking garage video clock was late by ten minutes (and had not been adjusted for the fall time change).

ON JUNE 12 AND 13, 2009, the defense finally kicked off its presentation with the star witness everyone had been waiting for, Amanda herself. She arrived in court dressed in jeans and a white blouse, looking as virginal as ever but with a large cold sore on her lip, apparently from the stress of preparing for her big moment. With Curt behind the defense tables fiercely whispering "Focus, Amanda, focus" like the soccer dad he'd once been, Amanda repeated her sequence of events without deviating from the e-mail she'd sent to friends on November 4, a year and a half before. Speaking in strongly accented but grammatically correct Italian that she had perfected during her nineteen months in prison, she parried with Mignini so confidently that some observers thought she was impertinent. For the first time, she publicly accused police of hitting her twice in the back of the head during the night of November 5. She said she had given them Patrick Lumumba's name because they were insisting that she remember seeing something at the house and because they were fixated on her "see you later" text message to him. With Napoleoni glaring at her from the prosecution side of the room, her lawyers had never advised her that she could earn herself a slander suit for her comments about the police. By the end of the year, the Kerchers' lawyer Maresca would have a new civil case, with eight police officers claiming *diffamazione*.

After she'd sparred with Mignini for a day and a half, the civil lawyers got to question Amanda. Maresca asked her how she knew that death comes slowly to those with slit throats.

"I've seen *CSI*," she replied. "I know how people die when their throats are cut." She then proceeded to make gurgly, gagging sounds before the unnerved judge, jurors, and press corps.

"It's disgusting," she said.

To the *colpevolisti*, the sound effects were a chilling, unconscious display of guilt.

The press corps and the world at large followed Amanda's two days of testimony with a speeded-up cycle of fascination and analysis, and finally the consensus was that she had done herself no favors with her frisky defiance of the prosecutor. She hadn't shown sufficient *pietà*, the spiritual sense of pity or mercy associated with the Madonna. She had not apologized to the Kercher family, let alone Lumumba.

Why had she felt compelled to explain that she had "scootched" on a towel from the shower to her room in the morning after the murder to keep the floor dry, unless she was trying to give a plausible reason for the prosecution theory that the floor had been swiped clean? Why couldn't she remember the first panicked call to her mother in Seattle, at barely 3 A.M. Seattle time, waking her mother up before she supposedly knew Meredith's body was in a pool of blood behind a locked door? Why had she been so panicked on the phone but seemed so cool and calm toward the arriving police around the same time?

Amanda's testimony kicked off a summer break that lasted six weeks. When the trial resumed in September, the defense would try to disassemble, piece by complicated piece, the narrative of the crime that the prosecution and police and press had been refining for eighteen months. The story had been burrowing into the international psyche for almost a year and a half, and the Perugia jurors and judges had never been sequestered.

Taken separately, the individual elements of the theory were illogical and easy enough to dispute. The defense convincingly showed that the large knife was not the murder weapon based on its not matching a bloody print of the actual murder knife on the sheet on Meredith's bed. They forced the state forensic scientist to concede that the DNA on it was "low copy number," that it did not meet the minimum standard recognized by most courts. Absent scientific testing proving they were in blood, the small bare footprints showing up in luminol in the hallway could have been from a cleaning agent from the shower; absent scientific proof that Amanda's blood—rather than DNA shed from skin or other body fluids—was in the so-called mixed blood spots on the sink and bidet, the combined DNA in Meredith's blood spots in the bathroom was easily explained by the fact that the girls shared the bathroom. The bra clasp with Raffaele's DNA on it was tainted evidence because its path from the murder scene to the lab had been inexplicably delayed by six weeks, discovered and tested only after police had determined that the bloody Nike shoe prints leading out the door of the murder house were Rudy's and not Raffaele's.

Raffaele's rich and powerful family was a second bogeyman in the trial, after the "American PR machine." Dott. Sollecito was a urologist—and because of his personal connections to powerful people and mostly because of where he was from, southern Italy, the land of the Mafia, the joke during the trial was that he was "urologist to the dons."

Dott. Sollecito claimed that his wealth was overstated and that he was bankrupting himself. His apartment on the Puglia coast was certainly not lavish. He tensed up at the mention of his son's name. With Raffaele incarcerated four hundred miles to the north, he could not discuss his feelings about his son. He had to leave the room when people did so, to keep his jaw from quivering. He could, though, speak for many hours with restrained fury on the ways the police had failed to make their case.

Besides urology, he had a degree in forensic science, allowing him to critique the case against his son knowledgeably. To his great frustration, that knowledge was useless to him when he needed it most. He watched from the sidelines in utter helplessness and paid experts huge sums of money to do what he might have done himself. He personally micro-analyzed the crime scene photos and created a PowerPoint presentation about the shoe prints—clearly showing a tiny triangular flaw in the bloody shoe's tread print that he posited was a piece of glass picked up when the killer had jumped down into Filomena's room—that never made it into evidence.

Highly paid defense experts and defense lawyers explained some of that, persuasively, in court. Defense witnesses, however, in Italian court are not sworn in, and they are presumed to be lying. To make their case, defense lawyers needed not only to contest the elements of the prosecutorial evidence but to offer another narrative—a story as compelling as the interesting notion that Amanda Knox had been the central figure in the murder and that female rage or envy, rather than male sexual aggression or simple robbery, was the motive. By fall 2009, Amanda Knox simply made a more fascinating criminal than the nearly forgotten Rudy Guede.

Italian law originated in ancient Roman law; was refined over the centuries and made more inquisitorial in the Catholic, papal centuries; was altered by the Fascists in the 1930s; and then altered again in 1988 with constitutional additions to more closely resemble the accusatory U.S. system. Italian commentators took great offense at Americans' claims that their system was unfair, pointing out that, first of all, they don't have the American death penalty, and second, that the defendants had stopgaps and safety checks against prosecutorial misconduct at every step of the investigation. That is indeed theoretically true: eighteen judges reviewed Mignini's evidence against Amanda and Raffaele before the case went to trial. But it is also true that the system is more inquisitorial and the changes put into place in 1988 are not yet common practice. Preventive detention is allowed (Amanda and Raffaele were in jail for a year before being charged), there is no voir dire—the preselection of jurors by defense and prosecution—and the standard of "proof beyond a reasonable doubt" is not adhered to. On the contrary, the jury is expected to pronounce judgment even if it has doubts. "Only God has no doubts," assistant prosecutor Comodi reminded the jurors in her closing arguments.

A peculiarity of Italian law—by Anglo-Saxon standards—is that judges and prosecutors are technically on the same side, while judges are also asked to impartially weigh evidence. They come out of the same training program, and it is not uncommon to find judges and prosecutors lunching together during trials—"ex parte" meetings that are strictly forbidden in American courts. Furthermore, Mignini's job was to be both investigator and prosecutor, but, like other Italian magistrates, he had no training in criminal investigation.

Defense lawyers working in the Italian system are also at an institutional disadvantage. Some of the basic rights defendants have in the United States were removed from the Italian system in the early 1990s to strengthen and protect the judicial system from violence and corruption, after the brazen Mafia assassinations of the so-called superprosecutors Paolo Borsalino and Giovanni Falcone. Since then, defendants do not have the right to face witnesses, and although prosecutors must theoretically share evidence with the defense, in practice they do not. Police surveillance and wiretapping are endemic, requiring little oversight. Lawyers meet with journalists outside their offices, in the streets, where they are safe from wiretapping, if they have anything sensitive to discuss.

In the United States, since a 1963 Supreme Court ruling, prosecutors must turn over any potentially exculpatory evidence to the defense team. Withholding of these so-called Brady materials is grounds for dismissal of a case. No such precedent exists in Italian law. Amanda's and Raffaele's lawyers didn't receive all the evidence against their clients at once but acquired it piecemeal and sometimes only by formal request as they learned during the trial that it existed. For example, Patrizia Stefanoni had scrawled "low copy number"—in English, apparently the lingua franca of DNA technology—on the results relating to the kitchen knife Mignini was presenting as the murder weapon. She also had noted that she tested specifically for blood on the knife and the small bare footprints in the hallway with TMB and found none, but dismissed the significance of that test in Rudy's trial and simply did not mention it in her testimony at Raffaele and Amanda's trial. The prosecution turned over her notes documenting these potentially exculpatory facts only after a special request halfway through the trial.

Defense lawyers are still not sure whether other crucial pieces of potentially exculpatory evidence exist. The Perugia authorities have always insisted they never taped the interrogations of November 5–6, even though they were surreptitiously taping every conversation the two students uttered on their phones and in the questura. The defense never received all those recordings either.

Another difference between the U.S. and Italian systems is that in Italy, civil cases, with their lower standard of proof and looser rules of evidence, can be tried simultaneously—in the same room—as the criminal cases. Because Patrick Lumumba was suing Amanda for slander, the jury was allowed to consider her questura "vision" statement putting herself in the house, even though the Italian Supreme Court had disallowed the statement in the criminal case because of the dodgy way it was obtained, without an attorney and without any recording. The judge also admitted into evidence something that in the United States would certainly have been barred as highly prejudicial: an animated film of Amanda, Raffaele, and Rudy killing Meredith Kercher, narrated by Prosecutor Comodi.

Defense experts raised doubts about the validity and meaning of most of the material evidence presented by the prosecution and police. Defense lawyers demanded to see the raw data on which the scientists had based their work. The prosecution refused, and the defense asked the judge to appoint forensic experts not aligned with the police or the defense to reconsider all the evidence behind hotly disputed matters such as the DNA on the knife, the "mixed blood," and the footprints.

Comodi, in charge of explaining the tediously complicated scientific evidence, fought back. By the ninth month of the trial, September 2009, as the defense put on its case, she had lost all patience, often arguing with a cigarette in hand and stalking out the side door while the defense was still cross-examining or redirecting witnesses, her lighter already igniting the Marlboro. Sure of her position and of the fact that the case had triumphed in the public square, she finally dispensed with all pretense to fussy detail in favor of more personal tactics.

"The defense has been overly dramatic about this," she explained, arguing against the defense request to toss out the case based on the fact that the crime lab hadn't turned over all the paperwork involved in the DNA analysis. "No defense right has been threatened. We decide if documents are necessary or not. I didn't even look at their request of July 30 [for the superwitness]. I opened it and closed it right away. It was so useless. No law says the scientific police have to produce all that's requested. It's not proof, and we didn't need it to support our case. The prosecutor's office decides what is useful and what is distraction. You can tell me that Stefanoni has to get another degree, but telling us that not producing the documents warrants tossing out the case is like asking the postal police to explain how they found a hooker online. The important thing is that they found the hooker!"

She reminded the jury that the defense's scientific witnesses were not trustworthy anyway. They had testified "with their eyes fixed on a certain point in the courtroom"—the defense table—from which they were, she implied, being coached. In the end, the *results* were what mattered, not the incomprehensible details of how the scientists had obtained them.

Finally, she offered up a kitchen analogy tailored to the three female jurors and the female judge in case any of them had surrendered to the *dubbio*—doubt—that the defense team was planting by maligning the police work and questioning forensic evidence. "It's like cooking pasta," she suggested. "When you prepare the spaghetti, for example, some people weigh it first, and some people don't. In any case, the pasta gets cooked and still tastes delicious."

The judge denied the motion for an independent witness to consider the science, to no one's surprise.

According to defense lawyers who practice in Perugia, it is common practice for defense lawyers to go to trial without having access to evidence against their clients, no matter what the national Constitution says. "Prosecutors have all the power over the evidence. Theoretically, the prosecutor must give all the evidence to the defense before the trial," said one Perugia lawyer. He added, with a wry smile, "In Italy, everything is theoretical."

THERE COMES A DAY in late September, around the autumn equinox, when all Italian women simultaneously don their boots. The temperature has little to do with it; it can be quite warm outside, but everyone understands that the time has come to put away summer sandals and get down to the business of autumn.

Inside the Tribunale in September 2009, every female, from the reporters milling in the smoke-filled hallway to the backup female lawyers on the defense and prosecution teams to the jurors themselves, had slipped into high-heeled Gucci boots if they had the money and, if not, into black or brown leather or colored suede facsimiles thereof. Manuela Comodi started wearing a pair of black cowboy-style boots under her pantsuit; Napoleoni pulled some chunky-heeled, towering pale leather motorcycle boots over her skintight white jeans. During lunch breaks, the two women and a third member of their posse, a lissome brunette crime reporter from the local office of *La Nazione,* sometimes returned together from the boot stores on the corso toting massive shopping bags.

The lone fashion holdout in the room, in her summery sea-green canvas sneakers, was Amanda Knox, slouched at the defense table. She did have one new item of clothing, though, a red hoodie with "Beatles" printed on it in black. Her UW student friend Madison Paxton, who had become Amanda's staunchest supporter on American, British, and Italian television, had delivered it during a summer visit. With the weather finally cooling off, Amanda put it on and wore it to court every day until the final days of the trial. Usually Italian prison guards confiscate hoodies, as they are believed to be perfect for concealing contraband, but by the fall of 2009, Amanda's jailers were getting soft on her. In the end, when she cried in public as Mignini called her an aggressive narcissist and Lumumba's lawyer called her a she-devil, they huddled around with looks of grave concern in their eyes, shielding her face from the eager eyes of reporters, who were furiously scribbling the next day's headline: "Defendant Finally Shows Emotion."

The trial convened two days a week through most of the fall, and the defense put on witnesses rebutting the science, rebutting the psychology, rebutting the phone call and computer timing. Reporters listened and scribbled down some of the more memorable exchanges, but as the weather outside cooled and the courtroom got stuffy and hot, it became clear to everyone but members of the Knox family that the case was already decided.

Every day, the guards led Amanda in by the elbows, and the girl clad in her red hoodie, like a magic coat, smiled broadly at her lawyers and whichever family or friends were sitting behind her that day. During breaks in the action, everyone except the accused and their guards scurried upstairs and outside onto the piazza for a shot of espresso and a cigarette. At the close of each day of trial, the lawyers would emerge, with their secretaries and clients beside them, from the great, griffon-embossed Tribunale doors. Lit cigarettes in hand, they would hold court with groups of reporters huddled on the cobblestones. Television camera lights illuminated each little discussion group in the early-evening darkness of October and November, until the final good quote had drifted from the lips of the players like smoke.

During the last days of the trial, Mignini, who had been preparing his eight-hour-long closing argument throughout the summer, preferred to discuss more weighty historical matters, such as the slaughter of the Templars in the 1500s and how they—not, he pointed out, the pope—had been responsible for the Christian *reconquista* of Spain from the Muslims before the French decided they had to be excommunicated and exterminated. He loved sharing information about his hometown's history. During a break in the action after a particularly heated exchange between Comodi and one of the defense's DNA experts, Mignini wanted to chat about the Etruscans and how the Estruscan language had been more Basque than Indo-European. He recounted how, in A.D. 40, Marcus Aurelius's brother had come to Perugia and destroyed the Etruscan town, stabbing the nobles to death at the precise spot where now stands the Caffè Turreno, a watering hole beside the duomo where Amanda's lawyer Luciano Ghirga—a Mason in good standing sitting not twenty feet away—often held court. "They did pagan sacrifices right there," Mignini observed, noting that the duomo was on the site of a pagan temple.

Trial observers came to relish dramatic moments of conflict—catfights—between Raffaele's lawyer Giulia Bongiorno and Manuela Comodi. Both women had riveting styles. Comodi had a flair for the outrageous and feminine transgression: she brought an actual white bra of her own into the courtroom and wound it around the microphone stand in what she claimed was a demonstration of how Meredith Kercher's bra had been torn; later she cast the trial in terms of the Three Little Pigs, with the defense case the house of straw and the prosecution case the invulnerable structure of brick. Bongiorno—the only professional woman in the courtroom never wearing boots, always pants and a pair of running shoes—was tiny and intense, her air-chopping Neapolitan hand gestures a riveting nonverbal accompaniment to her staccato speaking style. Conventional wisdom had pegged her to be the best lawyer on the defense team. Her closing argument, in which she portrayed Amanda Knox as the flighty and eccentric but utterly benign "Amélie of Seattle," was probably Amanda's best shot at winning the jury.

That fall, the tough, well-educated women in the courtroom—the policewomen, the lawyers, the reporters, the judges—were contending with the ever more cartoonish, disgusting, and humiliating public image of successful womanhood just outside the courtroom, on Italy's streets, on television, and in the government of Silvio Berlusconi in Rome.

The nation's minister of equality was a former *velina*—one of the legion of mute TV showgirls who had been a hallmark on Italian state television since the 1980s. Even the prime minister's wife, a former actress herself, was fed up and had filed for divorce earlier in 2009, after accusing her husband of having an affair with a teenager. Before that he had earned his wife's public wrath by selecting thirty-odd of his favorite showgirls to be groomed as candidates for the European Parliament representing Italy. Few of them had any political experience; the one with the most media savvy had been a weather girl. His seething wife, Veronica Lario, publicly called the women "trash without shame . . . who offer themselves like virgins to the dragon in order to chase after success, fame, and money."

In late November 2009, as the lawyers in the Kercher murder trial delivered closing arguments, a prostitute published a book called *Gradisca, Presidente* (*Take Your Pleasure, Mr. President*). The call girl Patrizia D'Addario wrote that she had been hired to service Berlusconi by a Puglian businessman seeking health care contracts with the government. The scenes she described were straight out of the ancient Roman Saturnalia, without the sadism. In one memorable scene, she was hired to participate as one of twenty almost identically dressed young women who serviced the prime minister simultaneously at one of the bacchanalian events he hosted in his Roman palazzo, within yards of the Forum and Colosseum. "He wants to be adored by all the women who are here, he likes being touched, caressed, by many hands at once," she wrote in her memoir. "I was watching the whole thing with curiosity and my first thought was that I'd found myself in a harem. . . . He was on the couch and all of us, twenty girls in all, were at his disposal. The younger women were in fierce competition with each other as to who could sit closest to the Prime Minister. . . . Having been an escort I thought I'd seen a lot, but this I'd never seen, twenty women for one man. Normally in an orgy you have roughly the same number of men and women, otherwise people get upset. But here the other men had no say. There was just one man with the right to copulate and that was the Prime Minister."

One of Berlusconi's former supporters had started calling the state of affairs under his former boss a "whore-ocracy." And indeed, a whore-ocracy may have ruled the rest of Italy, but its source was distant from the pure mountain air of Perugia, with its starched, tradition-bound residents. In a public room dominated by frescoes of the Virgin Mary nursing her child, the booted-up professional women of the Knox case had in their sights the disgusting spectacle of a sexually liberated, cartwheel-flipping, grief-resistant, pale-eyed American Barbie doll, now perhaps the most famous non-Italian *velina* in Italy. In the press, Amanda had come to represent the most vile, unforgiveable aspects of a certain popular version of womanhood: beautiful, sexual, manipulative, narcissistic to the point of fame-loving, and jealous to the point of murder. They knew that Amanda had never cried as a human, innocent woman would have, had never apologized, never evinced *pietà*. On the contrary, she had smiled for the cameras almost every single day.

Her female prison mates at Capanne had nicknamed her "Bambi" for her bizarrely pacifistic behavior under attack. "Because she's like a helpless animal," Edda explained about the nickname before gushing tears. Led every morning into the courtroom by stern women in uniform, judged and found wanting by the females in law enforcement, the press, and a jury of men and women who were hardly her peers, in fall 2009, "Bambi" Knox was like Iphigenia in Perugia, deerlike, sacrificial, an irresistible, maybe necessary scapegoat.

THE TIME FOR CLOSING arguments arrived. Mignini went first. He stood on his feet for eight hours, resting for only the smallest of breaks, and, in a blizzard of verbiage peppered with archaic Latinisms, delivered the state's case against the two students. He had altered the theory of the crime slightly to fit a new timeline more in line with Antonio Curatolo's bench-view memories. Amanda and Raffaele, he said, had been anxiously waiting in Piazza Grimana until 11 P.M., looking over the wall periodically because they were waiting for Rudy, with whom Amanda had made a date, maybe to share drugs, maybe just to party. Mignini called the three young killers *cannabinomani*—users of cannabis—adding that, according to one of Amanda's statements, Raffaele was also a former cocaine and acid user. Citing two websites about cocaine, he suggested that Raffaele was suffering from lasting depression due to prior cocaine use.

He started out by courteously praising the defense lawyers for their work but then criticized their "circus of experts" and accused the Americans of staging a "parallel trial" in the media. He thanked the Kercher family for staying above the fray.

He said that Amanda must have known Rudy Guede, since Rudy's professed lust for her would have made her aware of him. "It's hard to believe Amanda Knox would not know Rudy Guede by more than sight," Mignini argued. "He played basketball in Piazza Grimana, he had been at the apartment downstairs, and he told people he liked her."

By the second hour of his statement, it was clear that he still considered Amanda Knox and a sexual game the primary motives behind the killing. "The three of them, under the influence of drugs and the fumes of alcohol, decided to act on the project they had, to involve Meredith in a *pesante gioco sessuale*"—a heavy sexual game. "They were looking for strong emotions, and Amanda Knox now had an occasion to take revenge on this too-serious English girl, whose ties with her British friends were too close; they had this little group, and this English girl had been accusing her of not cleaning up in the house and of bringing home too many boys. Now for Amanda the moment for revenge against *quella smorfiosa* [this spoiled brat] had finally come. And now Mez begins her *calvario* [Calvary], her death ordeal."

As noted earlier, Mignini moved the hour of death from Medical Examiner Lalli's 10:00 P.M. estimate to about 11:30 P.M., the better to match Curatolo's memory. The problem with that new timing was that Meredith's cut-off call to her mom occurred at 8:56 P.M. and the mysterious call to her bank was logged at 10 P.M., which would seem to indicate that her killers were already in charge of her phone long before 11:30.

In Mignini's final scenario, Amanda had brought Rudy and Raffaele into the house, and Meredith didn't want the boys there. Amanda had had the kitchen knife, she had held it to her roommate's neck, and she had driven in the killing blow while Sollecito held one of Meredith's arms and Guede penetrated the poor victim with his hand from behind. "Amanda was the most violent one. After knifing Meredith, she grabbed her by the neck."

At that point in his delivery, Amanda was visibly agitated, squirming in her chair, shaking her head, holding her lawyer's hand. Chris Mellas, the only family member in the room, without an interpreter nearby, was utterly oblivious to what was being said in Italian; he sat behind her, furiously BlackBerrying with someone. By the first break, she was crying into her lawyer's arms.

"An expert has spoken of the blanket," Mignini continued. "Putting it on the body is a gesture of respect and pity for the victim. A person who came into the house for thievery would never have done this. It would have been someone who knew her, and that person would be Knox. Putting up the scene is proof that they are murderers."

Finally he went to the mat for the honor of the police and especially the interpreters.

"After her 'fantasy' of Lumumba, she slanders the police? I am disgusted by the accusations against Mrs. Donnino and Mrs. Colantone. Mrs. Donnino has incredible humanity and would never have done anything against Amanda. I am scandalized! She broke down and cried when I questioned her because her back was against the wall. She tells us this story in between fantasy and reality, of trying to imagine Lumumba in the house. She imagined Lumumba instead of Rudy Guede because they have something in common: both are black. Why didn't she tell us the message was generic? Why didn't she just say we had no meeting? Her answer is 'I was confused.' So the only way to justify slander is to blame police pressure."

A day later, Comodi rose and narrated the little animated movie about the murder, in a sweet Minnie Mouse voice. The defense objected, but the judge overruled. Dark went the room, and the film started, opening with a Google Earth map of Perugia, zooming in on the little cottage at 7 via della Pergola. Raffaele's avatar wore glasses, Rudy's was black, Amanda's was curvaceous. All together they cornered Meredith, but Amanda alone clawed at the poor English girl's face and stabbed the kitchen knife into her neck. Then the two white students scampered off with Meredith's cell phones while Rudy, in a gesture of pity, stayed behind to get towels and try to stanch the bleeding. Later the students came back to mop up the blood.

After the movie aired in court, the newspaper *La Stampa* published a headline encapsulating the prosecution's concluding theory: "Amanda Knox Hated Meredith." "As in a Tarantino film, a twenty-year-old girl manipulated two adult men."

Raffaele's lawyers presented pictures of the murder house after the scientific police—the CSI team—had done their work. Meredith's belongings were heaped on the floor and on her desk in piles—shoes and clothes, papers, trash, all helter-skelter. The photos left the impression that the police had been so sloppy that the fact that their single piece of evidence against Raffaele had been extracted six weeks after the photos were taken made it dubious. Assistant Prosecutor Manuela Comodi rose and interjected that the mess in Meredith's bedroom was nothing more than "proof of good police work."

In the waning hours of the final day of their arguments, for the first time in the trial, defense lawyers asked the prosecution to present a picture of the glass on top of Filomena's clothes, a key element in the state's claim that what looked like a robbery attempt was really a staged scene the two students had created during a night spent covering up their bloody deed. The prosecution and police had always contended that Filomena had securely locked her shutters before leaving on November 1 and that her room was closed up tight as a drum, impossible for anyone to break into from the outside. Interrogation records indicate that that was not true.

"How did you leave the windows of your room?" Mignini asked her on December 3, 2007.

"I think I left the inside shutters open. The window was closed, and the external shutters—I think I had pulled them in."

"So you locked the shutters?"

"No, locked, no, because they had a problem. Of the two shutters, I would use the left one, the right one wouldn't pull completely, so I pulled them both as hard as I could and let it be."

"Could they have reopened?"

"I don't know."

By the end of the trial, Mignini was insisting that the last best piece of proof of the students' guilt was the fake break-in and robbery. He and the police said that the defendants had made one little mistake in their carefully staged scene: they had tossed around Filomena's clothing first, and then thrown a rock at the window from inside, spraying glass *on top of* the clothes when it should have been under them. Police had described this in trial testimony but never shown it. It was determined that the Kerchers' civil lawyer, Francesco Maresca, was the only lawyer in the room who knew how to find the picture in his copy of the massive, unorganized digital case archive. His laptop was beamed onto the wall screen, and his motocross screensaver came up, a bike at right angles to a spray of dirt. The dapper Florentine with the gold-embedded shark's tooth dangling beneath his bespoke shirt collar smirked and then clicked the mouse again to bring up a picture of Filomena's bed as it had looked on the morning of November 2, 2007. The defense lawyers insisted that what was supposed to be glass on top of a blue dress on the bed was actually a white dot pattern in the fabric. No one denied that or even bothered to explain what could have happened to the damning glass on top of the clothes in Filomena's room. In the last minutes of the trial, it was clear that no photographic proof of "glass on top of clothes" even existed and that it didn't matter anyway.

. . .

ON THE MORNING OF December 5, some observers were certain that justice had been done for Meredith Kercher. The Kercher family held a press conference in a hotel in Perugia on the other side of town from the luxury Hotel Brufani Palace, where the Knox "clan" was holed up, doing interview after interview about how they planned to fight on.

Meredith's parents and three siblings filed in and sat in chairs at the front of the room. They all had tight little smiles on their faces. A representative from the British Consulate translated for them. Their lawyer, Maresca, sat to one side.

Meredith's brothers spoke first, in strong north London accents. "We would like to thank our legal team, the prosecution team, the police and the legal authorities who worked very hard," said John Kercher, Jr. "I think the best way to say it is we are very satisfied with the verdict," said his younger brother, Lyle Kercher. "Ultimately we are pleased with the decision. But it's not a time for celebration. We are gathered here because our sister was brutally murdered, taken away from us. But there are young people yesterday who were sent away for a long time behind bars."

The room was packed with Italian and British reporters and a few Americans. John Hooper, a Rome-based reporter for *The Guardian*, asked the family, "Did you at any time have qualms about the fact that your legal team endorsed so thoroughly the prosecution's case? In your minds, are you convinced beyond a reasonable doubt that Knox and Sollecito were responsible?"

Lyle responded by suggesting that the family had more knowledge about the case than the press. "We are not the lawyers or judges, but we were obviously privy to information that you guys aren't," he said. Then he backtracked. "Sorry, when I say that, I couldn't describe information when the case was ongoing, about six months ago, two weeks ago, but there has been a verdict now and you have seen it."

Arline Kercher spoke for the first and only time: "I would say if the evidence has been presented then yes, you have to agree with that."

Another British reporter asked, is this verdict "justice for Meredith"?

Meredith's sister, Stephanie, a dark beauty who looked a lot like pictures of her younger sister, took that one. "As much as it can be really, yeah, we can only be as satisfied as we can be. It does bring just that little bit of justice for us and for her, and that's all we can say, really."

16

CAPANNE

"Some ask me to have faith in God. Others bash the Italian justice
system. The majority comment on how beautiful I am. . . . If I
were ugly, would they be writing me, wishing me encouragement?
I don't think so. . . . And geez, I'm not even that good-looking!
People are acting like I'm the prettiest thing since Helen of Troy.
Which makes me think of D.J."

—*Amanda Knox,* about the fan letters she was receiving in jail, *Il Mio
Diario Prigione,* November 2007

"How can I grow from this? I don't think I'm ever wandering round
alone after dark because of this. I also hope I'm not scared to be alone
I don't want to be traumatized because of this. I want to live happily,
like I was, if understandably a little more cautious I guess I've
grown up a bit and I'm not even sure what that means. . . . I might
even become a more spiritual person, because someone helped me

---

Madonna delle Grazie, in Perugia's Duomo San Lorenzo, by Giannicola di Paolo, a follower
of Perugino.

remember, it was all gone and now it is here, safe and sound, secure
in my clearing mind. I am safe because at least I know."

—*Amanda Knox,* in her *Il Mio Diario Prigione,* November 2007

"After this experience, believe me, I will never never
touch the pipe again in my life."

—*Raffaele Sollecito,* writing to his father from jail, November 7, 2007

INMATES AT CAPANNE PRISON ON the flats below Perugia cannot see over
the thirty vertical feet of beige concrete that surrounds the compound.
The wall hides the majestic Umbrian scenery, and the incarcerated cannot watch the mist every morning slowly evaporating and revealing
the tips of Perugia's rust and ocher bell towers first, until finally the
whole medieval city on the hill appears five miles away. The inmates'
view is limited but not entirely devoid of amusement. Several acres of
healthy grass surround the barred windows, an inviting green expanse,
extending all the way to the high walls. This meadow is inhabited not
by humans—who are confined to fenced exercise yards—but by hundreds of rabbits. No one seems to know how they got into the prison
yard. Perhaps their forebears were already living on the field when
it was enclosed and excavated in the 1980s, when the Italian government built a modern incarceration compound to replace the Perugia
dungeons.

The Capanne bunnies, of course, are oblivious to blood, guilt, or
incarceration. They live the free-est of lives, within walls of which they
are only dimly aware. They know nothing of guilty children, man's
original sin, the implacable envy of women, and the splitting of women
into madonnas and whores, certainly not the murder of innocents. They
live and die in a rabbit dreamland, eating and procreating on acres of
sweet green grass, warm in summer, cool in winter, safe from predators

beyond the high walls. And prisoners and guards alike enjoy watching them hop, eat, and proliferate.

On the morning of November 6, 2007, Amanda moved into Capanne, destined to become its most famous resident. She was twenty, young enough, maybe, to remember that in junior high, she had a habit of drawing bunnies on all her homework papers. For the first few days, she was isolated and her only visitors were nuns in full habit, members of the same order that had ministered to incarcerated females in the Torcoletti dungeon since 1908. The sisters of Jesus Christ Redemptors are hired by the Italian government to counsel inside women's prisons. A few generations ago, members of the same order had ministered to the tormented child murderer Caterina Forte, across the wall from Magistrate Mignini's boyhood bedroom.

A sister visited Amanda on her second day in isolation. The American was lying in bed, wearing the clothes she'd had on through the night of her interrogation forty-eight hours prior, alternately sobbing and consoling herself singing, over and over, the Beatles' "Let It Be." After the night at the questura, she had lost track of what she had previously thought she was doing on the night of the murder. "I still couldn't remember exactly what I had been doing at my boyfriend's apartment. This was my great mystery," she wrote later. With the sister at the door of the cell, she suddenly regained clarity. "She told me God would provide the answer. I nodded along, but as she talked I remembered what I had done when I was with Raffaele at his apartment." She thought she was living the "Let It Be" lyrics: "In my hour of darkness, she is standing right in front of me. Speaking words of wisdom, let it be."

A few hours later, Padre Don Saulo Scarabattoli, a meek, diminutive bearded priest who ministers to both male and female inmates at Capanne, knocked on her cell bars. Don Saulo, who speaks no English, brought her an English Bible, in which, at some point, she underlined all the passages in the Gospel of Mark. He also brought her books in English about Christianity.

After two days and nights in jail, she asked for paper and began writing what she called "My Prison Diary" or, as she subtitled it, *"Il Mio Diario Prigione,"* in her never-changing, meticulously rounded script. The diary looked like an extreme class project, with exercises in Italian sprinkled in between digressions on home, love, and pep talks to herself. "I'm writing this because I want to remember," she wrote at the top of the first page. "I want to remember because this is an experience that no one else could ever have." When she had filled more than seventy pages, at the end of November, the Italian authorities entered her cell and took the prison diary, translated it into Italian, and put it into the investigative record, and into the hands of reporters, providing new raw material for the black chronicle.

In her first month in prison, she was denied all reading material except for prison-approved religious tomes from the ministry. The first English book Don Saulo gave her was called *How to Be Born Again.* She wrote in her diary that she read it out of respect for the nuns and priest, but found it "an insult to my intelligence." She launched into a four-page point-by-point argument against the ideas presented in the book's first four chapters. The author, calling himself "Billy," she found "bigoted" for criticizing Eastern religions. "I don't know how the universe is made, nor do I know where 'I' will go when I die. What is important to me is to live well, to help others, to create, to love. The priest and the nuns are not satisfied with this answer. One nun even told me that a person without religion is no better than an animal, but I disagree."

Her family was not religious. Despite her Jesuit education, she was agnostic. She had nearly flunked a religion class her junior year of high school for arguing about faith with the instructor. She was assigned to do summer school penance for it.

Agnostic Amanda soon came to rely on Padre Don Saulo for moral support. In interviews with reporters, he always had a sad expression, sometimes even breaking into tears, when he talked of her moods and how she passed her time. He would never discuss what he thought of her guilt or innocence, but he was one of the first people to meet with her in prison, before her mother arrived.

On the third page of her diary, in the first entry after she'd been given paper and pen, she wrote, "I talked with the father here just a moment ago. He is a very sweet man." He told her a parable about a bird flying in and then out of the room. "He said this was the great question of life, where did the bird come from and where did it go. This man, who doesn't know me, I told him I was happy because I was able to give what I knew, finally, to the police, and this man cried. This man told me to do what I felt was right in my heart."

On early mornings in Perugia when trial was not in session, Don Saulo could sometimes be found sipping coffee with Mignini at the bar near the *procura*, before the mist had burned off the hollows down below.

REPORTERS PLUNGED INTO THE diary, marveling at its childishly rounded, perfect script, so incongruous for a sex murderess. English translations of Italian translations of Amanda's original English bolstered the psychopath theory. A typical example was a passage Amanda wrote after she heard of her and Meredith's DNA on Raffaele's kitchen knife: The exact words in the diary are: "Raffaele and I have used this knife to cook, and it's impossible that Meredith's DNA is on the knife because she's never been to Raffaele's apartment before. So unless Raffaele decided to get up after I fell asleep, grabbed said knife, went over to my house, used it to kill Meredith, came home, cleaned the blood off, rubbed my fingerprints all over it, put it away, then tucked himself back into bed, and then pretended really well the next couple of days, well, I just highly doubt all of that."

The Italian translation of that section, which appeared in much of the Italian and British press, offered the exact opposite of her meaning, inserting the idea that she actually thought it "possible" Raffaele was the killer: "That night I smoked a lot of marijuana and I fell asleep at my boyfriend's house. I don't remember anything. But I think it's possible that Raffaele went to Meredith's house, raped her, and then killed. And when he got home, while I was sleeping, he put my fingerprints on the knife. But I don't understand why Raffaele would do that."

Reporters cherry-picked sections from the diary where she mentioned fan letters from anonymous men who thought she was pretty. They ignored ample evidence that the girl was uncomfortable with at least some male attention. In an entry dated November 17, noted as "11th day?" Amanda wrote that a "'vice-capo' guy" was "getting kind of weird." He was, she wrote, "very interested in my sex life. And he's constantly telling me I'm pretty. I don't trust people who are constantly commenting on my looks." She listed six incidents with the "vise capo," describing an incrementally more threatening situation for any woman in prison. The unnamed capo winked at her when delivering letters from unknown male admirers who saw her on TV, told her not to cry because it made her "ugly," repeatedly commented on her body, and "blatantly gives me a stare up and down when he sees me."

Eventually, he asked her if she dreamed about sex, and then asked her if she was "good at sex." Ever the agreeable girl, Amanda wrote: "At first I chalked it up to cultural difference, but I talked to my roommate [actually, cellmate] later about it and she said that was an incredibly rude thing to do." Later, when he approached her again, asking if she dreamed about sex, she wrote: "I don't tell him he's rude, though I'm dying to. My mind says, 'Because you're a dirty old perv,' but my mouth says 'I'm not ashamed of my sexuality, and it's my own private business.'"

Italian police and prosecution translators summarized her description of the conflict with the vice-capo as *"battibecchi"*—squabbles—implying triviality. Following complaints from the family, an offending guard was transferred.

The last pictures of Amanda Knox for a long time were snapped as she was being driven away after her midnight conviction and sentencing. Photographers captured her tear-stained face, appropriately behind the bars of the penitentiary van.

As months passed, word drifted out from behind prison walls that she had cut her hair, that she was despondent and had lost her spirit. Italian Parliamentarian Rocco Girlanda went in and offered comfort, and published a book of his dialogues with her. Finally in the fall of 2010, the authorities delivered her before the public eye again, to face charges of defaming the police. The change from her first "perp walk" of September 2008 was stark. Her hair was brutally and unskillfully shorn, dull and greasy, her eyes were terrified, her face was pale, her skin somehow saggy, and she seemed not just smaller but literally cowering from the cameras that had once recorded her smiles.

In the intervening months, she had physically diminished but her fame had not. She had been discussed in Italian Parliament; Wikileaks indicated her name had come up between Obama's ambassador to Italy and Berlusconi. An American television movie was being made about her, with a rising starlet in her role. The judge that convicted and sentenced her had called her "a manipulative, promiscuous woman who clashed with Kercher." Now she was a neutralized witch, without capacity to either mesmerize men or to invite jealousy from women.

In prison, Amanda continued to write so much that Chris Mellas hurt his back carrying boxes of journals and books out to be mailed back to Seattle in 2010. She even won an award from a prison literary magazine for a short epistolary story that seemed to be a confession to witnessing the Kercher murder. The narrator seems to be describing a passed-out, undressed friend or lover at a smoke-filled party.

You remember that night, suddenly hot in November? How beautiful you were! . . . If I had another chance I would have helped you and would have been much closer to you. . . . I turned and you were gone. Swam in the waves of warm bodies and wet with sweat and drink. . . . I was opening a window to get some air when I saw from the door smoke coming out. . . . then I saw you lying on the ground, without a jacket and without shirt. At that moment I did not understand anything and while I was out of the house I remembered that with you there were other peo-

ple who smoked, that were piercing. I didn't understand, you must be-
lieve me.

She wrote that story in Italian sometime prior to her conviction, and Don Saulo entered it into a Catholic Charities prison writing competition, which eventually published it under the name Marie Pace. Someone leaked it to the Italian press a day after her conviction for murder. The story looked like another confused confession. Who else was the topless, passed-out body supposed to belong to? What people were doing the "piercing"? And was that "suddenly hot" November night not certainly the murder night? And: "My madness doesn't know surrender"?

Italian reporters who were disposed to view the prosecution case with some skepticism rolled their eyes when they saw this literary exercise in the local newspaper. It appeared that the American girl simply couldn't control the urge to confess, no matter how dubious the material evidence against her.

In a February 2010 letter to me, Amanda denied that the one-page story was "a confession," adding, "Granted, I reread it afterward and I felt . . . kinda stupid really for having never thought that it could have been taken the wrong way." She said the inspiration for it came from several events, including a Valentine's Day letter from Raffaele musing on "what could have been" and her own memories of a party in which she had helped a sick, drunk friend. "I mixed that feeling of 'what if' with my experience taking care of drunk friends at parties, and specifically one friend I once had to take care of while she sobbed and threw up into a fish bowl. I had found her sprawled and passed out, covered in sweat and tears. It was a party experience that has always remained really negative in my mind because I remember feeling both really worried about the sick, delirious state my friend was in, but also having felt sick of it myself. I remember feeling like all I wanted to do was to pick her up on my back and tromp on out, but there was no way I could."

Amanda, and her family and friends, often fielded questions about her shifty, strange way of expressing herself. She seemed to flirt with ideas about her own guilt. Edda would repeatedly say, "That's Amanda!" as if that explained everything. One adult friend, who grew close to Amanda after she went to prison, said she seemed "delusional." This person, who met with her and with whom she corresponded semiweekly, said, "I think that she looks at the world with different eyes from a regular person. It's very hard, sometimes you want to be objective, to say: Is she simulating? Acting? Is she living in reality, or is it all imagination? She's not a rational person, not one hundred percent. She believes she's an artist. And she believes she's a writer. She believes that her life is all a developing movie, a plot that is never—that is not designed yet. There's no screenplay. She's making the screenplay."

Apart from the three short stories on the web and in prison, nothing Amanda Knox wrote—that the world saw anyway—leaked the slightest inky trace of psychic darkness. On the contrary, her prison diary and her letters from prison to me, other journalists, and her friends were surreally breezy and cheerful. She decorated them with teddies, peace signs, smiley faces, and hearts, described birthday parties in jail, and shared little jokes and drawings. Some were irreverent in the extreme, given her circumstances: Two months before her conviction, she wrote one male journalist, joking about a "catalystic [sic] love triangle," and a year into her imprisonment, she sent a cartoon to a friend in Seattle of herself, tearful and in prison stripes, with the caption "Jail Barbie" underneath and the balloon thought "Why, oh God, why?" Next to it, she wrote about how hard life was in jail, then stopped herself and commented, "Negative Nancy, right?"

Taken together, the writings confirmed one thing only: the girl's absence of gravitas. Was she simply, as her Seattle friends and family always insisted, trustful, naive to an almost otherwordly level? Or was she, as those who assumed she killed Meredith believe, masking evil behind a screen of pink hearts and flowers?

The conundrum preoccupied everyone who came into contact with her, supporters and detractors alike, and none more so than the prosecutor, Mignini, who first reviewed her most important piece of writing ever, her "gift" to the cops, the *memoriale* of November 6, 2007.

"She has some way of expressing herself, Amanda," Mignini mused. "It's as if she mixes dream and reality. She doesn't know if things have really happened or if it's a product of her imagination. We don't even know if what she thinks is just her imagination is reality. So it goes both ways. Where does her dream start and where does it end? She doesn't understand and we can't either. She has always been like this."

Mignini might have been interested in the results of a psychological examination, but it wasn't his duty or legal right to order one up. "We cannot ask for psychological tests. The only thing we can request is psychological counseling when we have doubts that she's capable of understanding the charges."

To her college friend Madison Paxton, Amanda's inability to defend herself convincingly had to do with her friend's reflexive passivity in the face of conflict. "It is her coping mechanism to avoid the gravity of the situation. The lawyers shielded her from a lot. She isn't the type of person who enjoys a confrontation. She will avoid. She is not a bitchy gossip, and so she wouldn't think other people would be. She would be oblivious to what people thought of her. But, on the other hand if she learned she hurt someone's feelings she was horrified. She has certain strengths, one of which helped her deal with prison—tuning it out. On the other hand, she doesn't have the skills to fight back." She was so inclined to seek compromise that, even in her closing statement to the jury hours before her conviction, Amanda still couldn't attack the Perugia authorities—but rather expressed her gratitude. "I want to thank the prosecutors because they are only trying to do their job, even if they don't understand. They are only trying to bring justice to someone whose life has been taken from this world."

After the conviction, the defense tried again to create an alternative scenario to the prosecution theory. In March 2010, Raffaele's lawyer, Giulia Bongiorno, interviewed a convicted child kidnapper/murderer named Mario Alessi, who had been one of Rudy's cellmates in the jail at Viterbo. Alessi signed a document stating that Rudy told him the students had nothing to do with the murder, but that the real killer was an unnamed second man.

> *"Rudy Guede told me that he had come to know Meredith Kercher in a bar a few days before the murder, and that he was accompanied by a friend," Alessi stated. "On the night of the murder, Rudy and his friend surprised Kercher, that is they went to her place without her knowing. After a little while, Rudy asked Kercher to have a threesome. Kercher refused: she even got up and asked Guede and his friend to leave the house. At this point Guede asked where the bathroom was. He stayed in the bathroom for quite a bit, 10 to 15 minutes tops. When he got back to the room, he found this scene . . . so Kercher was lying there, stretched out with her shoulders on the floor, half-naked. His friend was holding her by the arms, and Rudy went to stand, like, astride her and he started to masturbate.*

Alessi named two other inmates who had supposedly heard the same story from Guede. Those inmates were swiftly moved from the jail after Sollecito's lawyers released the statement. He also named two religious people, Sister Annunziata and Father Antonio, who also heard Rudy's story. They are exempt under Italian law from answering questions, although Alessi said they encouraged him to "step forward toward the Truth." But Alessi's credibility was null, since he had in fact murdered the child he'd kidnapped.

Around the same time, Amanda's lawyers interviewed an incarcerated mafioso named Luciano Aviello, who told them that his brother, a small-time mobster in Perugia, had been involved in the murder. Aviello said his brother and Rudy had been looking to steal art from wealthy houses, and had stumbled into the wrong house—finding Meredith alone, they sexually abused and killed her. Aviello claimed he had helped his brother bury Meredith's never-found keys and the knife that killed her. Aviello had written three letters to Massei, the judge in the case, all of which had been ignored.

Rudy, through his lawyers, quickly denied both men's stories. The prisoners who had spoken out had been sequestered from contact with the press.

PEOPLE OFTEN WONDER WHY, since three suspects were convicted of killing Meredith Kercher, most can only remember the name of the woman. One, not the only, reason is the Italian attitude toward women. The story starts with a spirituality based in sex and the worship of the female. Our word "veneration" comes from Venus, goddess of fertility, called in Italian, *Venere*. The primeval object of "veneration" was the goddess with the power to call forth desire from men, and to make barren women fertile.

Despite the fact that the Pope resides among them, Italians are not as Catholic as one might expect. Italy remains, as the journalist Luigi Barzini, put it, "gloriously pagan." In Italy, "Christianity has not deeply disturbed the happy traditions and customs of ancient Greece and Rome" but is a "thin veneer over older customs."

Pagan pantheism survives in the Italian proliferation of saints. But in Italy, one feminine deity has always been venerated above the rest. Throughout Italy, one confronts images of a beatific young mother holding or nursing a baby, gazing down mysteriously from a roadside *edicola*—tiny shrine—or from a niche in a church, or from the walls of art museums.

There's a pagan element in the cult of Mary, the mother of Jesus. The young virgin is worshipped apart from God or Christ. The Mary cult is stronger in Italy than in any other European nation. Italy has the greatest number of Church-validated Marian "apparitions"—sightings of the Virgin—than any other nation throughout recorded Church history.

Italy is home to hundreds of regional Mary cults. The most common name for the local Madonna deities is, simply, Santa Maria delle Grazie—the Mary of thanks, the Mary who dispenses favors. Traditionally, favor seekers approach the icon of Santa Maria delle Grazie on their knees with *ex voto* objects, small pressed metal or painted tile offerings, usually depicting a body part—a heart, an arm, a pair of eyes—whose recovery will be attributed to the attention of the Madonna delle Grazie.

Favors, though, are not granted for free. Madonnas in the Italian Mary cult are not necessarily altruistic. Like the vengeful goddesses of ancient Rome, the Madonnas are jealous and fickle and demand veneration. "The madonnas and saints worshipped by Italian Catholics are seen to have the power to cure and protect, they are also seen as a source of danger," wrote a scholar of popular Italian Catholicism, Michael Carroll. "This danger has nothing to do with the punishment of sin, it derives from something much simpler: the saints and madonnas of Italy want to be worshipped, and it is toward this end, and the maintenance of their own cults, that they use their great power."

The flip side to Italian veneration of the female deity is wariness about her legendary insatiable neediness, the voracious desire and jealousy of females, embodied in the whore, who is also still very much a part of modern Italian culture. All women are assumed to be in possession of bewitching seductive powers, but proper women are assumed to know how to use control and limit those powers.

Modern young women visiting Italy might not recognize those limits, though, because the stripper or girly-showgirl was so mainstreamed in Italy, especially during the years of Silvio Berlusconi's control of Italian television and politics. The gusher of hard, sex-based commercial marketing, the nearly naked television dancers called *veline* jiggling on political talk shows, were just the visual element of a political structure that officially degraded women.

Their schizophrenic status had subtle effects on Italian women. The nation had a large and growing class of professional women who were not *veline*. Female lawyers, police, judges, and forensics experts played key roles in the Amanda Knox trial. While most media focused on the male judge, prosecutor, and lawyers, all of these men had female lieutenants who did most of the heavy lifting in the case. The best lawyer in the case was a woman, Giulia Bongiorno, a powerful Parliamentarian who had, inexplicablly, used her wits to help womanizer Berlusconi stay in power.

But Italy was ranked 74th out of 128 nations in the World Economic Forum's 2010 global index of gender equality, lowest in the EU and behind Ghana and Kazakhstan. For professional women like the lawyers and policewomen involved in the Kercher murder investigation and trial, the years leading up to and during the murder trial were a time of massive disconnection between their apparent and their real status. Italian professional women like Bongiorno and the other female lawyers and police in the Knox case put up with their *veline* sisters and the national girl-ogling sport, but uneasily. Many were divorced or single. The ancient Madonna/whore split poisoned their private lives, not to mention their attitudes toward other women—including the American college vixen Amanda Knox.

Two popular Madonnas reside in Perugia. One is the Madonna del Verde, a very old fresco from the mysterious round hilltop Tempio Sant' Angelo, dating to the Dark Ages, whose background color green represented hope. The temple, located at the highest point in Perugia, is locally believed to have originated as a temple to Venus or Vesta. The site was probably also important to the Etruscans, who kept spiritual sanctuaries and tombs on hilltops adjacent to, but separate from, the city centers reserved for the living.

The other Perugia Madonna is the Madonna delle Grazie in the Duomo. Mignini kept her image hanging on the wall behind his desk and spoke of how she had helped his uncle escape from certain death at the hands of the Russians in the 1940s. The icon is a larger-than-life, clearly pregnant young woman, painted in 1515 by Giannicola di Paolo, one of Perugia's Renaissance greats. She wears a brocade blue dress, and her pale eyes are strangely distant and slightly uneven. Perugians hundreds of years ago adorned her image with a real crown. Every day, parishioners can be seen kneeling before her. Over the centuries, they have appeased or thanked her with thousands of ex voto offerings— silver hearts and other body parts tied with small red ribbons—tucked in the glass case behind her.

Both Perugia's Madonnas have pale, heart-shaped faces, tiny pert noses, light distant eyes, small perfect mouths. Amanda Knox bears an uncanny resemblance to both of them. The hippie soccer player from twenty-first-century Seattle could have been the Renaissance artist's model.

WAS THE AMERICAN GIRL, the star of the trial, guilty as charged or culpable in some other way? Amanda's behavior looked suspicious, even though the police were not able to pull together convincing material evidence. She was unable to show sorrow after the murder, and in many instances afterward, when she might have shown empathy for her dead friend, she did not. Listening to her make gurgling death sounds during her trial testimony was chilling. At that moment, it was easy to understand what the *colpevolisti* saw behind the pretty blue eyes.

British psychoanalyst Coline Covington, writing after the conviction on a U.K. news aggregator called *The First Post*, diagnosed Amanda as psychopathic. "Our deepest fear is that the 'girl next door,' whom we trust and see as innocent and loving, turns out to be a vampire or a murderer. This is the stuff of horror movies and we all want to believe that in real life these horrors don't occur. We also want to believe that we are not capable of doing evil deeds. Evil is something that is done by others—not one of us. Knox's narcissistic pleasure at catching the eye of the media and her apparent nonchalant attitude during most of the proceedings show the signs of a psychopathic personality. Her behaviour is hauntingly reminiscent of Eichmann's arrogance during his trial for war crimes in Jerusalem in 1961 and most recently of Karadžić's preening before the International Criminal Court at the Hague."

A girl monster of that stature is truly something to behold, and—contrary to Covington's assessment—people *do* want to believe that in real life "these horrors" walk among us. In fact, so many people wanted to believe Amanda was one of "these horrors" that many spectators and investigators involved in the Kercher murder refused to believe it wasn't so, even when presented with convincing evidence. Like the head of Medusa, the image was too fascinating to turn away from.

Over time, as I learned more about Rudy, Amanda, and Raffaele and the facts of the case against them, I realized that what people like Covington and the rest of the *colpevolisti* saw in Amanda was not psychopathy but something that I and most women are familiar with: the secret dislike that young women on the cusp of adulthood develop for one another. In dormitories all over the supposedly post-feminist world, young single women are driven by competitive jealousy and a desire to triumph cloaked in such a sickish sweetness that one must look closely to see it.

Meredith Kercher didn't like Amanda Knox very much and, maybe someday, in a parallel universe, Amanda will be able to admit that the feeling was mutual. Amanda was insecure, on her own, and perhaps jealous of her sophisticated roommate. She was probably afflicted with a case of twenty-year-old-female envy that women know well, tension cloaked under smiles and air kisses.

Is my hair pretty? Do I look fat? Can I borrow those cute jeans? Do you like me? Can I steal your boyfriend? Are you hotter than I am? Who am I? Am I not loved?

And: *"I like Giacomo too, but you can have him."* Every woman knows that type.

Both girls were entering womanhood and navigating their effect on men, and on each other.

In a letter to me dated December 17, 2009, thirteen days after her conviction and sentencing, Amanda tried to answer a question about the way she and Meredith had been experiencing the world, and how she thought the world perceived them.

How young women experience the world and how the world experiences young women . . . It's an age-old question, isn't it? One that doesn't quite mutate but at least has peaked [sic] its head out from beneath its shroud to grow and blossom under the direct light of the sun. I guess any and every young woman can become a story, because I feel like I'm not really so special, other than having to experience a rather exceptional range of experiences the world has felt coming full circle in regards to not only me, but also to Meredith. It's like we're both in this together and I'm really baffled sometimes by how something so big and exceptional could have happened to the both of us, how different our lives became, how horribly hers ended, all of a sudden without us even seeing it coming. It's so big, and so sad.

Before she was murdered, Meredith, more sophisticated, was already getting bikini waxes and wearing lacy underthings, smiling for cameras with her back arched and tongue between her teeth. Amanda, before she was arrested, was calling herself a hippie, wearing no makeup, but maybe realizing for the first time, with the example of her feminine, sophisticated roommate in close proximity, that there was something more to be gained by the feminine wiles than she'd previously understood. And that the rules of the game played on the green soccer fields of the West Coast were different from those that applied to worldly women. Dead, of course, Meredith Kercher had finally garnered all the attention, a state of affairs that Amanda could never abide for long.

But if envying a roommate produced sexual killers, the world would be soon short of young women.

The scenario presented by the prosecution was not very plausible. One had to suspend disbelief to buy the theory that Amanda Knox and Raffaele Sollecito killed Meredith Kercher without leaving a trace of themselves in the bloody room, and then spent the night putting up a false scene in the burgled room. There was no believable material proof that they did either.

Nothing in either of the students' prior behavior indicated a predis-position to aggression, let alone murder. Raffaele's blog, from which the prosecutor and press cherry-picked a single reference to "strong emo-tions," is filled with many more references to graduating, caring for his grandmother, doing homework, and helping the community. Amanda's own writing shows a basically healthy young woman constantly grap-pling to find the upside of her predicament. She was no vixen with kinky adult impulses. She had had sex with seven men in two years, hardly a record for American college women.

After Meredith was murdered, the two students did not behave like guilty people. The sequence of phone calls alone on the morning of November 2 reflects the slowly rising panic of two students who went from hungover and blasé to alarmed and finally worried enough to call friends, then family, then police. They stayed in Perugia, against fam-ily advice. They didn't contact lawyers. Raffaele showed up at the po-lice station for questioning with his penknife in his pocket. They were guilty of callous, blithe, and stupid behavior, maybe the stupidest being getting high before going into the police station on the night of Novem-ber 5, 2007.

On that night, the police misunderstood a text message to a *stra-niero* male, of a type who fit their habitual model of a male aggressor in Perugia. They wanted Patrick Lumumba to be the culprit, for that reason, and also because the timing of the phone message was perfect, and the police—to avoid further lawsuits, let's say—*gently persuaded* Amanda into having a "vision" that matched a scenario they had painted for her first.

Almost everyone except the prosecutors eventually agreed that the knife in the trial was not the murder knife. Besides the fact that it didn't match the murder weapon's print on the bed, the idea that they would carry it back to Raffaele's kitchen when they had access to numerous trash dumpsters was at odds with the alleged clever cover-up in the rest of the prosecution theory.

If the DNA on the bra clasp is in fact Raffaele's, it was either the result of contamination or something innocent and far more plausible than the group sex and cover-up theorized by the police. Who is to say Amanda didn't at some point before the murder do what female roommates and sisters have always done: secretly tried on, borrowed, or snuck off with another woman's pretty clothes. (Raffaele's father suggested this at one point, and was immediately silenced by lawyers.) The little bare footprints in the hallway illuminated by luminol may be Amanda's footprints, not in blood but in the luminol-reactive cleaning substance that the fastidious Italian girls used to scrub their bathroom clean. She stood in it during the morning shower she took, ignoring the strange signs around her in her cannabinoid hangover, her year-abroad state of mind in which normal life was suspended, and her rush to get back to her new boyfriend.

They did not clean the apartment, carefully removing only their traces and leaving only Rudy's fingerprints, bloody footprints, and DNA. Besides the impossibility of such a feat, the scientific police tested the household mop and bucket and apparently found not a trace of Meredith on either. If they had, the items would have been exhibits A and B.

Although it is impossible to know exactly what transpired without a confession from the killer or killers, all the evidence suggests that the house at number 7 via della Pergola was in the process of being robbed when Meredith Kercher came home from dinner with her friends on the night of November 1, 2007, interrupted a crime, and screamed. As her family pointed out, she had taken kickboxing and, though small, she would have fought for her life. The evidence of that fight is in the bruises on her body.

Meredith's physical training failed her when she needed it most, in the clutches of an athletic, larger man enraged at having been interrupted in the course of a fantasy of being alone, free to browse and take, and luxuriating in someone else's house, and now terrified of being arrested and imprisoned. The robber had no choice but to confront her, as he was locked in when Meredith came home and locked the door shut from the inside with her keys. He might have cut off her phone call to her mother at 8:56 P.M., but by 10:00 P.M., when a brief attempt was made to connect with her bank, he was certainly already in complete control of her phone. The robber took the $300 she had in her purse and her cell phones, wiped off the most visible blood on the door handle, washed his foot, and loped out of the front door, using Meredith's house keys, which were never found, to lock her bedroom door and unlock the front door, letting himself out, hopping on one blood-soaked shoe and probably carrying the other.

The single bare right bloody footprint on the blue bathmat is the footprint of the killer, before he rinsed it off in the bidet—hence Meredith's blood on the bidet drain.

The killer's right Nike was drenched in blood and slipped off during his unspeakable act of dispatching Meredith into the underworld. Like the practitioners of the bloody mystery rites that Mignini was on the lookout for, Meredith's killer was slipshod when he left, leaving a single left shoeprint leading out the door.

The robber was someone who had not killed before, who usually worked alone, and who had the habit of breaking in and padding around vacant premises, feeling secure under cover of night, making himself at home, rummaging, eating, drinking, going to the bathroom, maybe even sleeping.

Rudy Guede might have told the truth about what he saw and did in that house if he hadn't lawyered up before the Perugia police got to him. The part of him that was raised by Mrs. Tiberi was the part of him that felt deep remorse about Meredith Kercher. The good Catholic Italian boy in him knew the difference between right and wrong and knew compassion. That's why he tried to stanch the blood with towels and that's why he covered her body with a duvet. That's why he still sees red when he closes his eyes. What the police mistook as feminine *pietà* was the remorse of a man, horrified by the sight of blood, who had never killed before.

The part of him that was locked in the bathroom, left to wander the streets alone, and beaten bloody as a small boy, and welcomed and then abandoned as "a mistake" by the aristocratic Caporalis, the part of him welcomed and shunned by Italian society, remains silent in the face of an injustice he could have stopped.

The jury and judges that eventually convicted Amanda and Raffaele apparently bought parts of Rudy's story. They called him "the author of the evil," but also perpetuated the notion, repeatedly put forth by prosecutors and his friends, that Rudy was a benign, albeit lost, young man, who usually operated within the predictable norms of society. They flatly dismissed the theory that Rudy, even with his known burglary habit, would break into the via della Pergola house to steal, because, the judge wrote, Rudy associated the location with "friendship and fun."

It has already been stated that Rudy Guede was acquainted with the inhabitants of via della Pergola and that he had a good relationship of friendship and fun with them (with all of the boys downstairs; with Amanda, in whom he had actually shown some interest; and with Meredith). It thus seems unlikely that Rudy decided to enter this house in the illicit and violent matter shown by the smashing of the window.

During the investigation and trial, Italian criminologists and psychologists in the U.K. offered many theories about the mind and pathology of convicted murderess Amanda Knox. Besides Covington, the British psychiatrist who diagnosed her as a psychopath and compared her courtroom demeanor to that of genocidal world figures, a young woman with a degree in social media from Bath, England, would pose as a forensic psychiatrist on the Internet and publish what she presented as expert analyses of Amanda Knox's psychopathy. No one ever offered to analyze the exceedingly complicated psyche of sleepwalker Rudy Guede—or if anyone did, neither the press nor the prosecution took advantage of the expertise.

Biscotti was right to surmise that Americans would have no problem assuming Rudy was the lone killer, and one ugly reason for that has to do with institutionalized racism. Forty-four percent of male prisoners in U.S. jails in 2010 were black. The truth is that Italian racism is no less virulent than American racism; it just manifests differently. Because the number of foreigners in homogeneous white Italy rose dramatically only recently, the racist bogeyman of a dark-skinned criminal underclass that infects white America had not taken hold. Italian jails were not filled with black males. But Italians were certainly no more friendly to blacks than Americans were, and probably even less so in an institutional sense. Italian culture simply excluded and ignored its black residents. Unlike in the United States, blacks were not represented in Italy's government or educational institutions, nor in its professions.

Americans might have accepted a revised theory of the crime once forensics experts found Rudy Guede's fingerprints and DNA in the murder room. The Perugia jury accepted the more convoluted logic of the manipulative white female at the center of the killing. The conviction of Amanda Knox perversely gave Italians a very public reassurance that in spite of their deep distrust of the dark *stranieri* hordes, they are not racist.

One could argue that Rudy's defense—*I was there, but Meredith wanted me there and I tried to save her*—made no sense, but Biscotti had made it work, especially as his client slowly matched his memories to the prosecution theory involving the students. Rudy's story had the perverse advantage of its illogic, which satisfied the Italian insistence on complicated theories. His story was also far more interesting than the theory the students' lawyers presented: Our clients were asleep. The students' lawyers couldn't offer a competing version of events at the murder house if that were so. And the logical inconsistencies of Rudy's account and his ever-changing story could always easily be parried with the logical inconsistency of Amanda's recanted "vision" and her and Raffaele's changing stories about the night of November 1 while being interrogated on the night of November 5.

The Perugian authorities', the civil lawyers', and the media's refusal to look more closely at Rudy—to learn about his psychology, his trances, his sleepwalking, his fears, his childhood, his prior criminal life, his mental state in the months before the killing, a great, enduring mystery of the case—is simply a symptom of the fact that people like Rudy are mostly invisible in Italian and European society. In the extremely rare cases where they seem to be accepted in a community, they are so completely "other" that average Italians, like the judge and jury in Perugia, can't even ascribe normal standards of human behavior to them.

After the 2009 verdict and sentencing, American supporters belatedly mobilized in a way that did resemble the expensive PR machine American reporters in Italy and the Italian authorites had incessantly—and mistakenly—complained about during the investigation and trial. Prominent American defense lawyer Ted Simon began advising on the case. Retired FBI expert Bruce Budowle, a world-renowned DNA expert, was brought on board. Elaborate websites were created debunking the forensic evidence. And behind it all, there was Donald Trump, bellowing for a boycott of Italy.

In the end, though, not even those best efforts, the collapse of the forensic evidence, and a convincing appeal persuaded everyone that Amanda's inculpatory statement and callous, flip behavior were not proof of a murderess, but the reaction of an emotionally stunted young woman faced with a terrifying tragedy inside her own house, and simultaneously afflicted with an ugly, suppressed, garden-variety case of college roommate envy. Despite the lack of evidence, police and prosecutor—and multitudes of media consumers in Italy, the U.K., and the United States—believe her to be complicit.

The material evidence against the students was weak to nonexistent, but circumstantial evidence exists. Their whereabouts at the time of the murder can never be determined beyond doubt. Their phones stopped receiving signals at the same time, within an hour or so of the murder. They were evasive about the sequence of events on the night of the murder, and about what time they woke up in the morning. Although these anomalies can be explained by the fact that they spent not just the night before but days—and in Raffaele's case, years—smoking hash several times a day, their inability to be clear on their doings on the night of and morning after a gruesome murder has only perpetuated the enigma.

For those who knew what to look for, there were many signs of witches' sabbath on the scene. It was a Thursday night, and All Souls' Night, when the dead mingle with the living, a time of year ritualistically marked in Europe for millennia. There was the slipshod bloody shoe track out the door. The person who entered through the high broken window seemed to have had magical powers of flight and, even more uncanny, the power to leave no trace of self on the windowsill. The American girl looked like the town Madonna and, in some photographs from November 2, even had a spot on the center of her throat, where the Madonna delle Grazie has a tiny cross. She had enchanted numerous men. Rudy Guede had advertised himself in public as a vampire. He really had a penchant for waking up in the night and finding himself far from home. He had a lame leg, with a scar on it, a known symbol in pagan spirituality. He had claimed he had a Florentine connection, which would surely have reminded Mignini of his nemeses in the Masonic conspiracy centered there. Taken together, it all suggested the age-old rites, the dark practices, represented by the pentacle on the floor of the strange, round temple at the top of Corso Garibaldi, with its mysterious backward Etruscan writing on the columns, and its round hollows on the floor, perfect for the erotic, bloody Dionysian death revels the Etruscans favored.

The modern American religion of science was tested in the trial and found dispensable by the judge and jury. The jurors could hardly have cared less about the mysterious, invisible chemical substances that proved and disproved blood on the knife and in the footprints. In some sense the substances and what they purported to reveal were as real or unreal as the body and blood of Christ in the Eucharist. You either believed or not. They went with another sort of criminal analysis and used the science testimony only as a kind of "possibility" indicator. Thus, the judge could write in the final sentencing report, that even though TMB (the blood-detecting chemical) had indicated there was no blood in footprints, and even though the low-copy-number DNA (material amounts considered below most courtroom standards of proof) on the knife made the material evidence dubious, it was still certainly "possible" that blood had been there, and that the big kitchen knife had been at least one of an unknown set of other knives used to kill Meredith.

It is easy to say that the jury, the judge, and maybe even Mignini were wrong to ignore modern science, but they had their reasons for doing so, reasons that may in fact be as valid as our own faith in it. As Hamlet reminded the rationalist Horatio, "There are more things in heaven and earth, Horatio, than are dreamt of in your philosophy."

On the afternoon of November 2, 2007, Magistrate Mignini found himself in the presence of inexplicable evil. In his worldview, evil is a primary force, and it is made manifest in many forms. In America, we might explain evil as the product of child abuse and mental illness. For Mignini, and others, there are older, other ways of explaining the vilest acts of men.

What was Amanda's role on the night of November 1, 2007? Besides the supersition, there is the sex.

The young American had attracted sexual desire and attention from men—willfully and not. Scampering around Perugia, she was only doing what liberated, athletic, self-absorbed young American girls do: having fun. And that fun—boisterous, brazen maybe—was read by Italian men like Rudy and the others, including Mignini and the police, in the only context by which they had to understand female behavior: she was the witch, the deliberate player of men.

Amanda was put through an extreme version of every young woman's greatest test. She was arrested at a time and in a place where young, sexually active women are endowed in the minds of grown men, and maybe women, too, with propensities for fantastic adult kink that few possess. At twenty, she was passing through the crucible through which all young women must pass: realizing the world no longer sees you as the girl you were, but as an unfamiliar creature with compelling powers over men that you either can or cannot control. She was unable to defend herself because she didn't understand the role herself and had not perfected it in the world. That the scapegoatish prosecution—and media celebration around it—focused on her sexuality suggests that civilization really has not advanced far beyond the primeval era when female power was classified, worshipped, and feared in the form of terrifying, all-powerful Madonnas and Dianas.

The Meredith Kercher murder hooked into the global psyche because the story is filled with ancient female archetypes—rewarded good girls, punished evil girls, virgins and whores, the monster of insatiable female sexual desire—that people across many cultures instantly recognize. Amanda Knox inadvertently fed these archetypes by the ways she behaved in public, and advertised herself on the web, and, eventually, in her own compulsive writings from prison. Despite her short lifetime of writing exercises, and her outwardly confident mien, she didn't possess the language, the words, the maturity, the style, the true self-confidence that comes from being emotionally whole, to define, let alone defend herself. Meanwhile, others—stronger, smarter, older, more eloquent— were eager to define her. Locked up, she might have all the pencils and notebooks she wanted and still not match the authority of other people's words.

The Perugians didn't know what to make of this unusual, slightly damaged girl with the inappropriate emotional responses, whose over-confident exterior masked a person with a deep aversion to conflict. Needing to solve the high-profile crime, they made a deduction about her and extracted a statement that put her at the scene. Everything in the investigation evolved from that, including the subjective calls on low-copy-number DNA.

Then, the whole world was watching.

To admit they'd been wrong was not an option. "The imperative which they implicitly obey in all their decisions," wrote Barzini, of his fellow countrymen, is *non farsi far fesso*—not to be made a fool of. "To be *fesso* is the ultimate ignominy, as credulity is the unmentionable sin. The *fesso* is betrayed by his wife . . . falls for deceptions and intrigues.

The *fesso*, incidentally, also obeys the laws, pays the taxes, believes what he reads in the papers, keeps his promises and generally does his duty."

The *fesso* might be fooled by a pretty American girl who is, in fact, a murderess.

Those who recognized the mistake responded by circling the wagons. Others persisted in belief, and blustered on.

The timing of the release of the bra clasp DNA, immediately after the shoe prints were found to be Rudy's, and all the fraudulent embellishments that were never proven nor officially corrected but which so captured the media and public mind—sex game, googling bleach, the mop and bucket, "mixed blood DNA," Raffaele supposedly deviously calling police after police arrived, Amanda's bare footprints supposedly being made in blood—were elements of an injustice, of a sort sadly not uncommon in courts and police departments in the United States, only more fascinating because this one involved women, beauty, and sex in the Anglo-Saxon playpen called Italy.

By filing slander suits against not only Amanda Knox but also her parents, by kicking them while down, the Perugians reminded the world that *vendetta* is in fact an Italian word.

The spired settlement on the hill has been under siege countless times before. As it has for millennia, the walled city will hold out.

NOTES ON SOURCES AND METHODS

To research the book, I interviewed the Perugia authorities, defense lawyers, and friends and family members of the defendants. I engaged in written correspondence with Amanda Knox and Raffaele Sollecito. I reviewed the Perugia court's "digital archive" of the investigation, including wiretap audio and crime-scene video. I consulted experts in Italy and the United States on Italian law, forensic and DNA science, and psychology.

I attended trial hearings beginning in June 2009, and I lived in Perugia for nine months in 2009 and 2010.

My method was journalistic in that I interviewed people, many of them on several occasions, looked at primary documents, and followed leads to geographical locations and to sources living in those locations. Besides Perugia, I visited Amanda Knox's homes in Seattle; Raffaele Sollecito's home, friends, and family near Bari; and Rudy Guede's family and homes in Perugia, Lecco, and Milan.

I also used secondary documents, mainly newspaper articles and books.

I had technical assistance in interpreting the crime-scene video and the crime-scene analysis carried out by the Scientific Police from several legal and forensic officials in New York who prefer to remain anonymous, and from retired NYPD homicide detective Ron Dwyer and former New York prosecutor, now in private practice, Georges G. Lederman, who shared expertise gained from working on hundreds of murder cases.

I wrote to Rudy Guede in prison, a letter that I understood that I received. If he responded, I never received it. His lawyer, Valter Biscotti, accosted me in the street after that and insisted that I refrain from contacting his client by letter. Biscotti wanted to be paid for interactions with Rudy Guede, and to my knowledge he has never granted access to any journalist.

I wrote and sent several letters each to members of the Kercher family and to the young women who were Meredith's friends in Perugia and who testified at the trial. I also sent e-mails to those whose addresses were available. None of them ever responded, leading me reluctantly to rely solely on published material and trial testimony about Meredith Kercher's personality and history.

PROLOGUE: MEZZANOTTE

All quotes and anecdotes from the trial's closing arguments are from my courtroom notes.

CHAPTER 1: CRONACA NERA

Perugians' comments and other observations from my notes and journals, written during the summer and fall of 2009. Statistics on violence against women in Europe and Italy from *Report of the European Council Parliamentary Assembly* (2000).

CHAPTER 2: SLAVE

Descriptions of the events of the morning of November 2 from trial testimony and investigative interviews conducted by the Perugia magistrate and police, contained in the case file.

CHAPTER 3: SEATTLE

Amanda Knox's description of Seattle from a letter she wrote from prison to me in May 2010. Edda Mellas's comments and family history from my interviews with Edda in Italy in summer 2009. Descriptions of Amanda's behavior as a child, the family dynamic, and the problems related to the custody agreement from a source close to the family who asked to remain anonymous. Amanda was "Curt's boy" from my interview with Brett Lither in May 2010. Curt Knox's pastimes from my interviews with Curt Knox in Italy in 2009 and 2010.

CHAPTER 4: PERUGIA

Luigi Barzini on Italy's effects on outsiders from *The Italians* (New York: Touchstone, 1996), p. 42. Tips for American tourists, Seth Stevenson, "How to Be Invisible," *Newsweek*, April 9, 2010. Perugia saints and local history and Lalande quote from Francesco Dufour, *Perugia: City of Art* (Perugia: Effe Fabrizio Fabbri Editore srl, 2003), throughout.

CHAPTER 5: AMERICAN GIRL

Amanda's jobs in Seattle from interviews with family and friends and numerous published sources. "Amanda is a writer": Curt Knox to me, summer 2009. Curt telling Amanda about a "major editor" from transcribed prison wiretaps in the digital archive. Amanda on why she picked Perugia from a letter to me. Amanda as a child from Brett Lither to me in an interview, Seattle, May 2010. Kris Johnson's quote from James Ross Gardner, "School of Knox," *Seattle Met Magazine*, December 2010. Amanda's college choice due to her financial situation, from my interview with Kris Johnson, May 2010. Amanda's driving problems from interviews with Curt Knox and other family members in 2009 and 2010. Drunk YouTube video: www.youtube.com/watch?v=f2m5qSHU88A. Madison Paxton on Amanda from interviews with me in Seattle and Perugia, summer and fall 2010. Amanda's Myspace short stories taken from the web in 2007. Curt's comments about Amanda's therapeutic writing and his own attitude toward books and Italy as well as his surreptitious installation of GPS on his daughters' cell phones from my interviews, fall-winter, 2009–2010. Amanda's 2007 Myspace journal was preserved and widely disseminated in many newspapers and books.

CHAPTER 6: ROOMMATES

Filomena Romanelli on meeting Amanda and Meredith and her early observations of the two girls together from an investigative interview conducted with her by Mignini on December 3, 2007, in the digital archive. Descriptions of the family and life of Meredith Kercher from various British newspapers, including Gordon Rayner, "Amanda Knox Trial: Meredith Kercher Profile," *Daily Telegraph*, December 5, 2009. Filomena described her problems with the shutters to Mignini as early as the December 3, 2007, interview, when she told him she "didn't know" if she had closed her shutters before leaving on November 1, 2007. The quotes about shutters in this passage are from her trial testimony, February 7, 2009. Quotes from Valentina are from Malcolm Moore and Gary Cleland, "British Student Had Sex with Killer, Say Police," *Daily Telegraph*, November 5, 2007. Operation Girasole details from Frances Kennedy, "Umbria, Home of Art, Culture and Violent White Slave Trade," *The Independent*, April 15, 2001. Further background on the subjects of Perugia, the Mafia, and prostitution from my interviews with Vanna Ugolini in 2009. History of the *poderetto* from my interview with Marisa Orlandi in Rome, December 2009. Young women and competitition, Nancy Friday, *Jealousy* (New York: Evans), p. 369. Filomena on Amanda and Meredith's habits and friendship, from Mignini interview, December 3, 2007, in the digital archive. Details of pot plants growing downstairs in numerous published sources, including Tom Kington, "Students Flock to Perugia a Year After Kercher Killing," *The Guardian*, November 1, 2008, and the sentencing report written by Judge Giancarlo Massei of the Court of Assizes, Perugia (hereafter "Massei report"). Bonassi quotes from statements he gave to police on November 3, 2007, in the digital archive. Bonassi on "the Baron" from statement to police, November 4, 2007.

CHAPTER 7: THE BARON

"Amanda and Meredith looked alike": Bonassi, trial testimony, February 14, 2009. Italy's "racism emergency": Nick Squires, "Protests in Italy Against Escalating Racism," *Daily Telegraph*, October 5, 2008. Police racism, Italian political reaction to immigrants, and quote from Mayor Bitonci: Sylvia Poggioli, "Immigrants Forced to Margins of Italian Society," NPR, January 13, 2009. Rudy Guede's birth, childhood, and family history from my interviews with Roger Guede, Georgette Guede, Ivana Tiberi, and Ilaria Caporali, 2009. Paolo Caporali quote from Nick Pisa, "Rudy Guede: Portrait of Meredith's Murderer as He Begins 30-Year Sentence," *Daily Mail*, October 29, 2008. Rudy Guede's letter with references to Amanda in digital archive.

CHAPTER 8: THE VORTEX

Quotes from the "British girls" from statements to police dated February 8, 2008, in the digital archive, and trial testimony, February 13, 2009. Hicham Khouri quotes from statements to police, November 3, 2007, in the digital archive. Daniel Tartaglia interview, summer 2009. Spyros Gatsios comment from trial testimony, June 2009. Lumumba quotes from my interviews in 2009 and 2010. Amanda quote from prison diary, November 2007, in the digital archive. Daniele and Giacomo date-night anecdotes from Stefano Bonassi, statements to police in the digital archive, and Giacomo Silenzi, statements to police and trial testimony. Marco Marzan quote from statement to police, November 4, 2007, in the digital archive. Giacomo pretending not to know Meredith on the corso from pub manager Pisco in Candace Dempsey, *Murder in Italy* (New York: Berkley, 2010), p. 120. Amanda, "I'll let you have him," from "Secret Diary Reveals Foxy Knoxy Was 'Always Thinking About Sex,'" *Daily Mail*, November 30, 2008. Description of Raffaele's childhood, home, and family from my interviews with Francesco and Vanessa Sollecito and with Raffaele's high school friends in the Bari area. "I liked to play with dolls" and other quotes from Raffaele's letters to me, 2009–2010. Description of life at ONAOSI from a University of Perugia graduate who prefers to remain anonymous. Raffaele's blog writings from the digital archive. Raffaele's drug use from Amanda Knox, handwritten notes from questura, November 1–2, 2007; Sollecito's letters and writings in prison in the digital archive."My first impression" from Raffaele's letter to his father in the digital archive. Raffaele was a virgin from Peter Popham, "A Chance to Redeem Italian Justice," *The Independent*, October 27, 2008. "It was love at first sight" from letter to me, 2010. Filomena on Raffaele and Amanda in the digital archive. December 2008 statements to Mignini. Sollecito letter to his father from prison in the digital archive.

CHAPTER 9: VENDEMMIA

Opening quote from Rudy Guede, letter from prison in the digital archive. Rudy's Perugia activities and behavior during the summer of 2007 from my interviews with former student Victor Oleinikov in Seattle, May 2010. Ivana Tiberi and Gabriele Mancini quotes from my interviews in 2009. Quotes from Rudy's Ponte San Giovanni friend to Mignini from Francesca Bene and Giuseppe Castellini, *Meredith: Il Cronaca di un delitto*, pp. 77–81, translated by Candace Dempsey. Tramontano anecdote from January 7, 2008, statement to police, in the digital archive. Maria Del Prato anecdotes from my interview in Milan, December 2009. Brocchi law office anecdotes from trial testimony of Paolo Brocchi, June 26, 2009. Madu Diaz anecdote from my interview, January 2010. Items found in Guede backpack confirmed by Perugia carabiniere Francesco Zampa to me, spring 2010.

CHAPTER 10: HALLOWTIDE

Amanda Knox quotes to Mignini from interrogation of December 17, 2007, in the digital archive. Amanda's and Meredith's SMS texts, Candace Dempsey, *Murder in Italy*, pp. 15–16. Lumumba interview from Antonio Hoyle, "I Fired Foxy Knoxy for Hitting on Customers," *Daily Mail*, November 25, 2007. Lumumba being paid, Frank Sfarzo, Perugia-shock blog. The "British girls"' Halloween night from interviews with police, November 3, 2007, in the digital archive. Rudy Guede YouTube vampire clip: www.youtube.com/watch?v=C9P6KishWBA. Michele Fabiani arrest anecdotes from my interviews with Michael Gregorio and with Fabiani, January 2010. Amanda Knox's description of her doings on November 1 from statement to police, November 2, 2007, in the digital archive, and e-mail to family and friends, sent November 4, 2007, in the digital archive. Details about the phone message and the phones being turned off, as well as the computer activity, from my interviews with Mignini, trial testimony, and the Massei report. Meredith's last dinner from testimony of Sophie Purton, November 4, 2007, in the digital archive, and trial testimony, February 13, 2009. Meredith's phone activity from the Massei report.

CHAPTER 11: MIGNINI

Mignini's memories of November 2 and his personal and family history from several interviews with me, 2009–2010. Filomena's description of her activities on November 2, her distrust of Amanda, the glass on top of her clothes, all from statement to Mignini, December 3, 2007, in the digital archive. Description of the crime scene from crime-scene video. Anecdotes and quotes about the investigation into the Monster of Florence from my multiple interviews with Mignini and from Doug Preston with Mario Spezi, *The Monster of Florence* (New York: Grand Central, 2008). Carlizzi anecdotes and quotes from my interview with Carlizzi in Rome, summer 2009. Gramsci quote from Barzini, p. 215. History of Masons and Templars in Perugia from various secondary sources, including Francesco DuFour, *Perugia: City of Art*. Monica Napoleoni's memories of November 2, 2007, from her trial testimony, February 27, 2009.

CHAPTER 12: QUESTURA

Amanda's handwritten statement, November 6, 2007, in the digital archive. Local newspaper headlines and quotes from the public library in Perugia. Description of Mignini's office from several visits by me. Napoleoni's personal life recounted to me by Luciano Ghirga. Amanda's description of November 2 from statement to police, November 2, 2007, in the digital archive. Timing of Amanda's and Raffaele's phone calls from the Massei report. Explanation of problems with the timing of the arrival of the postal police from defense expert witness testimony and closing arguments, November and December 2009. The "British girls" on Amanda's strange behavior at the questura from statements to Mignini at Bergamo, February 8, 2008, in the digital archive, and trial testimony, February 13, 2009. Amanda's hitting herself in the head while going to be fingerprinted from Fabio D'Astolto, statement to Mignini, December 21, 2007, in the digital archive. Amanda on Shaky from statement to police, November 4, 2007, in the digital archive. Sophie Purton on Shaky from statement to police, November 3, 2007, in the digital archive. Sophie on Meredith thinking one of the boys "a bit weird" from statement to Mignini, November 5, 2007, in the digital archive. Hicham on the Da Gennaro pizza boys and Meredith from statement to police, November 3, 2007, in the digital archive. Stefano Bonassi and Giacomo Silenzi quotes, from statements to police, November 3 and 4, 2007, in the digital archive. Marco Marzan on Meredith's sexual habits from statement to police, November 3, 2007, in the digital archive. Amanda's "oopla" and swivel from Eduardo Giobbi, trial testimony, quoted in Ann Wise, "Amanda Knox to Take Stand in Murder Trial," ABC News International, May 29, 2009. Amanda on Meredith's non–drug use, statement to police, November 3, 2007, in the digital archive. Filomena apologizing for drug use, trial testimony, February 7, 2009. Sophie Purton on drug use, statement to Mignini,

November 5, 2007, in the digital archive. Bubbles anecdote from numerous published sources. Laura Mezzetti's recollections of the November 4, 2007, gathering and Amanda's odd behavior from statement to Mignini, December 5, 2007, in the digital archive. Amanda on Italian roommates from letter to me, summer 2010. Amanda's e-mail to family and friends, November 4, 2007, in the digital archive. Amanda and Raffaele's wiretapped questura conversation from transcript in the digital archive. Antonella Negri's memories of Amanda's Monday-morning behavior and her classroom letter to her mother from Malcolm Moore, "Meredith's Flatmate Told Mother, 'I Feel on Edge,'" *The Telegraph*, November 14, 2007, and my interview with Rector Stefania Giannini of the Università per Stranieri. Filomena on her final conversation with Amanda from trial testimony, February 27, 2009. Press knowing something was going to happen on November 5, 2007, Erika Pontini, interview with me, December 2009. Description of the interrogations of November 5–6 from letters to me from Raffaele and Amanda, interviews with Mignini, and police testimony at the trial. Amanda's statements to police, November 6, 2007, in the digital archive. Press conference scene from published reports and photographs, including Candace Dempsey, *Murder in Italy,* and Barbie Nadeau, *Angel Face: The True Story of Student Killer Amanda Knox* (New York: Beast Books, 2009). Gubbiotti and Finzi selecting and handling Raffaele's knife from Candace Dempsey, *Murder in Italy,* p. 212. Mignini's detention argument in the digital archive. Judge Matteini's confirmation of detention in the digital archive. Rudy Guede's travels in Europe from Paul Russell and Graham Johnson with Luciano Garofano, *Darkness Descending: The Murder of Meredith Kercher* (London: Pocket Books, 2009). Rudy Guede's Skype conversation with Giacomo Benedetti, November 16, 2007, transcribed in the digital archive.

CHAPTER 13: LA SIGNORA DEL GIOCO

Descriptions of Italian pagan rites and monosandalism from Carlo Ginzburg, *The Witches' Sabbath* (translator, Raymond Rosenthal, Chicago: University of Chicago Press, 1991). Details about Masonic ritual from a number of books and websites about Masonry, including H. Paul Jeffers, *Freemasons: Inside the World's Oldest Secret Society* (New York: Kensington, 2005). Mignini's comments on fourth person from my interview, fall 2009. Ghirga on policewomen and sex games from my interview, January 2010. Mignini and

Filomena exchange from police statement, December 3, 2007, in the digital archive. Amanda Knox HIV test from her prison diary, November 2007, in the digital archive. Marina Toschi comments from my interview, January 2010.

CHAPTER 14: THE DREAM TEAMS

Francesco Maresca background from my interview in Florence, July 2009. U.S. Embassy lawyer list from my interview with Chris Mellas, December 2010. Defense lawyers overruling complaint from my interviews with Edda Mellas, summer 2009. Valter Biscotti anecdotes and description from my interviews, July 2009. Nicola Gentile anecdotes from my interviews, 2009. Rudy, quote about Meredith accusing Amanda of stealing her money, from Richard Owen, "Meredith Kercher Killer Rudy Guede 'Saw Amanda Knox Fleeing Scene,'" *The Times*, November 19, 2009. Rudy's fingerprints in purse and rent money missing, Massei report. Rudy's *memoriale* from the German jail in the digital archive. May 2008 hearing from my interview with Carlo Dalla Vedova and from Candace Dempsey, *Murder in Italy*, p. 253. Rudy's associating the murder house with "friendship and fun" from Massei report. Biscotti predicting what Rudy would say from Barbie Nadeau, *Angel Face: The True Story of Student-Killer Amanda Knox*, p. 117. Rudy on Meredith accusing Amanda of stealing from Richard Owen, "Meredith Kercher Killer Rudy Guede 'Saw Amanda Knox Fleeing Scene.'" Rudy's statement about being unable to get the red out of his mind from my notes on Rudy's spontaneous declaration, December 22, 2009. Rudy wanting a signed basketball from my interview with CBS producer Doug Longhini. Biscotti's complaint about Americans from my interview, July 2009. Explanation of how confessions change investigations from my interview with Saul Kassin, November 2010. Barry Laughman case from Saul Kassin and the Innocence Project (www .innocenceproject.org). The Reid Technique from my interview with Kassin and further defined on www.reid.com. Amanda on her treatment the night of November 5–6 from letter to me, July 2010. Exchange between Dalla Vedova and Donnino from trial testimony, March 13, 2009. Giobbi trial testimony on his initial suspicions, May 29, 2009.

CHAPTER 15: TRIBUNALE

Amanda competed with her mother for men, from Sharon Churcher, "Foxy Knoxy, the Girl Who Had to Compete with Her Own Mother for Men," *Daily Mail,* November 10, 2007. Patrick Lumumba taking payments, Frank Sfarzo, Perugia-shock blog. Sollecito family criticism of the police from *"Indagiti i familiari di Sollecito Volevano manipolare le indagine,"* La Repubblica, June 21, 2008. Witness testimony from trial transcripts, January and February 2009. Quintavale's excuse for not recognizing Amanda for a year as told to reporter Bob Graham, summer 2010. Treatment of Francesca Bene from my interview, July 2009. Letters from Amanda to Raffaele from Beth Hale, " 'We Could Have Had Something Special,' " *Daily Mail,* June 14, 2009. Silenzi examined by Comodi from trial testimony, February 14, 2009. Summary of Stefanoni's testimony and the DNA evidence from Massei report. Cell phone and computer times from Massei report. The burning of the hard drives: my interview with Chris Mellas, December 2009, also discussed in court on numerous occasions. The digital clock's problems discussed in closing arguments, my notes. Amanda Knox's testimony from my courtroom notes. Comodi's behavior and comments in court from my courtroom notes, September–December 2009. Translation of D'Addario quote and "whore-ocracy" quote from Alexander Stille, "The Corrupt Reign of Emperor Silvio," *New York Review of Books,* April 8, 2010. Closing arguments to verdict from my courtroom notes. Kercher press conference from my notes.

CHAPTER 16: CAPANNE

Quotes from Amanda's diary throughout the chapter, and Raffaele's letter to his father, all from the digital archive. Quotes from the "Marie Pace" short story, from a copy given to me by attorney Ghirga. Coline Covington on Amanda's psychopathy, "Signs That Suggest Amanda Knox Is a Psychopath," *The First Post,* December 9, 2009. Luigi Barzini on *"non farsi fesso,"* from *The Italians,* p. 65.

ACKNOWLEDGMENTS

I am deeply grateful to Giulia Alagna, Pieter Vanhove, and Laura Neilson, without whose tireless and enthusiastic assistance this book would not exist. *Grazie* also to my agent, Deborah Clarke Grosvenor, and my editor, Charles Conrad, for their advice, support, and unfailingly good ideas.

The following people either agreed to speak with me when they didn't have to, provided crucial background for the book, shared expertise, offered friendship, and/or provided critical technical and basic assistance in Perugia and in the United States: Giuliano Mignini, Manuela Comodi, Luciano Ghirga, Carlo Dalla Vedova, Maria Del Grosso, Luca Maori, Francesco Maresca, Francesco Introna, Curt Knox, Edda Mellas, Chris Mellas, Madison Paxton, Andrew Seliber, Brett Lither, Vanessa Sollecito, Roberto Giuffreda, Alessandra Lanciotti, Marina Tiberi, Francesco Sollecito, Valter Patumi, Ivana Tiberi, Ilaria Caporali, Roger Guede, Maria Del Prato, Antioco Fois, Francesca Bene, Vanna Ugolini, Daniel Tartaglia, Zach Nowak, Howard Cohn, Bob Graham, Doug Longhini, Sabina Castelfranco, Dennis Redmont, Antonio di Bartolomeo, Paul Ciolino, Georges G. Lederman, Ron Dwyer, Candace Dempsey, Barbie Nadeau, Andrea Vogt, Douglas Preston, Tom Wright, Frank Sfarzo, Mark Waterbury, Elio and Antonella Villi, Eve Mongin, Mauro Tosti, Christina Mecucci, Iva Marchioni, Accademia Lingua Italiana in Assisi, Anne Robichaud, and the teachers at Scuola Elementare Enzo Valentini in Perugia, especially Maestra Margarita. Thanks to Matthew Martin and Mark McCauslin.

The late Gabriella Carlizzi was especially edifying on the esoteric mysteries, as were the writings of Carlo Ginzburg.

I am grateful to Raffaele Sollecito and Amanda Knox for corresponding with me.

Special thanks to Erik Freeland for the beautiful photographs.

ABOUT THE AUTHOR

NINA BURLEIGH is the author of *Unholy Business: A True Tale of Faith, Greed, and Forgery in the Holy Land*; *A Very Private Woman: The Life and Unsolved Murder of Presidential Mistress Mary Meyer*; and two other books. She has written for the *New York Times*, *The New Yorker*, and *Time* and is a contributing editor at Elle. She has resided in France, Italy, and the Middle East and now lives in New York. Visit her at www.ninaburleigh.com.